WHERE THE TRAINS ARE!

Wonderful North American Train Attractions for Kids of All Ages

HEATHER R. TAYLOR

PRIMA PUBLISHING

© 1996 by Heather R. Taylor

PRIMA PUBLISHING and colophon are trademarks of Prima Communications, Inc.

Library of Congress Cataloging-in-Publication Data

Taylor, Heather R.
  Where the trains are! : wonderful North American train attractions for kids of all ages / by Heather Taylor.
    p. c.m.
  Includes index.
  ISBN 0-7615-0408-7
  1. Railroad museums—Canada. 2. Railroad museums—United States. 3. Railroad travel—Canada. 4. Railroad travel—United States. I. Title
TF6.U5T39 1996
385'.074'73—dc20   96-223
                                                                  CIP

96 97 98 99 00 HH 10 9 8 7 6 5 4 3 2 1
Printed in the United States of America

How to Order

Single copies may be ordered from Prima Publishing, P.O. Box 1260BK, Rocklin, CA 95677; telephone (916) 632-4400. Quantity discounts are also available. On your letterhead, include information concerning the intended use of the books and the number of books you wish to purchase.

To my son, Taylor,
whose love of trains
inspired me to write this book

CONTENTS

CANADA

INTRODUCTION

LBC (long before children), my husband and I enjoyed years of vacation travel via plane, car, and foot. Then, in 1992, something happened to change all that: A train enthusiast was born to our family. By the time our son was two years old, it was clear that he considered trains to be the center of the universe. To really share in his nearly contagious enthusiasm, we reasoned, we needed to learn a lot more about trains. It dawned on us—what better way to expand our knowledge than to visit sites that feature trains?

Where the Trains Are! is the result of our pilgrimages. This book is designed especially for young train enthusiasts and those who love them—their parents, grandparents, and other caregivers who plan train-focused itineraries for vacations and short stays. The research for this book involved conducting field visits to many train attractions, but the bulk of information was retrieved from the sites themselves. To qualify as a train attraction for the book, the sites had to be open to the public, appropriate for children, and located within the United States and Canada. Entries range from scenic train rides, museums, model railroad exhibits, and static displays, to train hotels and restaurants with train-theme ambiance.

WHY A BOOK ABOUT TRAIN ATTRACTIONS FOR KIDS?

It's an undeniable fact. Kids of every age love trains. From California to Florida, Ontario to Texas, train attractions draw countless visitors, especially families with children. This book is designed to help families identify those sites and to provide them with pertinent information in advance, to help ensure that each visit is a successful one.

While tourist railroads, scenic excursions, and railway museums are often the best-known sources of trains, other train attractions provide similar enjoyment and have great appeal to children. *Where the Trains Are!* uncovers lesser-known sites in addition to the more popular entries.

WHAT'S SO GREAT ABOUT TRAIN ATTRACTIONS?

Even if you, the parent or care giver, are not a train enthusiast, visiting a train attraction with a child who is can provide a memorable experience. For example, the sheer excitement of seeing a full-sized steam locomotive, climbing on board, and getting a chance to sit in the engineer's cab and ring the bell can be a child's greatest thrill.

But there's more. One of the wonderful things about taking a child to visit a train attraction included in this book is that nearly every site offers an opportunity to educate *and* entertain. Whether visiting an authentic railroad complex like the one at East Broad Top in Rockhill Furnace, Pennsylvania, or enjoying any one of the many live steam trains operated in community parks, it's hard to measure the knowledge a child absorbs as a whistle blows and a locomotive clickety-clacks along its track.

USING THIS GUIDE

Train attractions in this book are arranged alphabetically by state or province and by city. The list is by no means exhaustive, but it includes many wonderful train attractions currently operating in the United States and Canada.

Specific subheadings are included under each listing to help visitors obtain easy access to train sites.

How to Get There

This information is to be used in conjunction with a road map to navigate the intricacies of reaching the train sites. For larger cities, instructions in this section, supplemented by a local map, should serve you well. For attractions in smaller towns and more remote areas, careful attention has been paid to provide detailed directions and guidance door-to door.

Hours and Fares

This section provides some of the most important information about the time of year, daily hours, and cost (if any) of admission. Many, though not all, of the operations run during the summer only, from Memorial Day through Labor Day. In addition, most offer group rates and charter specials at a discount (call for reservations).

Special Events

Special events days that coincide with holidays and other theme days are commonly offered by train operators; Easter, Halloween, and Christmas "express" train rides are typical offerings. During the summer season, special trains are often run during rail fan festivals or family days. Fall foliage excursions are popular, too. Scheduled to coincide with the spectacular changing of the leaves, these excursions seem perfectly suited to the ambiance of a train ride, with its leisurely pace and the opportunity for beautiful views. Dinner trains and murder mystery trains (entertainment trains with a murder mystery theme) are also offered, but are often geared to adult patrons, so are outside the scope of this book.

Other Important Information

Where applicable, special notes are also included about whether an attraction is handicapped accessible; recommendations for cooler climates; information about the availability of snacks or meals on site, and whether there's a gift shop or souvenir stand.

Although a train site may not be technically classified as handicapped accessible, at many the staff can assist with handicapped visitors. Call ahead for information.

KIDS AND TRAINS

ATTRACTIONS OF ALL KINDS

TRAIN RIDES AND EXCURSIONS

Tourist train rides, often called scenic excursions, are among the most popular train attractions to visit with children. That's probably because trains offer loads of fun with a minimum of effort: visitors need only look, listen, and feel the experience of clickety-clacking along the rail tracks in order to arrive at simple recreation. And often where the train is going is far less important than the experience of simply getting there.

What to Expect

Although each ride or excursion has its own distinctive character, a common thread runs through them. Often vintage locomotives—original steam or diesel locomotives that have been fully restored to near-prime condition—are the car of choice. Locomotives can carry visitors in open (roofless or canopied to allow the circulation of fresh air) or enclosed coaches on a schedule that often begins Memorial Day weekend and makes a last run on Labor Day.

The type of journey differs, and may include a ride along a short stretch of track with little in the way of breathtaking scenery. In other cases, the journey may extend along mile after mile of spectacular scenery: past mountainous terrain, over trestles, through tunnels, and past cascading waterfalls, wild-life, and lush forest.

The train ride may originate from a station (often a re-stored former depot) with a renovated interior filled with mu-seum-quality exhibits and artifacts for viewing. On board, a friendly conductor or member of the train crew is on hand to provide historical background about the train, describe the landscape, and answer passenger questions.

Try Them All

With the great variety of excursions in North America, trying out new trains is half the fun. The choices available include steam and diesel locomotives, streetcars or trolleys (including cable cars and interurbans), and miniature trains.

Some are managed and operated by preservation groups such as chapters of the National Railway Historical Society and are operating museums, providing visitors with a dose of recre-ation *and* history with every visit. Others are private operations with elaborate excursions on elegantly refurbished coaches with lounge cars, or domed cars to enhance the view from the train, and offer refreshments on board. Still others are very simple affairs traveling along a short track in a public park. Whatever the site, there's bound to be a train attraction to de-light every member of the family.

Kids Will Love the Ride and the Extras

One of the many wonderful features of the kid-friendly train attractions included in this book is that these sites cultivate children's interest in trains. For example, many rides will allow children to ring the train bell or to visit the engineer's cab to better explore the world of railroading. A few operations in-clude engineering lessons for a fee, enabling a family to climb aboard and operate a locomotive while supervised by a trained engineer.

Party, Anyone?

What could delight a train fan more than a special party held on a train? Many organizations offer just that. For a modest fee, children can enjoy a birthday party or other special occasion aboard a caboose or other railcar. Still others offer charter service.

Occasional Trains

In addition to regular excursions listed under "special events" for each city, other train trips are offered on an occasional basis (usually once or twice a year) by groups like the local chapters of the National Railway Historical Society (in the U.S.) and the divisions of the Canadian Railroad Historical Association. Train hobby shops and magazines can provide current information on offerings.

AMTRAK

Tourist trains from yesteryear aren't the only place to look for scenic train journeys. Consider America's national passenger service, the National Railroad Passenger Corporation, or AMTRAK, now celebrating its 25th anniversary. Created by Congress in 1970 to revive and preserve a weakened rail passenger system, AMTRAK began service in 1971 and today operates in nearly every state, providing intercity transportation for over 530 communities in 45 states on over 24,000 miles of track.

From the east to the west, AMTRAK operates trains that offer spectacular vistas in comfortable accommodations. Following are just a few of the many choices available.

Coast Starlight This train line connects Los Angeles, San Francisco, Portland, and Seattle. The ride features Santa Barbara beaches, Cascade mountains, and the Williamette Pass, complete with 22 tunnels and hairpin turns.

California Zephyr This train travels from Chicago to Denver, Salt Lake City, and Sacramento. Spectacular scenery includes the Rocky Mountains, Donner Pass in the Sierra Nevada, and Moffat Tunnel, a 6-mile tunnel that crosses the Continental Divide. An on-board guide program on local culture, history, and wildlife is offered by volunteers.

Adirondack From New York City, the Adirondack travels through the beautiful Hudson River Valley, past Bear Mountain and West Point, through the Adirondack Mountains, and along Lake Champlain in a serpentine route through tiny rock cuts that cross 100-foot trestles before reaching its final destination in Montreal.

Pennsylvanian Traveling between Johnstown and Altoona, the train takes visitors through a historic tour of the famous Horseshoe Curve and the Johnstown Floods. National Park Rangers are part of an on-board guide program providing background information for AMTRAK passengers.

Comfort on Board

A variety of accommodations are available on AMTRAK, including a Superliner fleet, a two-level coach with sleeping cars, diner, and lounge area. Some trains include a reading library with games for children and adults. Vacation packages, air-rail combinations, and an Autotrain are also offered.

Among the special features for passengers traveling with children are AMTRAK activity books (available by request on long-distance trips), choo choo chewies (children's special meals in dining cars), and a special play area and mother's nursing section at the Chicago Union Station.

For more information, contact AMTRAK at (800) USA-RAIL.

LIVE STEAM AND MODEL TRAINS

Adult train hobbyists may make up the largest segment of "live steam" train enthusiasts, but kids must come a close second. In this book, "live steam" refers to steam-powered train replicas that are built as small-scale versions of real, full-sized trains.

These trains are usually built to be ridden by adults and children alike, and while they're kid-sized, it should be noted that they are not toys and should be treated like the steam-powered mammoths they were built to resemble. Live steam clubs often offer rides to the public in recreational parks or in a specially designed track area.

Model trains may also be an adult hobbyist's passion, but children can find great enjoyment in watching the operation of model train displays. Some are offered to the public as part of museum exhibits to help illustrate a historic train route. Others are layouts presented by model railroading clubs and train hobby shops. They are fun to visit because the exhibits can be elaborate affairs, with intricate detailing, beautiful landscaping, and several trains in motion at the same time.

Live steam and model railroading clubs thrive throughout the country, and many offer rides or public viewings on a regular basis. Schedules vary and fees may be charged. Call ahead. One of the best ways to identify these activities is to scan magazines on model railroading and live steam trains.

LOCATING A "LOOSE" CABOOSE: TRAINS ON PUBLIC DISPLAY

Seeing a "loose" caboose, locomotive, or other railcar—on display in front of a public building, in a recreational park, or elsewhere, away from a railway yard or museum—can have the feel of an unexpected and welcome find. They re-create the excitement of life on board what was once called "Rolling Thunder."

TRAIN AND TRANSPORTATION MUSEUMS, STATIONS, AND DEPOTS

Children who might lack interest in a visit to other kinds of historical centers are often drawn to a train or transportation museum and its many fascinating exhibits and train artifacts.

Like rides and excursions, museums vary widely. Many are extensive outdoor complexes, providing rides on full-sized trains, and exhibits with artifacts and displays. These most often have walkways with unpaved gravel surfaces. Others are housed inside former train depots and concentrate more heavily on smaller train artifacts and photographs. Transportation museums often include a special wing or section devoted exclusively to rail travel. Interpretive centers help to describe the exhibits in detail and routinely offer guided tours and safety tips to school children and others upon request.

Train museums usually have nonprofit status, and many were created by rail enthusiasts who are concerned about preserving railroad heritage. These railway historical societies often were created to help save a locomotive from the scrap heap. Many such museums came into existence as preservation groups continued to acquire and restore rail items, and wanted to use the items to help educate the public about rail history and the need to preserve it.

For more information, contact the National Railway Historical Society in a community near you.

FINDING GREAT VIEWS OF ROLLING TRAINS

While spectacular views discovered on a train journey provide a great experience, for train patrons, spotting a train in motion offers a different kind of thrill. For many train enthusiasts, an important way of identifying where the trains are is the adventure of capturing them in motion. It might be watching the speedy movement of a locomotive against a beautiful mountain range, or the sunset against the billowing smoke of a steam engine.

Whatever the backdrop, finding those moments (or hours, depending on your enthusiasm) is usually time well spent. The key is to locate a safe place to watch trains pass (without trespassing on private property). Examples of some rewarding train-sighting spots are the Horseshoe Curve in Altoona, Pennsylvania, and Cajon Pass near Los Angeles, California.

KEEPING TRAINS ALIVE: THE IMPORTANCE OF PRESERVING RAILROAD HERITAGE

The rich histories of railroading in the United States and Canada began in the 19th century. The introduction of this new mode of travel dramatically influenced the social, economic, and political development of both countries.

Many factors have led to the decline of railroads in the last 40 years, among them the widespread use of automobiles and airplanes. But thanks to the efforts of rail preservationists, train enthusiasts, and others who recognized the importance of preserving this history, more train attractions than ever are available for visits.

The continued restoration, maintenance, and development of exhibits and programs of many of the nonprofit train attractions depend on donations from visitors because they are operated primarily by unpaid volunteers. Please give generously. Continued financial support is critical to their continued operation.

For more information on how to help and how to become a member, contact your local chapter of the National Railway Historical Society or division of the Canadian Railroad Historical Association.

TRAVELING WITH CHILDREN

SAFETY FIRST

The search and discovery of great train attractions can be an exciting experience for children and adults. The importance of safety, though, cannot be overstated. Tourist train rides, rail museums, and any other places where trains are in operation can pose particular hazards for young children and others if safety isn't made the number one priority.

Please be sure to take special safety measures when visiting train sites. Ahead of time, read the book listings closely for any notes about safety. At all train sites, be alert for posted safety tips and warnings, watch for possible hazards like steep stairs, and stick together as a family.

Operation Lifesaver, a national, nonprofit public information program, was founded in 1972 by Union Pacific Railroad to help reduce the rate of highway rail crossing-related injuries and fatalities. Since 1972, the number of these incidents has fallen dramatically. Independent Operation Lifesaver programs operate in every state except Hawaii, with many special workshops and programs offered at many of the train sites listed in this book. Main themes of the program include education, engineering, and enforcement. In addition, coloring and activity books are important tools used by Operation Lifesaver to help promote railroad safety to children.

In conjunction with the Operation Lifesaver program, every individual accompanying a child to a train attraction is advised to be aware that "any time is train time." Whether in a motor vehicle near a railroad crossing or walking through a rail yard at a train site, the potential for injury is present and people must take safety seriously.

For more information, contact Operation Lifesaver, 1420 King Street, Suite 401, Alexandria, VA 22314. Telephone (800) 537-6224 or (703) 739-0308; fax (703) 519-8267.

MAKING THE MOST OF YOUR VISITS

Taking a child to visit a train attraction should always be an enjoyable experience, but to guarantee successful outings, it is important for parents and other caregivers to keep a few things in mind before heading out to your nearest train excursion, museum, or other site. A good rule of thumb is to be flexible at all times, and to follow a few handy suggestions:

Call Ahead

In this book every effort has been made to provide up-to-date schedules, fares, and other information, but unexpected changes do occur. Be sure to telephone your destination beforehand. Ask when to arrive and whether reservations are required. Also, be sure to think about logistical concerns, such as where strollers may be stored and what can be carried on board (for train rides).

Time the Outing Accordingly

If a child is tired, hungry, or under the weather, visiting even the most appealing train attraction can result in an unsatisfactory experience for everyone involved. Selecting a time when a child is apt to get the most enjoyment out of a visit is important.

Take Along the Necessary Supplies

The youngest visitor still in diapers will need whatever number of changes the length of a visit requires. Snacks, a favorite toy, and a change of clothing can make the visit more pleasant. During colder months and in mountainous areas, a jacket, sweater, and blanket may be appropriate.

Dress Accordingly

If you're not wearing comfortable shoes and clothing for many of the train attractions offered, your visit could prove to be quite a challenge. For example, because many train museums' full-sized trains are exhibited outside, access is primarily on foot (wheelchair access is usually limited). And traveling to higher elevations may make even a summer train excursion a sweater or jacket affair.

Children Need Adult Supervision

The train attractions included in this book were selected because of their kid-friendliness. But it's a simple fact that while all children are warmly welcomed, implicit in that welcome is that all visitors be respectful and well behaved, to guarantee that a visit to a train attraction is enjoyable for everyone involved.

UNITED STATES

ALABAMA

GADSDEN

COOSA VALLEY MODEL RAILROAD
CENTER FOR CULTURAL ARTS

The Coosa Valley Model Railroad Club, housed in the Gadsden Center for Cultural Arts building, gives visitors a glimpse of Gadsden in the 1940s and 1950s. A 72-foot layout displays replicas of the four railroads that operated during those years: the Alabama Great Southern (AGS), the Tennessee, Alabama and Georgia (TAG), the Louisville & Nashville Railroad (L & N), and the Nashville, Chattanooga and St. Louis (NC & St.L). The exhibit has been open since 1990, but additions to the layout are ongoing. Train whistles help to create railway atmosphere.

How to Get There   Sixty miles north of Birmingham. Take I-59 north, exit 759 (Gadsden). Take U.S. 411 north, and exit U.S. 431 west. The Gadsden Center for Cultural Arts is downtown.

Hours   Monday through Saturday, 9 A.M. to 6 P.M.; Sundays, 1 P.M. to 5 P.M. (by appointment).

Fares   Nonmembers, $2; Tuesdays after 12 P.M. free.

Contact   Marvin Lynn, president, Coosa Valley Model Railroad Club, c/o Gadsden Center for Cultural Arts, 501 Broad Street, Gadsden, AL 35901. Telephone (205) 543-2787 (Center for Cultural Arts).

NOCCALULA FALLS PARK

The *Kiwanis Special* is a miniature train that travels one mile through beautiful Noccalula Falls Park, which was built to resemble a pioneer homestead. Visitors to the park pass through a pioneer village and have a view of the gorge and botanical gardens. The village, first begun in the late 1960s, now includes a statue of Native American Princess Noccalula (for whom the park is named), a log cabin and cook house, blacksmith shop, covered bridge, wishing well, schoolhouse, and many other items that illustrate pioneer life.

How to Get There   Sixty miles north of Birmingham. Take I-59 north, exit 186 (Noccalula Falls) onto Highway 211, which takes you right to the park at 1500 Noccalula Falls.

Hours   Both park and train open March through Labor Day (weather permitting) and holidays and weekends during good weather: 9 A.M. until dark.

Fares   Adults, $1; children, $.50.

Contact   Gadsden-Etowah Tourism Board, P.O. Box 8267, Gadsden, AL 35902-8267. Telephone (205) 549-0351 or (205) 549-4663; fax (205) 549-1854.

H U N T S V I L L E

HUNTSVILLE DEPOT
TRANSPORTATION MUSEUM

An 1860 depot houses the Huntsville Depot Transportation Museum. One of the oldest railroad buildings in existence, it was once part of the Memphis & Charleston Railroad line, a passenger station with connections to Nashville and Chattanooga, Tennessee. The museum provides tours, and children have the chance to get a taste of trains in a variety of ways. On display are: *Number 4*, a narrow gauge steam engine; an operating miniature station model that depicts the depot grounds in the 1860s; a ticket office operated with robotics; and the Train and Trolley Shop, full of souvenirs and memorabilia.

The Depot Trolley departs from the museum and takes visitors on a 30-minute tour of downtown Huntsville.

How to Get There   From Nashville, take I-65 south to I-565 east, exit 19C. The depot is adjacent. From Birmingham, take I-65 north to I-565 west, exit 19C.

Hours   March to December, Monday through Saturday, 9 A.M. to 5 P.M. (last tour begins at 4 P.M.).

Fares   Adults, $6; seniors, $5; children (ages 6 to 18), $3.50.

Contact   Huntsville Depot Transportation Museum, 320 Church Street, Huntsville, AL 35801. Telephone (205) 539-1860 or (800) 678-1819.

ALASKA

ANCHORAGE

ALASKA RAILROAD

The route for the Alaska Railroad was completed in 1923. Its construction was influential in the settlement of the state. Today the line covers hundreds of miles of breathtaking scenery and provides year-round passenger and freight service. Excursions are offered between Anchorage and Seward and between Anchorage and Fairbanks. In season, whales, moose, bears, eagles, geese, and other wildlife are visible against the spectacular backdrop of the Alaskan wilderness.

      Tour selections include four-hour trains from Anchorage to Seward, or longer 12-hour express train excursions between Anchorage and Fairbanks, complete with full-service dining cars, dome car, reclining seats, and wide-view windows. Featured on board are student tour guides equipped to answer questions on the railroad's history and landscape. A variety of combination rail/sightseeing tours are also offered.

How to Get There   Take the New Seward Highway to the Third Avenue exit and turn left at the end of the offramp. At E Street, turn right and drive to a fork in the road. Turn right at the fork. Turn left onto First Avenue. The railroad depot is the second building on the right.

Hours   Excursions are available daily, from May through the beginning of September, 6:45 A.M. and 10:00 P.M. Contact the Railroad for 12-hour excursions fares and schedules.

Fares   To Seward (round-trip): adults, $80; children (ages 2 to 11), $40. To Seward (one-way): adults, $50; children (ages 2 to 11), $25.

Contact   Alaska Railroad Corporation, Passenger Services Department, P.O. Box 107500, Anchorage, AK 99510-7500. Telephone (800) 544-0552; (907) 265-2494 (Anchorage); (907) 456-4155 (Fairbanks); (907) 265-2323 (fax).

S K A G W A Y

WHITE PASS & YUKON ROUTE

To take the White Pass & Yukon Route is to relive the 1800s and the days of the gold rush—when trains hauled gold, miners, and related supplies to the Yukon Territory. Today, the route's narrow gauge track is more than 110 miles long between Skagway and Whitehorse, Yukon. Scenic rides include a three-hour round-trip to the White Pass Summit, which follows the Gold Rush Trail and climbs over 2,800 feet above sea level.

Other trains offer longer trips, such as the Chilkoot Hikers' Train, which is especially designed for visitors hiking the 33-mile Chilkoot Trail, and the Skagway/Whitehorse, a

BARBARA KALEN, WHITE PASS & YUKON ROUTE RAILWAY

Vintage steam locomotive #73 proudly escorts trains out of town.

train traveling through Alaska and Canada and connecting with a motor coach.

NOTE: 30-day advance reservations are recommended. All trains are wheelchair accessible.

How to Get There   From Whitehorse, take the Alaskan Canadian Highway to the Klondike Highway to Skagway (about 110 miles total). The train station is on Second Street, just east of Broadway.

Hours   Departures begin at 8:45 A.M.

Fares   White Pass Summit: adults, $75; children, $37.50. Chilkoot Hikers': adults, $64; children, $32. Skagway/Whitehorse: adults, $95; children, $47.50. No charge for infants.

MICHAEL ANDERSON, WHITE PASS & YUKON ROUTE RAILWAY

Powerful diesel locomotive climbs the steep grade to the White Pass Summit.

Contact White Pass & Yukon Route, P.O. Box 435, Dept. B, Skagway, AK 99840. Telephone (800) 343-7373; (907) 983-2217; fax (907) 983-2734.

W A S I L L A

MUSEUM OF ALASKA TRANSPORTATION AND INDUSTRY

One of the most appealing features of the Museum of Alaska Transportation and Industry is access to indoor and outdoor exhibits on seven acres of land. Run by a nonprofit group with the goal of preserving Alaskan transportation and industrial history, the museum has a variety of displays, including railroad cars, military aircraft, mining equipment, and a train museum. The train museum is filled with three Alaska Railroad cars and photographs and tools from the railroad's heyday. Included are *Tillie's Caboose*, built in 1917, and the last wooden caboose used by Alaska Railroad.

How to Get There   Take Parks Highway 3 to Wasilla. Exit at mile 47 and turn onto Neuser Road. Follow it three-quarters of a mile to the museum, at 3800 W. Neuser Drive.

Hours   May to September: open daily, 10:00 A.M. to 6:00 P.M.; October to April: open Tuesday through Saturday, 9:00 A.M. to 5:00 P.M.

Fares   Adults, $5; seniors and students, $2.50; family, $12; children under eight years of age are free of charge.

Contact   Museum of Alaska Transportation and Industry, P.O. Box 870646, Wasilla, AK 99687. Telephone (907) 376-1211.

ARIZONA

CLARKDALE

VERDE CANYON RAILROAD

The Verde Canyon Railroad operates a 40-mile, three-and-a-half-hour round-trip excursion train between Clarkdale and Perkinsville, Arizona. The trip offers spectacular views of the Verde Canyon, a wilderness and protected habitat for bald eagles, herons, javelinas, and deer.

Visitors are offered the canyon view from the railroad's five open-air cars, or can enjoy year-round comfort in the heated and cooled, renovated New York Metro Line coaches, each holding up to 70 passengers.

How to Get There   Clarkdale is 16 miles from exit 287 off I-17, 22 miles west of Sedona and two hours north of Phoenix.

Hours   Open Wednesday through Sunday, beginning at 11:00 A.M. In October, April, and May, open every day except Tuesday. Two trains run on Saturday, beginning at 11:00 A.M.

Fares First class: adults and children, $52.95. Coach: adults, $34.95; children (ages 2 to 12), $19.95. Train and hotel packages are available with the Red Canyon Inn at Sedona.

Contact Verde Canyon Railroad, 300 North Broadway, Clarkdale, AZ 86324. Telephone (800) 293-7245 or (520) 639-0010; fax (520) 639-1653.

SCOTTSDALE

McCormick Railroad Park

A facility like McCormick Railroad Park offers visitors of all ages the chance to roam spacious grounds freely and to enjoy a variety of train exhibits and displays. Opened in 1974 and named after its benefactors, McCormick Railroad Park offers 30 acres and lots to see, including Arizona's Forty and Eight French Boxcar (one of the 48 gift-laden boxcars from France, sent to each state as an expression of gratitude to the U.S. for its help in World War II).

The park also features a train ride, railway exhibits including a Santa Fe Baggage Express car and the Roald Amundsen Presidential Pullman car (ridden by Presidents Hoover, Roosevelt, Truman, and Eisenhower), a snack bar caboose (serving hot dogs, yogurt and drinks), and the Peoria and Aguila Depots, built in 1895 and 1907, respectively. An antique carousel, arboretum, and two Hopi hogans are also part of the visitors' exhibits.

How to Get There From Tucson, take I-10 to U.S. 51 north. Exit Lincoln Drive and turn right. Continue driving east on Lincoln to Scottsdale Road. Turn right at Indian Bend; the park is at the southeast corner.

Hours Open daily, except Thanksgiving and Christmas. In 1996, the park may be closed from June to December to undergo major renovations. Call the contact number for operating hours.

Fares Adults, $1. Children under three years of age with a paying adult are free of charge.

Contact McCormick Railroad Park, 7301 East Indian Bend Road, Scottsdale, AZ 85250. Telephone (602) 994-2312.

T U C S O N

OLD PUEBLO TROLLEY, INC.

Electric streetcars serviced the Tucson area for more than 24 years, beginning in 1906. Their operation was reestablished in 1993 through the efforts of the University of Arizona. Today, historic electric streetcars journey from the shopping district to the University of Arizona on the Old Pueblo Trolley, a living museum depicting the history of Arizona transit. Two cornerstones of the museum's collection are car #10, formerly a Birney Safety Car, and car #255, a Hankai Electric Tramway Car from Japan. Old Pueblo Trolley's future plans include construction of a transportation museum and restoration shop, and extension of the rail line.

How to Get There From I-10, take the Speedway exit east to Fourth Avenue. Turn south (right) and look for the trolley track in the street at the intersection of University and Fourth. Follow the track either on Fourth Avenue or University to a car stop.

Hours Fridays, 6:00 P.M. to 10:00 P.M.; Saturdays, 10:00 A.M. to 12 midnight; Sundays, 12 noon to 6:00 P.M.

Fares One-way: adults, $1; children (ages 6 to 12), $.50. All day: adults, $2.50; children (ages 6 to 12), $1.25.

Contact   Old Pueblo Trolley, Inc., P.O. Box 1373, Tucson, AZ 85702. Telephone (602) 792-1802.

W I L L I A M S

GRAND CANYON RAILWAY

For a steam or diesel engine ride through one of America's most breathtaking landscapes—the Grand Canyon—this train is tough to beat. Passengers have the choice of three car classes: coach, club, and chief, all of which provide comfort, service, refreshments, and live entertainment.

But the steam trains aren't the only attractions. Visitors may tour the Williams Depot complex, built in 1908, which is on the National Register of Historic Places and is the site of the former Fray Marcos Hotel. Outside the complex are a locomotive built in 1910 and a Harriman coach car built in 1923. The 1920 Grand Canyon Depot, located not far from the rim of the canyon, is a National Historic Landmark; made of logs, it's the last one of its kind servicing a working railroad. The railway has a museum and a gift shop.

How to Get There   From Flagstaff, take I-40 to exit 163, then follow Grand Canyon Boulevard half a mile south to the Williams Depot.

Hours   Open daily, except Christmas Eve and Christmas. Departs Williams Depot at 9:30 A.M. and arrives at Grand Canyon at 11:45 A.M. Departs Grand Canyon at 3:15 P.M. and arrives at Williams Depot at 5:30 P.M.

Fares   Coach class: adults, $49; children (ages 3 to 16), $19. Club class: additional $12. Chief class: additional $50. State and local taxes and National Park Service fee are additional.

Contact   Grand Canyon Railway, 123 North San Francisco, Suite 210, Flagstaff, AZ 86001. Telephone (800) 843-8724.

ARKANSAS

MAMMOTH SPRING

MAMMOTH SPRING STATE PARK DEPOT MUSEUM

What better backdrop for a museum visit than the beauty of a forested state park with a natural spring? The Mammoth Spring State Park Depot Museum is all that's left of the former Frisco Railroad at Mammoth Spring, but railroad history is in large supply. Built in 1886 by the Frisco Railroad, the depot was one of the town's earliest. Restored in 1971, it includes a Frisco caboose and train memorabilia. Picnic areas, a fish hatchery, a visitor center, and walking trails are also on the site.

NOTE: The museum may be undergoing renovation in 1996. Call ahead.

How to Get There   From Little Rock, take Highway 67 north to Bald Knob exit. Then take Highway 167 north to Hardy, then U.S. 63 north for 16 miles to the visitor center entrance.

Hours   Open daily, April through October, 10:00 A.M. to 5:00 P.M.

Fares   Adults, $1; children, $.50.

Contact   Mammoth Spring State Park, P.O. Box 36, Mammoth Spring, AR 72554. Telephone (501) 625-7364.

R O G E R S

ROGERS HISTORICAL MUSEUM

Visitors to the Rogers Historical Museum have the opportunity to trace the history of this town, born in 1881 when the first steam train rolled into the area. Visitors can also explore a life-sized relic of the Frisco Railroad: a museum-owned caboose, circa 1939, donated by Frisco Railroad in 1981 for its centennial. The caboose is located at the corner of Walnut and First Streets. Also featured is another exhibit popular with children: a hands-on attraction called "The Attic," a permanent exhibit of life in the 19th century, which is housed in the Victorian Hawkins House, built in 1895.

How to Get There   From Fayetteville, take Highway 71 to exit 65 (Rogers).

Hours   The museum is open from 10:00 A.M. to 4:00 P.M., Tuesday to Saturday; it's closed on major holidays. The caboose is open for tours daily from May through October.

Fares   Admission is free.

Contact   Rogers Historical Museum, 322 South Second Street, Rogers, AR 72756. Telephone (501) 621-1154.

SPRINGDALE

ARKANSAS & MISSOURI RAILROAD

Two diesel excursion train rides are offered to riders of the Arkansas & Missouri Railroad: from Springdale to Van Buren and from Van Buren to Winslow. The Springdale to Van Buren route takes visitors to the top of the Ozark Mountains on a 134-mile round-trip ride that includes a ride through the Winslow Tunnel and over trestles. The trip includes complimentary buffet breakfast and refreshments along with a three-hour layover in Van Buren, providing an opportunity to visit the historic district and the restored **Old Frisco Depot,** built in 1901. The depot now houses the chamber of commerce and includes train artifacts and memorabilia.

The Van Buren to Winslow route is shorter (70 miles round-trip), and it includes complimentary snacks and beverages without a stopover.

How to Get There   From Little Rock, take I-40 west to Highway 540 north. Then take Highway 71 north to Springdale exit. Turn right onto Emma Street; the depot is on the right.

Hours   Springdale to Van Buren: open Wednesdays and Friday through Sunday; departs Springdale Depot at 8:00 A.M. and returns at 5:00 P.M.

Van Buren to Winslow: open Wednesday, Friday, and Saturday; departs Van Buren at 11:15 A.M. and returns at 2:15 P.M.

Fares   Springdale to Van Buren: Wednesday and Friday, $33; Saturday and Sunday, $38. In October, the fares are: Tuesday, Wednesday, and Friday, $38; Saturday and Sunday, $44.

Van Buren to Winslow: Wednesday and Friday, $19; Saturday, $21. In October, the fares are: Wednesday and Friday, $25; Saturday, $27.

Contact   Arkansas & Missouri Railroad, 306 East Emma Street, Springdale, AR 72764. Telephone (800) 687-8600 or (501) 751-8600.

CALIFORNIA

BISHOP

LAWS RAILROAD MUSEUM AND HISTORICAL SITE

Between 1883, when the railroad came to Laws, and 1959, when its depot closed, the town of Laws served the Carson, the Colorado, and the Southern Pacific Railroads as a narrow gauge line. In the early years, the railroad serviced the mines, but later carried freight and passengers.

In 1966, the Bishop Museum and Historical Society, a nonprofit organization, opened the Laws Railroad Museum, a 10-acre historical site that commemorates the Owens Valley and the eastern Sierra region. The museum featured a narrow gauge train called the *Slim Princess,* a host of railcars, oil and water tanks, a turntable, depot, and a train agent's house. The depot now contains railroad artifacts and a working model railroad.

Since 1966, the museum has acquired additional exhibits and buildings from the nearby area, including mining machinery, a restored barn, carriage house, and a country store.

LAWS RAILROAD MUSEUM AND HISTORICAL SITE

The *Slim Princess* was the final train to roll into Laws depot on its last day of operation.

All main buildings are wheelchair accessible. Refreshments and a picnic area are available.

How to Get There   From Los Angeles, take Highway 15 north to Bishop, then U.S. 6 north. Exit Silver Canyon Road and turn right; it's half a mile to the museum.

Hours   Open all year, except Thanksgiving and Christmas, from 10:00 A.M. to 4:00 P.M.

Fares   Donations are accepted.

Contact   Laws Railroad Museum and Historical Site, P.O. Box 363, Bishop, CA 93514. Telephone (619) 873-5950.

EUREKA

FORT HUMBOLDT
STATE HISTORIC PARK

Fort Humboldt State Historic Park, a 12.5-acre site, was formerly a U.S. Army military post and redwood logging center. In 1977, a nonprofit preservation group called the Northern Counties Logging Interpretive Association began working with the State of California to create a state logging museum. Acquisition and restoration efforts are ongoing.

Currently, the park houses an outdoor logging museum on two acres. The museum features logging equipment, interpretive panels, logging artifacts, steam donkeys (machines that replaced oxen in hauling logs from the woods), and two steam locomotives. The park also provides a self-guided trail of the various exhibits. The steam locomotives are operated during the season, offering visitor rides on a half mile of track.

The park is wheelchair accessible. Future plans include restoring the fort to its 1861 appearance.

Special Events   Rhododendron Festival; Donkey Days.

How to Get There   From San Francisco, take Highway 101 north to the south end of Eureka. The park is opposite Bayshore Mall.

Hours   The park is open daily, 9:00 A.M. to 5:00 P.M. Train rides are available the last weekend in April and every third Saturday, May through September.

Fares   Donations are welcome.

Contact   Fort Humboldt State Historic Park, 3431 Fort Avenue, Eureka, CA 95501. Telephone (707) 445-6567.

FELTON

ROARING CAMP & BIG TREES NARROW-GAUGE RAILROAD

Roaring Camp & Big Trees Narrow-Gauge Railroad offers a 6-mile round-trip (1 hour, 15 minutes) steam ride from Roaring Camp to Bear Mountain in Santa Cruz County. The scenic ride takes passengers through magnificent towering redwood trees, crossing trestles along a narrow gauge track first laid in 1880. Carrying passengers in open-air cars, it stops at Bear Mountain, where visitors can detrain for a hike, picnic before returning to Roaring Camp, or continue with the round-trip journey.

ROARING CAMP & BIG TREES RAILROAD

The *Dixiana Shay* crosses a trestle on the narrow gauge railroad.

Railroad equipment includes six steam locomotives, three diesels, and a host of railcars. In Roaring Camp, an 1880s-style general store sells railroad souvenirs and merchandise of the period. The Red Caboose Saloon operates when trains are running, featuring chuck wagon barbecue, lunch, and snack items.

Special Events   Great Train Robberies; Easter Egg Hunt; Civil War Reenactment; Rail Enthusiast Day; Music in the Mountains; Jumpin' Frog Contest; Handcar Races and Steam Festival; Summer Sampler; Harvest Fair; Halloween Ghost Train; Mountain Man Rendezvous; Pioneer Christmas.

How to Get There   Roaring Camp is 6 miles inland from Santa Cruz. From Highway 17, take Mt. Hermon Road exit at Scotts Valley. Go 3.5 miles to Graham Hill Road, then left half a mile to Roaring Camp.

Hours   April through December: open daily (except Christmas Day). January through March: open Wednesday through Sunday. One to five scheduled departures per day.

Fares   Adults (13 and over), $13; children (ages 3 to 12), $9.50; children (under 3), free.

Contact   Roaring Camp & Big Trees Narrow-Gauge Railroad, Graham Hill Road, P.O. Box G-1, Felton, CA 95018. Telephone (408) 335-4484; fax (408) 335-3509.

SANTA CRUZ, BIG TREES & PACIFIC RAILWAY

The Santa Cruz, Big Trees & Pacific Railway, operated by the Roaring Camp & Big Trees Narrow-Gauge Railroad (see the previous entry), takes visitors on a two-and-a-half-hour scenic diesel ride in turn-of-the-century passenger trains. A southbound train departs from the 1891 Roaring Camp Depot and proceeds to the San Lorenzo River Canyon through landscape that includes redwood and pine forests, tunnels, steel bridges and wooden trestles, Victorian-era homes, Santa Cruz Beach, and the original 1912 boardwalk with a carousel. Riders may explore the boardwalk or patronize the area shops and restaurants and return on a later train to Roaring Camp. Northbound, the train travels from the boardwalk to Roaring Camp.

Special Events   See the previous entry on the Roaring Camp & Big Trees Narrow-Gauge Railroad.

How to Get There   See the previous entry on the Roaring Camp & Big Trees Narrow-Gauge Railroad.

Hours   Mid-May to early June, and early September to November: open Saturday, Sunday, and holidays. June to early September: open daily.
    Trains depart at 10:30 A.M. and 2:30 P.M. (Roaring Camp to boardwalk) and at 12:30 P.M. and 4:30 P.M. (boardwalk to Roaring Camp).

Fares   Adults (13 years and older), $15; children (ages 3 to 12), $11; children (under 3), free.

Contact   Roaring Camp & Big Trees Narrow-Gauge Railroad, Box G-1, Felton, CA 95018. Telephone (408) 335-4484; fax (408) 335-3509.

F I L L M O R E

FILLMORE & WESTERN RAILWAY COMPANY

Nicknamed the "Movie Trains," the Fillmore & Western Railway Company features many trains that have been used in television shows and movies. The company operates one-hour and two-hour scenic steam and diesel excursions on the *Fillmore Flyer,* the *Santa Paula Limited,* and the *Sunday Scenic* from September through December. On these trips, the scenic views come in the form of beautiful citrus groves through Ventura County, past small farms, and across lovely countryside. The trains travel along portions of the old Southern Pacific line, which was built in 1887 and carried passengers between Los Angeles and San Francisco.

Passengers depart from the Central Park Depot in Fillmore or the Santa Paula Depot in Santa Paula. A 1906 Great Western Railway locomotive #51 is used for the *Santa Paula Limited* (two hours); 1949 locomotives are used for the *Fillmore Flyer* steam excursions diesel rides (one hour).

A luxury train with a historic Pullman car was introduced in 1995. Dinner trains are also offered.

Special Events   Spirit of the West Barbecue; Santa Claus Special; Haunted Express.

How to Get There   Fillmore and Santa Paula are an hour northwest of Los Angeles on State Route 126. To reach the depot in Fillmore, turn north on Central Avenue and drive one block. For the Santa Paula Depot, turn north on 10th Street and drive three blocks.

Hours   Steam trains operate in September, October, and November, with departures at 11:00 A.M., 12:30 P.M., 2:00 P.M., and 3:30 P.M. (call for exact dates). Diesel trains operate in September, October, and November, with departures at 10:00 A.M., 11:15 A.M., and 12:30 P.M.

Fares   Adults, $12.50 to $16; children (ages 4 to 12), $7 to $9; children under four years of age are admitted free of charge.

Contact   Fillmore & Western Railway Company, 351 Santa Clara Avenue, Fillmore, CA 93015. Telephone (805) 524-2546.

JOSEPH BISPO, YOSEMITE MOUNTAIN–SUGAR PINE RAILROAD

Shay locomotives #15 and #10, ready to steam through the Sierra Nevada.

FISH CAMP

YOSEMITE MOUNTAIN–SUGAR PINE RAILROAD

For a scenic trip through the Sierra Nevada Mountains, the Yosemite Mountain–Sugar Pine Railroad takes passengers on a 4-mile excursion along a narrow gauge track. The track was used between 1899 and 1931 by a logging company to transport over one billion pieces of timber.

Visitors can choose between two modes of transportation: a steam-powered antique Shay locomotive for a 45-minute narrated trip, or a gas-powered, trolley-like Jenny railcar (once used to transport track repair personnel) for a 30-minute trip.

The steam trains make a stop at Shady Slab Creek, where visitors may picnic before making the return trip.

Special Events   Moonlight Special.

How to Get There   Enter by the Yosemite Park South entrance on Highway 41.

Hours   Shay locomotives: daily from mid-May through September; weekends and holidays only in early May and October. Trains depart at 11:00 A.M. and 12:30 P.M. (additional trains run in June, July, and August).
   Jenny railcars: Trains run 9:00 A.M. to 3:30 P.M. from mid-March through October. Call for the November through February schedule.
   All schedules subject to change; call ahead.

Fares   Steam train: adults, $9.75; children (ages 3 to 12), $4.75. Railcars: adults, $6.50; children (ages 3 to 12), $3.50.

Contact   Yosemite Mountain–Sugar Pine Railroad, 56001 Highway 1, Fish Camp, CA 93623. Telephone (209) 683-7273.

F O L S O M

FOLSOM VALLEY RAILWAY

The Folsom Valley Railway is a 12-inch narrow gauge line that operates a 10-minute ride through Folsom City Park along a track adjacent to the Folsom Zoo. Built in 1950, the coal-powered miniature steam train operated in a Berkeley, California park for 20 years. It has been running in Folsom since 1970. The railway offers tours of its locomotive shop.

How to Get There   From Sacramento, take Highway 50 east to the Folsom exit. Turn left onto Folsom Street, which will become Liedersdorf. Turn right onto Riley, then left onto Natoma. The railway is next to the zoo, at 50 Natoma Street.

Hours   February through November: open Tuesday through Friday, 11:00 A.M. to 2:00 P.M., and Saturday, Sunday, and holidays, 11:00 A.M. to 5:00 P.M. December through January: open Saturday, Sunday, and holidays, 11:00 A.M. to 5:00 P.M.

Fares $1 per passenger.

Contact   Terry Gold, President, Golden Spike Enterprises, 121 Dunstable Way, Folsom, CA 95630. Telephone (916) 983-1873 (this is also a fax number—call before faxing) or (916) 955-1870.

FORT BRAGG

CALIFORNIA WESTERN RAILROAD

The California Western Railroad features the "Skunk" line— named after the early self powered railcars with gas engines, which ran along the former logging railroad line dating back to 1885. (Like skunks, a train's arrival could be detected by its smell long before it was actually seen.) Today's "Skunk Trains" offer historic diesel and steam logging trains, including *Old Number 45*, a 1924 Baldwin Steam locomotive, and motorcars.

The spectacular scenery includes redwood forests, 30 bridges and trestles, two mountain tunnels, a 1,700-foot summit, and rolling hills. The entire line runs 40 miles from the coast at Fort Bragg to Northspur and Willits on Highway 101. Visitors may opt for full, half-day, and one-way trips. Open observation cars are available to enhance viewing from the train, and refreshments are available. Five state parks are located within 15 miles of Fort Bragg.

How to Get There   From San Francisco, go north on Highway 101 to Willits, California. Go west on Highway 20 to Fort
Bragg. It's three-and-a-half hours north of San Francisco.

Hours   From early June to early September: train departs at
9:20 A.M. and 1:40 p.m. from Fort Bragg and at 9:00 A.M. and
1:25 P.M. from Willits.
    From early September to early June (off-season): train de-
parts at 9:20 A.M., 10:00 A.M., and 2:00 P.M. from Fort Bragg
and at 1:20 P.M. from Willits.

Fares   Half-day or one-way excursion: adults, $21; children
(ages 5 to 11), $10. Full-day excursion: adults, $26; children (ages 5 to 11), $12. Children under five years of age, not
occupying a seat, are free.

Contact   California Western Railroad, Highway 1 and Laurel
Street, P.O. Box 907, Fort Bragg, CA 95437. Telephone (707)
964-6371.

F R E M O N T

NILES CANYON RAILWAY

Established by the Pacific Locomotive Association, Inc. (PLA),
the Niles Canyon Railway is an operating railroad museum
concerned with preserving Pacific Coast railroad history. Niles
Canyon became an important railway center in 1869 when the
Central Pacific Railroad built a line through Niles Canyon en
route to Oakland. In 1984, after more than 80 years of railroading, the route was abandoned, and the PLA changed its
railway name from Castro Point Railway and Terminal Company (where it was then located) and established the Niles
Canyon Railway, relocating its equipment.

The PLA has a large and rich collection of locomotives and rolling stock. Ten steam locomotives (the oldest an 1882 Central Pacific and the largest a 1921 Southern Pacific), 14 passenger cars, internal combustion locomotives, rail motorcars, cabooses, and freight equipment make up its roster. Southern Pacific, Western Pacific, Santa Fe, Arizona Eastern, and El Paso & Southwestern Railroad passenger cars make up the collection.

How to Get There   Take Highway 84 west from I-680, or east from I-880 to Sunol. The station is at the corner of Main Street and Kilkare Road.

Hours   Open 10:00 A.M. to 4:00 P.M. on the first and third Sunday of each month.

Fares   Donations are requested.

Contact   Pacific Locomotive Association, Inc., P.O. Box 2247, Fremont, CA 94536-0247. Telephone (510) 862-9063.

GOLETA

SOUTH COAST RAILROAD MUSEUM AT GOLETA DEPOT

Visitors will enjoy the setting of the South Coast Railroad Museum at the Goleta Depot, a 1901 railroad station that was once part of the Southern Pacific line. The museum focuses on aspects of a rural railroad station and features hands-on exhibits, railroad memorabilia, displays, and photographs.

On Thursdays and Sundays, the museum theater runs free films and documentaries on travel and railroading. A gift shop and picnic area are on museum grounds.

Kids will enjoy visiting the telegraph office, where they can operate antique telegraph equipment and send a "Depot Gram" to family and friends. They can also take a ride on the *Goleta Short Line* (a miniature train that travels along one-third mile of track on the grounds of the Los Carneros County Park) and visit a 300-square-foot model railroad exhibit on display.

Special Events   Easter Bunny Express; Depot Day; Another Steaming Summer; Candy Cane Train.

How to Get There   From Santa Barbara, drive 7 miles north on U.S. 101 to the Los Carneros Road exit.

Hours   Open Wednesday through Sunday, 1:00 P.M. to 4:00 P.M. The train is closed on Thursdays from September through June.

Fares   Admission is free. Donations are requested.

Contact   Goleta Depot, 300 North Los Carneros Road, Goleta, CA 93117. Telephone (805) 964-3540.

KING CITY

MONTEREY COUNTY AGRICULTURAL AND RURAL LIFE MUSEUM

The Monterey County Agricultural and Rural Life Museum gives visitors a chance to learn about how Californian pioneers lived at the turn of the century. A school, farmhouse, blacksmith shop, and 20 barn exhibits help depict the development of Monterey County agriculture.

Train enthusiasts will particularly enjoy visiting the 1887 depot, situated in San Lorenzo Regional Park near King City. The depot is one of the few remaining stations built to serve the Southern Pacific Railroad and its expansion of Salinas Valley. Saved from demolition, the depot has been moved from its original location and restored to reflect the turn-of-the-century style. Original and reproduction furnishings are housed in and around the depot, including a caboose, baggage cars, and railroad communication equipment.

How to Get There   The museum is in San Lorenzo Regional Park, just outside King City. King City is 45 minutes from Salinas and 70 miles from San Luis Obispo. Take I-101, exit at Broadway, and follow the signs.

Hours   Historic buildings: from March through October, open Saturday and Sunday, 1:00 P.M. to 3:00 P.M.
    Main exhibit barn: Open daily year round, 10:00 A.M. to 4:00 P.M.

Fares   Park: $3. Museum admission is free.

Contact   Monterey County Agricultural and Rural Life Museum, San Lorenzo Regional Park, 1160 Broadway, King City, CA 93930. Telephone (408) 385-8020 or (408) 755-4913 (administrative office).

L O M I T A

LOMITA RAILROAD MUSEUM

The Lomita Railroad Museum, housed in a replica of the 19th-century Boston & Maine Greenwood Depot at Wakefield, Massachusetts, was commissioned in 1966 by Irene Lewis in honor of her husband. Dedicated to the steam age, the museum features a re-created passenger depot, with railroad memorabilia, a station agent's office, and outdoor displays of a 1902 Southern Pacific steam locomotive and a 1910 Union Pacific caboose (both open for exploration).

The museum annex includes a 1928 Union Oil tank car and a 1913 Southern Pacific wood boxcar. The museum annex park is available for picnicking, and a gift shop is on the site.

Future plans include expansion of the museum into a 32,000-square-foot site, with a 77-seat auditorium, conference rooms, library, and educational hands-on exhibits describing railroad history and operation.

How to Get There   From Los Angeles, take Highway 405 south to Highway 110 west. Exit at the Pacific Coast Highway offramp and turn right (west). Turn right on Narbonne and right on 250th Street.

Hours   Open year-round, Wednesday through Sunday, 10:00 A.M. to 5:00 P.M.

Fares   Adults, $1; children, $.50.

Contact   Lomita Railroad Museum, corner of Woodward and 250th Street, Lomita, CA 90717. Telephone (310) 326-6255.

LOS ANGELES

TRAVEL TOWN TRANSPORTATION MUSEUM

Travel Town Transportation Museum, created in 1952, is a combination museum and recreation center dedicated to preserving American railroad heritage, particularly that of Southern California. Owned and operated by the City of Los Angeles Recreation and Parks Department, Travel Town is located in Griffith Park. The facility is the creation of the late Charley Atkins, a former employee of the Recreation and Parks Department, and other rail enthusiasts, who wanted a facility that included railroad locomotives and other vintage transportation equipment for display. Their efforts led to generous donations of train and other transportation stock, including narrow gauge equipment that brought a steam train excursion ride to the park.

Today, the museum has a variety of train offerings: full-sized equipment running on the museum grounds; a miniature railroad ride chugging along a perimeter track; model railroad layouts in operation on weekends; and rides on a caboose or a tour of first-class passenger cars sponsored by preservation groups the first weekend of every month. In addition, the museum has a large collection of transportation displays, including steam and diesel locomotives, freight and passenger cars, interurbans, and motorcars. A special attraction is the *Little Nugget*, a former Union Pacific club-dormitory car built in 1937 by the Pullman Company.

Future plans include creation of a 2-mile standard-sized rail line to the Los Angeles Zoo and the Autry Museum; establishment of a research and exhibit facility; and construction of a new entrance and pavilion.

How to Get There   In Los Angeles, take I-5 north to freeway 134. Get off at Forest Lawn.

Hours   April through October: Monday through Friday, 10:00 A.M. to 5:00 P.M.; Saturday, Sunday, and holidays, 10:00 A.M. to 6:00 P.M. November through March: Monday through Friday, 10:00 A.M. to 4:00 P.M.; Saturday, Sunday, and holidays, 10:00 A.M. to 5:00 P.M.

Fares   Adults, $1.75; children (ages 12 and under), $1.25.

Contact   Travel Town, 5200 Zoo Drive, Los Angeles, CA 90027. Telephone (213) 662-5874.

LOS GATOS

BILLY JONES WILDCAT RAILROAD

Billy Jones Wildcat Railroad is named after a former Southern Pacific railroad employee who built a children's railroad for

Santa Clara Valley in the 1940s, using a locomotive from the
Venice Miniature Railway. After his death, a nonprofit group
purchased the line and moved it to Oak Meadow Park, where it
has operated since 1970.

Today, the railroad offers steam and diesel rides through
Oak Meadow and Vasona Parks and crosses a 40-foot, curved
wooden trestle. In 1980, a merry-go-round, the W. E. "Bill"
Mason Carousel, was added to the site.

How to Get There   From San Jose, take Highway 880 south.
Exit Highway 9 to Saratoga/Los Gatos. The Railroad is in Oak
Meadow Park, at Blossom Hill Road.

Hours   Open March through November: 11:00 A.M. to 3:00
P.M. (winter and spring); 10:30 A.M. to 4:30 P.M. (summer
and fall).

Fares   Train and carousel rides are $1 each (children under
two years old are free with paying adult).

Contact   Billy Jones Wildcat Railroad, Inc., P.O. Box 234, Los
Gatos, CA 95031-0234. Telephone (408) 395-RIDE.

O R L A N D

ORLAND-NEWVILLE &
PACIFIC RAILROAD

The Orland-Newville & Pacific Railroad is the centerpiece
of Heritage Trail, a historic complex operated by the Orland
Historical Society and Glenn County Fair, presenting the culture, architecture, and experience of early-20th-century life in
California.

The steam locomotive that operates on the railroad is a 5-
to-12 scale replica of an 1876 three-foot gauge locomotive,

ORLAND-NEWVILLE & PACIFIC RAILROAD

This steam locomotive is headed east through the Heritage Trail.

Sonoma, created by railroad enthusiast Frank Allen and volunteers. It began operating in 1993. Visitors ride along half a mile of track through landscape that includes farms, woods, orchards, and a tunnel. Heritage Trail also features a Southern Pacific Depot built in 1880; a Southern Pacific steam locomotive #2852; a caboose; a house museum; and other historic structures and artifacts.

The Heritage Trail is on the Glenn County Fairgrounds, and picnic areas are available at Dead Owl Station when the train is operating.

Future plans include landscaping and expanding the track.

Special Events   Easter Egg Hunt; Harvest Festival; Ghost Train.

How to Get There   Orland can be reached via I-5. Take the Highway 32 exit toward Chico and follow signs to Glenn County Fairgrounds.

Hours   Open 12:00 noon to 5:00 P.M. early April through mid-May (weekends only), Father's Day, July 4, and Labor Day weekend through October 13.

Fares   Admission is $1. (Fairground admission is additional during special events).

Contact   Orland-Newville & Pacific Railroad, P.O. Box 697, Orland, CA 95963. Telephone (916) 865-9747.

PERRIS

ORANGE EMPIRE RAILWAY MUSEUM

In 1975, the merger of two preservation groups (the Orange Empire Trolley Museum and the California Southern Railroad Museum) resulted in the creation of the Orange Empire Railway Museum, the largest railway museum in the western United States. The nonprofit museum tells the story of public transportation in Southern California and the West through displays of historical artifacts, exhibits, and railway rides and demonstrations.

Railway exhibits in the museum's rich collection date from 1870 to the 1960s. Several historic buildings house rail history exhibits, and trolley and locomotive yards contain early streetcars, electric railway cars, steam and diesel locomotives, narrow and standard gauge trains, and scale model railroad cars, trucks, and autos. In 1992, the museum added the Grizzly Flats Railroad, an 1880 three-foot narrow gauge railroad collection.

The museum offers narrated rides on city streetcars, suburban and interurban cars, and locomotive trains on weekends.

Refreshments, a book and gift shop, and a ticket office are located in Pinacate Station.

Special Events   Spring and Fall Rail Festivals.

How to Get There   The museum is 17 miles south of Riverside on I-215.

Hours   Grounds and gift shop: open daily, 9:00 A.M. to 5:00 P.M. Trolleys and trains: open Saturday, Sunday, and holidays; and weekdays around Christmas and Easter.

Fares   All-day pass: adults, $6; children (ages 6 to 11), $4; children under 6 are free of charge.

Contact   Orange Empire Railway Museum, 2201 South A Street, P.O. Box 548, Perris, CA 92572-0548. Telephone (909) 657-2605.

P O R T O L A

PORTOLA RAILROAD MUSEUM

One of the most exciting features of the Portola Railroad Museum is its user-friendly atmosphere. Situated in the Sierra Nevada Mountains and housed in what was once a diesel shop building, the museum is on 37 acres of land. This includes 2.5 miles of track, a collection of over 80 freight and passenger cars, and more than 30 diesel locomotives, making it one of the world's largest collections. The museum encourages visitors to tour the interior of all the cars—even to sit in the engineer's seat.

Train rides on cabooses and vista flats are given on weekends only. In addition to touring the cars, the museum offers train enthusiasts the "ultimate" experience: to rent and drive a diesel locomotive for one hour (with the supervision of a skilled engineer). Up to four visitors can operate it at a time. The museum is run by the Feather River Rail Society.

How to Get There   From Sacramento, take I-80 east to Truckee. Exit Quincy Road north (Road 89). From Quincy Road, take Highway 70 west to Portola. This goes right into Portola. The museum is at 700 Western Pacific Way.

From Reno (Nevada), take Highway 395 north and make a left onto Highway 70, straight into Portola.

Hours   Open Memorial Day through Labor Day, 10:00 A.M. to 5:00 P.M. Train rides are available from 10:00 A.M. to 4:00 P.M. on weekends.

Fares   Individuals, $2; families, $5.

Contact   Feather River Rail Society, P.O. Box 608, Portola, CA 96122. Telephone (916) 832-4131.

P O W A Y

POWAY MIDLAND RAILROAD

The Poway Midland Railroad is located in Old Poway Park, five acres of land developed to replicate a historic village, circa 1900. The village, newly opened in 1993, was first envisioned by a retired army colonel interested in revitalizing Poway. The park offers much that will appeal to train enthusiasts: a 1907 Baldwin steam engine, one-third mile of railway track, four passenger-carrying ore cars, a replica narrow gauge passenger coach, an 1894 trolley, and a large train barn that houses railroad equipment. In addition, the park provides a special program for young children on trains and train safety. Train rides are offered through the Heritage Museum and Nelson House.

Other park offerings include artist demonstrations of crafts and trades of the period, a reenactment of local historical events, the Heritage Museum, a farmers' market, and other exhibits that reflect turn-of-the-century American life.

How to Get There From San Diego, go north on I-15 to Poway Road. Go east on Poway Road to Midland Road. Turn left onto Midland to Old Poway Park.

Hours Park: open Saturday, 10:00 A.M. to 4:00 P.M.; Sunday, 11:00 A.M. to 2:00 P.M. (No operation on second Sundays of the month or on holidays.)

Fares Ore cars: adults, $1; children, $.50. Locomotive: adults, $2; children, $.50.

Contact Old Poway Park, 14134 Midland Road, P.O. Box 789, Poway, CA 92064-0789; telephone (619) 679-4313 or 679-4342. Midland Railroad Volunteers, telephone (619) 679-1252.

REDWOOD CITY

GOLDEN GATE RAILROAD MUSEUM

Dedicated to preserving San Francisco-area railroad history, the Golden Gate Railroad Museum has successfully restored a high-speed train that travels up to 100 miles an hour. Locomotive #2472 was built in 1921 and served as part of the Southern Pacific Railroad until 1956. A 16-year volunteer restoration effort, "Project 2472" led to the train's revival and to the creation of the museum. The museum offers excursion rides on locomotive #2472 three or four times a year.

For families of would-be railroad engineers, the museum has a special rent-a-locomotive program for learning about and operating a real locomotive. Adults and children alike have the opportunity to sit in the engineer's seat, operate the controls, and roll down the track right in the museum yard, in either a steam or diesel locomotive.

NOTE: Contacting the GGRM office prior to arrival is required to receive entry pass.

Special Events   Santa Train, Garlic Festival, Hunter's Point Steam-up.

How to Get There   From San Francisco, take Highway 101 south and exit Third Street east. Then turn right (south) onto Evans. Stay on this road for about a mile; the museum is located in the Hunter's Point naval yard.

Hours   Open weekends, 9:00 A.M. to 5:00 P.M. Call ahead for weekday visits.

Fares   Admission is free (for security, valid driver's license, current vehicle registration, and proof of insurance required at time of arrival at the naval yard).

Contact   Golden Gate Railroad Museum, P.O. Box 3315, Redwood City, CA 94064. Telephone (415) 363-2472.

SACRAMENTO

CALIFORNIA STATE RAILROAD MUSEUM

The California State Railroad Museum reflects the state's rich railroad history through two complexes, one in Old Sacramento and the other in Jamestown. From California's 19th-century involvement in railroading and the completion of the first transcontinental railroad up to the present day, the museum showcases the important role of the railroad in the development of California through permanent exhibits, displays, and special events.

The museum is composed of six buildings: a combination of reconstructed and new structures, including a wood passenger station, a freight depot, and a roundhouse. On its more than 225,000 square feet of space—divided between Old Sacramento and **Railtown 1897 State Historic Park** in Jamestown—the museum features interpretive exhibits and meticulously restored cars and locomotives.

The Jamestown site displays 47 locomotives and cars; 105 are housed in Old Sacramento. Three featured trains at the museum are the Union Pacific #4466, an operating coal-burning steam locomotive built in 1920; Canadian National Railways' *St. Hyacinthe*, a 1929 open-section sleeping car; and the museum's newest permanent exhibit, the Atchison, Topeka & Santa Fe's *Cochiti*, an elegantly appointed dining car built in 1937.

Train rides are offered at both sites. The Sacramento Southern Railroad reflects 1920s-style train travel; the Sierra Railway at Railtown 1897 provides five-mile countryside trips between Jamestown and Hatler's Quarry.

The museum has a souvenir shop and is wheelchair accessible. Future plans include construction of the Museum of Railroad Technology.

How to Get There   The museum is located at Second and I Streets in historic Old Sacramento. From I-5, exit J Street and drive east. Turn left onto Fifth Street, then left onto I Street, which goes straight into Old Sacramento.

Hours   Museum: open daily, except Thanksgiving, Christmas, and New Year's Day, 10:00 A.M. to 5:00 P.M. (last admission at 4:30 P.M.).

Sacramento Southern Railroad: departures on the hour, Saturday and Sunday. April through September: 10:00 A.M. to 5:00 P.M.; October through December: 12:00 noon to 3:00 P.M.

Sierra Railway: departures on the hour, weekends only year-round: 11:00 A.M. to 3:00 P.M.

Fares Museum and train rides (separate admission): adults, $5; children (ages 6 to 12), $2; children under 6 are free of charge.

Contact California State Railroad Museum, 111 I Street, Old Sacramento, CA 95814. Telephone (800) 417-7245 or (916) 324-4950 (Old Sacramento) or (209) 984-3953 (Railtown 1897 in Jamestown).

SAN DIEGO

SAN DIEGO MODEL RAILROAD MUSEUM

This nonprofit museum opened its doors to the public in 1980 and now has one of the largest permanent indoor model railroad exhibits in the U.S. The more than 24,000 square feet of space is used to display California railroads through four permanent scale models, visiting exhibits, and two operating exhibits in the museum's "Toy Train Gallery." Volunteer model railroad clubs create each exhibit, which range from N to O gauge size. The museum has a gift shop.

How to Get There In San Diego, take I-5 to Pershing Drive exit. At Florida Drive, make a left, and another left at Zoo Place. Look for the San Diego Zoo sign at the end of the street. At Park Boulevard, make a left and go south. Make a right on Space Theatre Way, and park near the Ruben H. Fleet parking lot. The museum is west of the lot.

Hours Tuesday through Friday, 11:00 A.M. to 4:00 P.M.; Saturdays and Sundays, 11:00 A.M. to 5:00 P.M.

Fares   Adults, $3; children (under 15 years old), free of charge.

Contact   San Diego Model Railroad Museum, 1649 El Prado, San Diego, CA 92101-1621. Telephone (619) 696-0199.

SAN DIEGO RAILROAD MUSEUM

Vintage depots, train rides, and an extensive collection of railroad rolling stock and artifacts all preserve the history and educate the public about the rich railroad heritage of San Diego County. An important part of that history is the San Diego & Arizona Railway, completed in 1919, which initiated transcontinental links with the East.

Today, the San Diego Railroad Museum has three facilities. The **Santa Fe Depot,** built in 1914, is a beautifully refurbished station on the National Register of Historic Places that currently serves rail and bus lines and contains a research library and administrative office. In the future, it will become a downtown display center for the museum. **La Mesa Depot,** also a historic landmark, was built in 1894 and contains a freight train display and artifacts. The Train Operations and Visitor's Center at **Campo Depot** includes a 1916 station situated on the former San Diego & Arizona Railway line, a restoration facility, and car barn containing 90 pieces of rolling stock. This collection includes steam and diesel-electric locomotives, passenger and freight trains, cabooses, trolleys, and other work equipment.

A 16-mile round-trip (1 hour, 30 minutes) train ride from Campo to Miller Creek is offered twice daily on weekends and select holidays. A steam ride on locomotive #2353, a Southern Pacific Railroad engine built in 1912, was inaugurated in 1995. The rides are followed by a guided walking tour of the museum, including a look at ongoing restoration work and historical background on the equipment and the area. Day-long rail trips are also available.

The museum operates a gift shop in the Campo Depot and sells souvenirs and light refreshments. Visitors may bring along a lunch for the train ride or use picnic tables.

Future plans include a new building on the Campo site, a display museum in Santa Fe Depot (expected 1997), and expanded train operations.

How to Get There   From San Diego, take Highway 8 east to Buckman Springs Road. Follow it south for 11 miles, where it will dead-end into Highway 94. Bear right, go around the meadow, and turn left after crossing the railroad tracks. Follow the large signs for the museum.

Hours   Train Operations and Visitor's Center at Campo Depot: Saturday, Sunday, and select holidays, 9:00 A.M. to 5:00 P.M.

La Mesa Depot: Saturday and Sunday, 1:00 P.M. to 4:00 P.M.

Santa Fe Depot: weekdays, 9:00 A.M. to 5:00 P.M. (administrative office); Saturdays (and by appointment), 10:00 A.M. to 4:00 P.M. (research library).

Fares   Adults, $10; children (ages 6 to 12), $3. Discounts for seniors and active military personnel.

Contact   San Diego Railroad Museum, Santa Fe Depot, 1050 Kettner Boulevard, San Diego, CA 92101. Telephone (619) 595-3030 or (619) 697-7762 or (619) 478-9937 (Campo Depot on Saturday and Sunday).

SAN FRANCISCO

SAN FRANCISCO CABLE CAR MUSEUM

Cable car rides in San Francisco have been operating since 1883, when Andrew Hallidie created the first cable car. The

San Francisco Cable Car Museum, operated by the nonprofit group Friends of the Cable Car Museum, Inc., is a tribute to the cable car's rich history. The museum, housed in the Cable Car Barn and Powerhouse, was newly renovated and restructured in 1984, and all cable car track and machinery were completely rebuilt.

From the museum gallery and the Sheave Room, visitors can learn how cable rope, wheels, channels, and gears all combine to pull the cars along the line. The cable operation is identical to the 19th century operation, with the exception of its power source. Instead of steam, the Powerhouse uses electric motors.

Other features of the museum are a video presentation and information stations; a photo exhibit of the Barn renovation effort; and cable car exhibits, including the first cable car from 1873 and a Sutter Street dummy and trailer. The museum also has a gift shop.

The cable car system operates 39 vehicles on three lines: Powell-Mason; Powell-Hyde, and California Street. Rides are offered daily and cost $2 one way; $6 for a day pass; $10 for a three-day pass; $15 for a one-week pass.

How to Get There   The best way to the museum is by cable car itself. Take the Powell-Mason line toward Fisherman's Wharf and exit at Mason and Jackson. Walk one block to the left; the museum is at the corner of Mason and Washington.

Hours   Open daily, except Thanksgiving, Christmas, and New Year's Day. April through September: 10:00 A.M. to 6:00 P.M.; October through March: 10:00 A.M. to 5:00 P.M.

Fares   Admission is free.

Contact   San Francisco Cable Car Museum, Cable Car Barn and Powerhouse, 1201 Mason Street, San Francisco, CA 94108. Telephone (415) 474-1887.

SAN JOSE

SAN JOSE HISTORICAL MUSEUM AND KELLEY PARK TROLLEY

A trip to San Jose means a chance to take the Kelley Park Trolley. Thanks to the contributions of volunteers, six trolleys are currently under restoration. Visitors can tour the Trolley Restoration Barn along with sites on 25 acres of land in Kelley Park. The park is part of the San Jose Historical Museum complex.

How to Get There   From downtown San Jose, take Highway 280 south and exit 10th Street. Turn right onto 10th, then left onto Keyes Street and right onto Senter Road. Kelley Park is on the left side.

Hours   Open Saturday and Sunday, 12:00 noon to 4:00 P.M.

Fares   Adults, $4; seniors, $3; children, $2.

Contact   Kelley Park Trolley, 1600 Senter Road, San Jose, CA 95112. Telephone (408) 293-2276 (Trolley Restoration Barn) or (408) 287-2290 (museum).

SONOMA

TRAIN TOWN

Illusion is the key at Train Town, a miniature railroad featuring a 20-minute ride through the tiny, make-believe town of Lakeview. The 10-acre site was founded in 1958 by model railroad enthusiast Stanley Frank, and features an elaborate model steam train that takes passengers in open-air cars along a 1.25-mile, 15-inch-wide track. The landscape includes small-scale forests, hills, a 15-foot waterfall, two tunnels, five bridges, and more than two acres of lakes and streams. The train makes a stop in the "town" where visitors can touch and feed real farm animals and get a closer look at town buildings, including a hotel, a newspaper office, and a fire department.

The entrance to Train Town features full-sized cabooses for exploring, a station, and clock tower. Visitors can purchase refreshments and souvenirs. A wheelchair accessible railroad car is available.

How to Get There Train Town is in Sonoma, 45 minutes north of San Francisco and 1 mile south of Sonoma Plaza on Broadway (Highway 12).

Hours October through May: open Friday, Saturday, Sunday, and holidays, 10:30 A.M. to 5:00 P.M.; June through September: open daily, 10:30 A.M. to 5:00 P.M.

Fares Adults, $3.50; seniors, $2.50; children, $2.50.

Contact Train Town, P.O. Box 656, Sonoma, CA 95476. Telephone (707) 938-3912.

WOODLAND

YOLO SHORTLINE RAILROAD COMPANY

The Yolo Shortline Railroad Company takes passengers on a scenic journey along track built in 1912 by the Sacramento and Woodland Railroad. The original line first carried trolleys, then locomotives, and eventually became a Union Pacific line. A portion of the original line was purchased by Yolo Shortline in 1992, and today the railroad provides both freight and passenger service.

The Woodland to West Sacramento trip (2 hours, 20 minutes round-trip) takes passengers through lush fields and farmland and along the Sacramento River, which includes a 20-foot-high, 8,000-foot-long trestle crossing and view of the beautiful Sacramento Valley. A second, three-hour round-trip excursion is offered monthly between West Sacramento and Clarksburg, a rustic farm community. This trip includes live music and a staged "train robbery." Refreshments are sold on the train, and visitors are welcome to bring along a picnic lunch.

Tourist excursions use both steam and diesel locomotives. The steam train, #1233, was built in 1918; the diesels were built in the 1940s and 1950s. Passenger cars include open observation cars and stainless-steel coaches. Cabooses are also available.

NOTE: The train is not designed for handicapped access. Contact the line for assistance. Baby strollers and infant seats are not allowed on the train.

Special Events   Saturday Clarksburg Special; Yolo County Fair; "Stroll Through History"; West Sacramento Port Fest.

How to Get There   Woodland is 20 minutes from Sacramento. From either Interstate 5 (Sacramento) or Highway 113 (Davis), take the Main Street exit. Turn left onto Main Street toward downtown Woodland. Follow signs to the passenger loading area at Thomas and East Main Street, across from Cracchiolo's Market.

Hours   Open mid-May through mid-October on Saturday, Sunday, and holidays. Train departs at 10:00 A.M. and 2:00 P.M. (from Woodland) and at 1:30 P.M. (from West Sacramento).

Fares   Diesel: adults, $11; seniors (age 65 and over with current AARP card), $9; children (ages 4 to 14), $6.

Steam: adults, $12; seniors (age 65 and over with current AARP card), $10; children (ages 4 to 14), $8.

Clarksburg Special: $17.50 per person.

Children under three years of age are free of charge on all trains.

Contact   Yolo Shortline Railroad, P.O. Box 724, West Sacramento, CA 95691; telephone (916) 372-9777. Or, 1965 East Main Street, Woodland, CA 95776; telephone (916) 666-9646; fax (916) 666-2919.

Y R E K A

YREKA WESTERN RAILROAD COMPANY

The Yreka Western Railroad Company offers both freight and tourist train service on a short line track between Yreka and Montague first operated in 1889. The tourist excursion is a

YREKA WESTERN RAILROAD COMPANY

The *Blue Goose Excursion Train* steams along the track between Yreka and Montague.

three-hour round-trip journey on the *Blue Goose Excursion Train*. Pulled by a 1915 Baldwin Steam Engine, the train takes passengers through the Shasta Valley, past sawmills, wood processing plants, and cattle ranches, and across the Shasta River—in view of majestic Mount Shasta, more than 14,000 feet high.

A one-hour layover in Montague gives visitors a chance to visit the 1887 depot museum, or to have lunch and tour the town. A 1,000-square-foot model railroad display can also be seen before or after the excursion ride.

How to Get There   Yreka is 35 miles south of Ashland, Oregon, and 35 miles north of Mount Shasta. From I-5 (north or south) take the central Yreka exit. The depot is visible from the exit, at 300 East Miner Street.

Hours   Opens 10:00 A.M. Spring: open weekends Memorial Day weekend to first weekend in June; summer: open mid-June through early September (Wednesday through Sunday); fall: open weekends through October.

Fares   Adults, $9; children (ages 3 to 12), $4.50.

Contact   Yreka Western Railroad Company, P.O. Box 660, Yreka, CA 96097. Telephone (916) 842-4146.

COLORADO

CUMBRES & TOLTEC
SCENIC RAILROAD

The Cumbres & Toltec Scenic Railroad takes passengers on a spectacular 64-mile Rocky Mountain journey through valleys, tunnels, and gorges and across trestles between Chama, New Mexico, and Antonito, Colorado. One of the longest and highest narrow gauge steam lines in the U.S., the railroad is a Registered National Historic Site. It began construction in 1880 and once served mining areas of the San Juan Mountains.

An open sightseeing car and coaches with operable windows provide passenger seating. The day-long trip departs from one of two depot locations, and passengers have several options for round-trip and one-way excursions. Trips provide a midday stop in Osier for lunch. Restrooms, snacks, and souvenirs are available aboard the train.

NOTE: Passengers are urged to dress warmly since the train is unheated. Special cars for the disabled are available, but requests must be made in advance.

How to Get There From Alamosa, take I-285 south to Highway 17. Drive west on Highway 17 for 28 miles to Antonito. To Chama, continue on Highway 17 west past Antonito and look for the station along the highway.

Hours Open Memorial Day weekend through mid-October. Departures: 8:00 A.M., 9:15 A.M., 10:00 A.M., and 10:30 A.M. Returns: 4:30 P.M., 5:00 P.M., 5:30 P.M., and 6:35 P.M. Both departures and returns depend on city and type of trip.

Fares Adults, $32 to $50; children (ages 11 and under), $16 to $26.

Contact Cumbres & Toltec Scenic Railroad, Antonito Depot, P.O. Box 668, Antonito, CO 81120; telephone (719) 376-5483. Or, Cumbres & Toltec Scenic Railroad, Chama Depot, P.O. Box 789, Chama, NM 87520; telephone (505) 756-2151.

C A N O N   C I T Y

ROYAL GORGE SCENIC RAILWAY

The Royal Gorge Scenic Railway offers a 30-minute ride with a panoramic view of the scenic Royal Gorge Canyon and a suspension bridge. The line was created by a rail enthusiast in the late 1950s and became a companion site to Buckskin Joe, a rebuilt 19th century Colorado mining town and tourist attraction. On the premises is a steam train and car museum with precision-scale, model turn-of-the-century trains.

How to Get There Canon City is one hour southwest of Colorado Springs via Highway 115 south. Exit Highway 50 west; drive through Canon City and continue about 8 miles. Take the Royal Gorge exit to the railway.

Hours   Open March through November, 8:00 A.M. to 8:00 P.M. Hours are shorter during the off-season.

Fares   Adults, $5.50; children (ages 4 to 11), $4.50; children under four years of age are free of charge. Museum admission is $2.

Contact   Royal Gorge Scenic Railway, P.O. Box 1387-RRB, Canon City, CO 81215. Telephone (719) 275-5485 or (719) 275-5149.

DENVER

FORNEY HISTORIC TRANSPORTATION MUSEUM

The Forney Historic Transportation Museum offers visitors a chance to see the largest steam locomotive in the world, *Big Boy #4005*, model train displays, and elegant antique railroad coaches, trolleys, and cabooses. The museum also provides examples of other vehicles, including bicycles, motorcycles, wagons, carriages, cars, and planes. Among the exhibits are vehicles operated by famous figures in history. The museum serves refreshments.

How to Get There   The museum is four blocks west of downtown Denver. Take Interstate 25 north or south to exit 211. Go east on Water Street. It is half a mile to Platte Street.

Hours   May through September: Monday to Saturday, 9:00 A.M. to 5:00 P.M.; Sunday, 11:00 A.M. to 5:00 P.M. October through April: Monday to Saturday, 10:00 A.M. to 5:00 P.M., Sunday, 11:00 A.M. to 5:00 P.M. Open holidays, except Thanksgiving, Christmas, and New Year's Day.

Fares   Adults, $4; youth (ages 12 to 18), $2; children (ages 5 to 11), $1; children under five years of age are free of charge.

Contact   Forney Historic Transportation Museum, 1416 Platte Street, Denver, CO 80202. Telephone (303) 433-3643.

THE SKI TRAIN

Skiers and nonskiers alike can enjoy the scenic trip on the quarter-mile-long Ski Train, which has been in operation since 1940. Sponsored by the *Denver Post* newspaper, the two-hour excursion starts at the downtown Union Station and travels past beautiful rock formations, called the Flatirons, and on through South Boulder Canyon toward the Continental Divide.

For skiers, the train stop is convenient to ski lifts; nonskiers can take free shuttles to the ski resort of Winter Park and the town of Fraser. There they can enjoy mountain sightseeing trips in heated snow cats, or sledding at Fraser Valley Tubing Hill.

NOTE: Advance purchase is recommended. Lift tickets are available at a discount rate on the train.

How to Get There   In Denver, take I-25 to the 20th Street exit (212c). Turn toward Coors Field downtown. Turn right on Wazee Street, and take another right on 19th Street. Make a left on Wynkoop Street to Union Station. The Ski Train is at 17th and Wynkoop.

Hours   Open mid-December to March 31, Saturday and Sunday; additional holiday trips are available in December. Train departs Denver at 7:15 A.M. and arrives back in Denver at 6:15 P.M.

Fares   Coach class: $35. Club class: $50.

Contact   The Ski Train is managed by Ansco Investment Company, 555 17th Street, Suite 2400, Denver, CO 80202. Telephone (303) 296-I-SKI.

D U R A N G O

DURANGO & SILVERTON NARROW GAUGE RAILROAD

The Durango & Silverton Narrow Gauge Railroad, a Registered National Historical Landmark, operates on a line built in 1882 for the Denver & Rio Grande Railway. The line was designed to transport silver, gold, and other minerals from the San Juan Mountains. Today's railroad travels on a 45-mile stretch of that track, between Durango and Silverton.

Coal-fired steam locomotives from the 1920s haul vintage coaches and open gondola cars. Traveling north, the trains stop twice to replenish their water supply, and again on the return trip.

In addition to summer trips to Silverton (90 miles round-trip), the line also offers Winter Train journeys (52 miles round-trip) that travel to Cascade Canyon, a wilderness area. The railroad also operates an 1880 parlor car, an 1886 caboose, and other historic private cars.

Some of the most spectacular scenery in the world awaits visitors along the route. A favorite area for fishing, hiking, backpacking and skiing, the San Juan National Forest contains beautiful vistas and wildlife.

Durango rail yard tours are also available from May through October for an additional charge. Souvenirs and light refreshments are available at the Durango Depot and on all trains. Handicapped-equipped restroom and a seating area are available.

NOTE: A dark-colored warm sweater or jacket is recommended to accommodate the changing weather and the cinders from the burning coal. A picnic lunch is recommended for the trip.

How to Get There   From Denver, take I-25 south to Walsenberg. Exit U.S. 160 west to Durango and exit Highway 550. Turn right on College Drive, then right on Main Street. The entrance is two blocks down.

Hours   Durango Depot: January to April, 8:00 A.M. to 5:00 P.M.; late April to June, 7:00 A.M. to 7:00 P.M.
     Silverton Depot: mid-May to September, 7:45 A.M. to 4:25 P.M. Winter Train: late November 27 to late April, 10:00 A.M. to 3:00 P.M.

Fares   Round-trip: adults (ages 12 and older), $42.70; children (ages 5 to 11), $21.45; parlor car, $73.40; caboose, $67.85. Children under five years of age not occupying a seat are free of charge.

Contact   Durango & Silverton Narrow Gauge Railroad, 479 Main Avenue, Durango, CO 81301. Telephone (970) 247-2733.

F O R T   C O L L I N S

FORT COLLINS MUNICIPAL RAILWAY

The Fort Collins Municipal Railway is an authentic restored city street car operation, the only one of its kind in the western United States. The railway originally encompassed a 7-mile system and ran six cars in Fort Collins between 1919 and 1951. Today, visitors can take a ride on the restored Birney Car 21 for a trip along 1.5 miles of track along Mountain Avenue, a historic area of Fort Collins.

How to Get There   From Denver, take I-25 north for 65 miles. Take the Colorado 14 intersection west about 4 miles to reach Fort Collins.

Hours   May through September: open weekends and holidays (weather permitting), 12:00 noon to 5:00 P.M.

Fares   Adults, $1; children (ages 12 and under), $.50.

Contact   Fort Collins Municipal Railway Society, P.O. Box 635, Fort Collins, CO 80522. Telephone (970) 224-5372.

GEORGETOWN

GEORGETOWN LOOP RAILROAD

The original Georgetown Loop Railroad, first built in the late 1800s, serviced the mining camps between Denver and Silver Plume, carrying both freight and passenger cars. Though only 2 miles separates the two towns, the elevation is more than 600 feet. To ease the railroad's climb, the Georgetown Loop Railroad was created. Considered an engineering marvel in its day, the line made a spiral, or "loop," crossing over itself to reach its destination. The looping was helped by the construction of the Devil's Gate, a 300-foot-long, 100-foot-high iron bridge. The track and bridges were sold for scrap in 1939.

Through the efforts of the Colorado Historical Society and the new Georgetown Loop Railroad, the line and bridges were reconstructed; in 1975, the railroad reopened. Steam locomotives pull open-air coaches past old mining areas and past spectacular mountain scenery on a journey that lasts 1 hour and 10 minutes. The railroad also offers an additional tour (1 hour, 20 minutes) of the Lebanon Silver Mine and combination mountain bike tours.

Two boarding areas are available: at the Silver Plume Depot, a fully restored 1884 station, and at Devil's Gate. The Old Georgetown Station is the headquarters for the railroad and houses a ticket office, cafe, gift shop, and information center. The train is handicapped accessible.

Note: The mine walking tour temperature is 44°F, so a jacket or sweater and comfortable shoes are recommended.

How to Get There From Denver, take I-70 west and exit #228. Turn left off the exit and follow signs to the station.

Hours Memorial Day weekend to the beginning of October: open daily.

Silver Plume: departures at 9:20 A.M., 10:40 A.M., 12 noon, 1:20 P.M., 2:40 P.M., and 4:00 P.M. Devil's Gate: departures at 10:00 A.M., 11:20 A.M., 12:40 P.M., 2:00 P.M., and 3:20 P.M.

Fall schedule (September): limited departures on weekdays; full schedule on weekends.

Lebanon Mine Tour: offered from Memorial Day weekend to the Sunday before Labor Day.

Fares Railroad: adults, $10.95; children (ages 4 to 15), $6.50. Mine tour: adults, $4; children (ages 4 to 15), $2. Prices are expected to rise in 1996.

Contact Georgetown Loop Railroad, Inc., c/o Old Georgetown Station, P.O. Box 217, 1106 Rose Street, Georgetown, CO 80444. Telephone (800) 691-4FUN or (303) 569-2403 (local) or (303) 670-1686 (Denver); fax (303) 569-2894.

G O L D E N

COLORADO RAILROAD MUSEUM

The Colorado Railroad Museum presents a rich history of the railroads and the settlement of Colorado. Gold and silver mines spurred the development of both narrow and standard gauge rail lines—at their peak, over 2,000 miles of track had been laid on the mountainous terrain. Visitors to the museum, operated by the Colorado Railroad Historical Foundation, can view over 50 narrow and standard gauge trains and equipment outside on 12 acres of land. Inside the museum building, an 1880 depot replica displays more than 50,000 historic materials. The Denver HO Model Railroad Club also has a 45-feet-by-20-feet railroad model layout of Colorado railroads housed in the basement of the museum.

One of the most interesting and popular attractions at the museum is Denver & Rio Grande Western #346, the oldest operating steam locomotive in Colorado. Built in 1881, the train has been restored and on special occasions runs at 20-minute intervals over a one-third mile line on the museum grounds. The *Galloping Goose*, a 1930s rail motorcar, is also operated at these times.

How to Get There   From Denver, take I-70 west to exit 265. From the east, take exit 266 to West 44th Avenue.

Hours   Open daily, except Thanksgiving and Christmas, 9:00 A.M. to 5:00 P.M. (open until 6 P.M. in June, July, and August).

Fares   A nominal admission is charged. A special family rate is also available.

Contact   Colorado Railroad Museum, P.O. Box 10, 17155 West 44th Avenue, Golden, CO 80402-0010. Telephone (800) 365-6263 or (303) 279-4591; fax (303) 279-4229.

L E A D V I L L E

LEADVILLE, COLORADO & SOUTHERN RAILROAD

To gain greater access to the rich mineral deposits in the mountains of Colorado, the former Denver, South Park & Pacific Railroad (DSP & P) created the "High Line Extension," a route between Denver and Leadville in 1884. Today, the Leadville, Colorado & Southern Railroad takes passengers along a 14-mile portion of the original line between Leadville and Climax.

The railroad departs from the Leadville, Colorado & Southern Railroad Depot, built in 1893 for Union Pacific (which at the time owned the DSP & P), for a two-and-a-half-hour diesel journey. Beginning at an elevation of 10,200 feet (Leadville was nicknamed "Cloud City"), the railroad climbs more than 900 feet near the summit at Fremont Pass. Spectacular views include evergreen forests, wildlife, and the mountain peaks of the Continental Divide.

The railroad is wheelchair accessible.

NOTE: Sweaters and jackets are recommended during all months, due to altitude changes.

How to Get There   From Denver, take I-70 west to Highway 91 south. It takes you right into Leadville.

Hours   Late May to mid-June: departure at 1:00 P.M.; mid-June to Labor Day: departures at 10:00 A.M. and 2:00 P.M.; the rest of September: departure at 1:00 P.M.

Fares   Adults, $22.50; children, $12.50.

Contact   Leadville, Colorado & Southern Railroad, 326 East 7th Street, Leadville, CO 80461. Telephone (719) 486-3936.

L I M O N

LIMON HERITAGE MUSEUM AND RAILROAD PARK

In its heyday, Limon was a busy railroad town, with seven passenger trains running daily. The museum and park help capture the town's pioneer history in a museum complex featuring the 1920s-era Limon Depot, which once served the Rock Island and Union Pacific Railroads. The museum and park feature a lunch counter diner, a Union Pacific caboose, an 1890 boxcar full of western artifacts, antique farm machinery, an operating N-scale model of Limon rail yards, and other related exhibits. The railroad park is located two blocks east and four blocks west of the museum and has train-themed playground equipment and family picnic areas.

How to Get There   From Denver take I-70 east to exit 361. The museum is downtown, housed in an old depot behind town hall.

Hours   June through August: open Monday to Saturday, 1:00 P.M. to 8:00 P.M.

Fares   Admission is free.

Contact   Limon Heritage Museum and Railroad Park, Box 341, Limon, CO 80828. Telephone (719) 775-2373.

M A N I T O U   S P R I N G S

MANITOU AND PIKE'S PEAK RAILWAY COMPANY

For mountain beauty and scenery, the Manitou and Pike's Peak Railway Company train ride is hard to beat. In fact, its exquisite beauty was the inspiration for the song "America the Beautiful." Unlike standard trains, the railway offers diesel-driven cog trains that operate with gears that hook like teeth underneath the engine. This helps pull the trains up tracks in high elevations in a way that conventional trains cannot.

In enclosed rail cars, visitors travel 8 miles per hour on a 9-mile track, climbing nearly 8,000 feet. The varied landscape includes cascading streams, boulders, and towering snow-capped mountains. The trip takes 3 hours and 10 minutes. This includes a 35-minute stop at the Summit House, which houses a curio shop, lobby, restrooms, information desk, and a refreshment booth.

Special Events   An original steam locomotive and coach are operated on special occasions.

How to Get There   From Colorado Springs, take highway 24 west about 7 miles to the Manitou Springs business exit. Turn right off the exit, drive 2 miles, and turn left on Roxton Avenue. The station is a mile down on the left.

Hours   From late April to October: open daily; train departs every 80 minutes, 8:00 A.M. to 5:20 P.M. (schedule varies from mid-June to August).

Fares   Adults, $22; children (ages 5 to 11), $10; children under five years of age are free of charge (if held in lap).

Contact   Manitou and Pike's Peak Railway Company, P.O. Box 351, Manitou Springs, CO 80829. Telephone (719) 685-5401; fax (719) 685-9033.

M O R R I S O N

TINY TOWN

A kid-sized village and railway in a scenic mountain canyon make Tiny Town the perfect place to visit with children. Three steam locomotives with open-air cars currently operate along a 1-mile loop that takes rides around the town and up a canyon. Tiny Town is about one-sixth the size of a life-sized town. Visitors will find 100 kid-sized buildings, hand-crafted by Colorado volunteers, including everything from a fire station and toy store to a movie theater. Some structures even have crawl spaces that can be explored by the youngest visitors.

Built in 1915 by a businessman for his daughter, Tiny Town was most recently restored in 1988.

How to Get There   Tiny Town is 30 minutes southwest of Denver off I-285 south. Exit South Turkey Creek Road and turn right to get to the park.

Hours   Memorial Day weekend to Labor Day: open daily, 10:00 A.M. to 5:00 P.M. In May, September, and October: open weekends, 10:00 A.M. to 5:00 P.M.

Fares   Admission: adults, $2.50; children (ages 3 to 12), $1.50. Children under three years of age are free of charge.

Train rides: $1.

Contact   Tiny Town, 6249 South Turkey Creek Road, Morrison, CO 80465. Telephone (303) 697-6829.

CONNECTICUT

EAST HAVEN

SHORE LINE TROLLEY MUSEUM

The Shore Line Trolley Museum, operated by the nonprofit Branford Electric Railway Association, is dedicated to the preservation of the trolley era. The museum collection exceeds 90 streetcars and includes a rich mixture. Among them are horsecars, cable cars, streamliners, interurbans, rapid transit cars, subway cars, and trackless trolleys. Photographs, books, and memorabilia on electric railways housed in the Sprague Building are also part of the museum's exhibits.

Visitors may also take a 3-mile round-trip trolley ride. The journey includes crossing a trestle, quarry, woods, and meadow. The area's trolley operation has been in regular service since 1900, and trolley property is on the National Register of Historic Places.

Special Events: Santa Days (ask for special events flyer).

How to Get There From Bridgeport, take I-95 to exit 51. At the second traffic light, make a right. Go approximately two blocks to reach East Haven Green (at River Street). Make a left onto River Street to number 17.

Hours   The museum opens at 11:00 A.M., with the last trolley at 5:00 P.M. Trolleys leave approximately every 30 minutes.
   Memorial Day through Labor Day: open daily. All other months, open some weekends and holidays; call ahead for schedule.

Fares   Adults, $5; seniors, $4; children (ages 2 to 11), $2; children under two years of age are free of charge.

Contact   Branford Electric Railway Association, 17 River Street, East Haven, CT 06512. Telephone (203) 467-6927.

EAST WINDSOR

CONNECTICUT TROLLEY MUSEUM

Year-round trolley rides through beautiful New England countryside are offered to visitors to the Connecticut Trolley Museum. During the 3-mile excursion on antique open-air or closed cars (depending on the season), a museum volunteer provides an informative narration describing the trolley era in New England.
   Trolley fans will appreciate the unlimited trolley rides, available for the cost of a single daily fare. The museum also offers walking tours of the trolley barn, restoration shop, visitor's center (featuring a stationary locomotive), gift shop, snack bar (open seasonally), and trolley artifacts.

Special Events   Halloween Festival; Little Pumpkin Patch (for children ages 3 to 12); Winterfest.

How to Get There   The museum is 10 minutes from Springfield, Massachusetts or Hartford, Connecticut. From I-91 exit

45 east. The museum is on the right, about three-quarters of a mile off the exit.

Hours   January and February: by reservation; open for charters, parties, and special events. Memorial Day to Labor Day: open Monday to Friday, 10 A.M. to 4 P.M.; Saturday, 10 A.M. to 6 P.M.; Sunday, 12 noon to 6 P.M.

Fares   Adults, $6; seniors, $5; children (ages 5 to 12), $3; children under five years of age are free of charge.

Contact   Connecticut Trolley Museum, Route 140, P.O. Box 360, East Windsor, CT 06088. Telephone (203) 627-6540; fax (203) 627-6510.

ESSEX

VALLEY RAILROAD COMPANY

The Valley Railroad Company, which began tourist excursions in 1971, offers visitors a one-hour-long excursion on the Essex Steam Train through the Connecticut River Valley, a two-and-a-half-hour train and riverboat combination ride along the Connecticut River, and dinner trains. Also featured are a working railway yard, where locomotive and coach restoration is performed, and a freight depot gift shop listed on the National Register of Historic Places.

Special Events   Easter Eggspress; North Pole Express.

How to Get There   From New York, take I-95 to exit 69. Take Route 9 north to exit 3. Turn left off the exit; the railroad is on the left, about a quarter of a mile from the exit.

Hours   May 4 to June 7: Wednesday to Friday, departures at 2:00 P.M. and 3:30 P.M.; Saturday and Sunday, departures at 12 noon, 1:30 P.M., 3:00 P.M., and 4:30 P.M.

June 8 to September 2: Monday through Friday, departures at 10:00 A.M., 12 noon, 1:30 P.M., 3:00 P.M., and 4:30 P.M.; Saturday and Sunday, departures at 12 noon, 1:30 P.M., 3:00 P.M., and 4:30 P.M.

September 4 to October 27: Wednesday through Sunday (and Columbus Day), departures at 10:00 A.M., 12 noon, 1:30 P.M., 3:00 P.M., and 4:30 P.M.

Fares   Train only: adults, $8.50; children (ages 3 to 11), $4.25. Train and boat: adults, $14; children (ages 3 to 11), $7. Children under three years of age are free of charge.

Contact   Valley Railroad Company, 1 Railroad Avenue, Essex, CT 06426. Telephone (203) 767-0103.

DELAWARE

L E W E S

QUEEN ANNE'S RAILROAD

Queen Anne's Railroad offers a tourist steam train excursion (1 hour, 45 minutes round-trip) in vintage 1920s and 1930s open-window coaches. Longer excursions are available on a variety of *Royal Zephyr,* climate-controlled dinner trains that combine music or theater offerings.

How to Get There From Route 1 in Delaware, take Route 9 east 1.25 miles to Lewes town limits. Go left on the road marked "To Downtown Historic District." The railroad station is on the left on Kings Highway.

Hours Excursion trains: open May to October (call for schedule). Dinner trains: open May to December (call for schedule).

Fares Excursion train: adults, $7; children (ages 3 to 12), $5; children under three years of age (not occupying a seat) are free of charge.

Contact   Queen Anne's Railroad, 730 King's Highway, Lewes, DE 19958. Telephone (302) 644-1720.

WILMINGTON

WILMINGTON AND WESTERN RAILROAD

The Wilmington and Western Railroad began operating more than 120 years ago, and in its heyday carried both passengers and freight over 20 miles of track between Wilmington and Landenberg, Pennsylvania. Today, the railroad is owned and operated by Historic Red Clay Valley, Inc., a nonprofit group that offers both steam- and diesel-powered scenic excursions from Greenbank Station to the towns of Mt. Cuba and Hockessin. Special dinner trains are also offered.

Special Events   Easter Bunny Special; Santa Claus Special; Wild West Robbery; Civil War Skirmish; Halloween Ghost.

How to Get There   From I-95, take Route N 141 to W 2 to N 41. Turn right at Greenbank Park; the station is at the bottom of the hill on the right.

Hours   Open April to December (call for schedule).

Fares   Adults, $7 to $12; seniors (ages 60 and over), $6 to $10; children (ages 2 to 12), $4 to $5; children under two years of age are free of charge.

Contact   Wilmington and Western Railroad, P.O. Box 5787, Wilmington, DE 19808. Telephone (302) 998-1930.

DISTRICT OF COLUMBIA

SMITHSONIAN INSTITUTION

The National Museum of American History of the Smithsonian Institution contains "Transportation Hall," an exhibit area devoted to the development of rail transportation. The room is divided into three major sections: street railways, cars, and locomotives. Scale models dominate the exhibit, but standard-sized pieces are also on display. Full-sized equipment includes an 1888 cable car from Seattle; an eight-wheel Camden & Amboy passenger car, circa 1836; the 280-ton Southern Pacific locomotive #1401; and relics of the first steam locomotive in North America, the *Stourbridge Lion*.

The world's oldest working locomotive, the *John Bull*, was built in 1831, and is on display outside the transportation hall; the *Jupiter*, built in the same year as the American centennial (1876) by Baldwin Locomotive Works, is a re-creation that can be seen at the Arts and Industries Building.

How to Get There　　From the south, take I-95 north to I-395. Take I-395 toward the Mall, cross the 14th Street bridge, and turn right onto Constitution Avenue to 12th Street.

Hours   Open daily (except Christmas), 10:00 A.M. to 5:30 P.M.

Fares   Admission is free.

Contact   Smithsonian Institution, National Museum of American History, 12th and Constitution NW, Washington, DC 20560. Telephone (202) 357-2700; TDD (for the hearing-impaired) (202) 357-1729.

FLORIDA

DADE CITY

PIONEER FLORIDA MUSEUM

The Pioneer Florida Museum celebrates the Sunshine State's pioneer past. Operated by the nonprofit Pioneer Florida Museum Association, the museum was founded in the 1960s and includes several historic buildings that illustrate the development of 19th- and early-20th-century Florida. The Association has been successful in acquiring historic buildings and structures which now include a one-room schoolhouse from the 1930s, an 1860s two-story farmhouse, a 1903 church, and a 1913 shoe repair shop. Two modern structures built in the 1970s and 1980s are also on display and house collections of historical artifacts and memorabilia.

Special attractions at the museum are the Trilby Depot, an 1896 train station, which contains model trains and operating model train displays, and the Number 3 Cummer steam locomotive, which once hauled cypress trees for the logging industry.

Special Events Civil War Reenactment; Quilt and Antique Show; Picnic-N-Pops; Christmas Open House.

How to Get There   Take U.S. Highway 301 north to Pioneer Museum Road (1 mile north of Dade City).

Hours   Tuesday through Saturday: open 1:00 P.M. to 5:00 P.M.; Sunday: open 2:00 P.M. to 5:00 P.M.

Fares   Adults, $2; children and students, $1. Children under six years of age are free of charge.

Contact   Pioneer Florida Museum, 15602 Pioneer Museum Road, Dade City, FL 33526; telephone (904) 567-0262. Or, Pioneer Florida Museum, P.O. Box 335, Dade City, FL 33525.

F O R T   M Y E R S

RAILROAD MUSEUM OF SOUTH FLORIDA AND TRAIN VILLAGE

Visitors to the Fort Myers area can enjoy two special train attractions, the Railroad Museum of South Florida and the Train Village at Lakes Park. The museum features photographic exhibits of Florida railroading and the rescue of a 1905 Atlantic Coast Line locomotive.

Ten minutes from the museum is the Train Village at Lakes Regional Park, built by museum volunteers. The 1.5-mile miniature train ride takes passengers on a scenic journey through old world villages, past replica Florida railroad stations, through a 100-foot tunnel, and over a 22-foot truss bridge. The oldest-known Atlantic Coast Line switch engine #143, a steam locomotive built in 1905, was added to the village in October 1995 and is currently undergoing restoration.

Future plans include the complete restoration of locomotive #143. The village has wilderness trails, a picnicking area, a children's playground, and other activities. The museum has a gift shop.

Special Events   Valentine Special; Easter Bunny Express; Halloween Express; Holiday Express.

How to Get There   The museum is off U.S. Highway 41 on Colonial Boulevard in Metro Mall. The village is on Gladiolus Drive between Summerlin Road and U.S. 41.   .

Hours   Museum: Tuesday through Friday, 10 A.M. to 4 P.M.; Saturday, 10 A.M. to 2 P.M.
    Train Village: closed Mondays (except Monday holidays); Tuesday to Friday, 10 A.M. to 2 P.M.; Saturday and holidays, 10 A.M. to 4 P.M.; Sunday, 12 noon to 4 P.M. Weekends only during August and September.

Fares   Train ride: adults and children, $2.50; children three years old and under are free of charge. Museum admission is free.

Contact   Railroad Museum of South Florida, P.O. Box 7372, Fort Myers, FL 33911-7372. Telephone (941) 275-3000 or (941) 275-3331.

SEMINOLE GULF RAILWAY

The Seminole Gulf Railway operates a diesel electric train along a historic rail line built by Fort Myers Southern Railway beginning in 1922. This line extended tracks first constructed by the Florida Southern Railroad and Atlantic Coast Line. The railway runs two-hour scenic train trips between Metro Mall, Fort Myers, and Old Bonita Springs in southwest Florida. Dinner and murder mystery trains are also offered.

How to Get There   From I-75, take exit 22 and drive west for 3 miles. The railroad is on the right behind the Metro Mall Shopping Center.

Hours   Open year-round. Excursion trains depart Wednesday and Saturday at 9:30 A.M. and 12 noon; Sunday at 12 noon and 2:30 P.M.

Fares   Adults, $11; children (ages 3 to 12), $6. Children under three years of age are free of charge.

Contact   Seminole Gulf Railway, 4110 Centerpointe Drive, Fort Myers, FL 33916. Telephone (941) 275-8487.

H I G H   S P R I N G S

HIGH SPRINGS STATION MUSEUM

The High Springs Station Museum contains hundreds of railroad artifacts from various railroads, including the Atlantic Coast, Seaboard, and Pennsylvania, and railroad cars built between 1928 and 1986. It also has a large gift shop.

How to Get There   From I-75, take exits 80, 79, or 78 to the High Springs city center.

Hours   Wednesday and Thursday, 10:00 A.M. to 5:00 P.M.; Friday, 10:00 A.M. to 6:00 P.M.; Saturday, 10:00 A.M. to 5:00 P.M.; Sunday, 12 noon to 5:00 P.M.

Fares   Call for information.

Contact   High Springs Station Museum, Inc., 20 NW Railroad Avenue, P.O. Box 2008, High Springs, FL 32643. Telephone (904) I-LIKE-RR (454-5377).

J A C K S O N V I L L E

JACKSONVILLE ZOOLOGICAL GARDENS

In 1995, the Jacksonville Zoological Gardens unveiled two new sets of trains (donated by the CSX Corporation), which were custom-designed and built in New Brunswick, Canada. The narrow gauge railroad carries 110-foot-long trains, each consisting of a diesel locomotive, tender, and three passenger coaches. One train set is a replica of the *General,* a Civil War steam engine. The second train, *Victoria,* resembles trains typical in turn-of-the-century colonial Africa. Currently, the trains operate around zoo grounds along 0.6 miles of track, including an open-deck trestle that crosses a lake, and five road crossings. Future plans include expansion to total a full mile of track.

NOTE: Wheelchair and stroller rentals are available.

How to Get There   Take I-95 to Heckscher Drive (exit 124-A). From Arlington, take 9A over Dames Point Bridge to the Heckscher Drive exit and follow the signs.

Hours   Open daily (except major holidays), 9:00 A.M. to 5:00 P.M. Trains operate every 30 minutes.

Fares   Prices do not include tax. Adults, $3; seniors (age 65 or older), $2; children (ages 3 to 12), $2; Zoo members, $2; children of members, $1.50.

Contact   Jacksonville Zoological Gardens, 8605 Zoo Road, Jacksonville, FL 32218-5799. Telephone (904) 757-4463; fax (904) 757-4315.

L A K E   W A L E S

LAKE WALES DEPOT MUSEUM/ SEABOARD AIR LINE DEPOT

The railroad was introduced to Lake Wales in 1911; in 1928, the former Atlantic Coast Line Railroad Depot was built to accommodate rail service. It was donated to the city in 1976 by a successor company, the Seaboard Coastline Railroad.

The depot is situated along a highway parallel to the CSX Historic Corridor, which includes buildings prominent in the early history and development of Lake Wales. The one-story, hollow tile and stuccoed building features a model railroad display, caboose, engine and Pullman car, photographs, and artifacts.

The Seaboard Air Line Depot offers visitors the chance to explore a second railroad exhibit while in Lake Wales. Built in 1916 and located north of the Depot Museum, the building escaped demolition and was moved to the Corridor in 1993. A children's museum is also located nearby.

How to Get There   From Winter Haven, take Cypress Gardens Road to U.S. 27 South. Make a left on Central Avenue. Go four traffic lights, and make a right on Alternate 27 South. Proceed for two blocks; the museum is in a pink building on the left.

Hours   Depot Museum: Monday to Friday, 9:00 A.M. to 5:00 P.M.; Saturday, 10:00 A.M. to 4:00 P.M. Closed Sunday and on national holidays.

Fares   Admission is free.

Contact   City of Lake Wales, Historic Lake Wales Society, 325 South Scenic Highway, Lake Wales, FL 33853. Telephone (941) 678-4209.

M I A M I

GOLD COAST RAILROAD MUSEUM

For animal-loving train enthusiasts, the Gold Coast Railroad Museum provides the ideal location—it's right next to Miami's Metro Zoo. The museum is an outdoor facility featuring self-guided tours of historic railroad cars. Among them are the *Ferdinand Magellan,* the only Pullman car custom-built for a 20th century president, and the *Silver Crescent,* an elegant stainless steel train with a vista dome, bedroom, bar, and observation lounge. Visitors can also take a diesel train ride. Restroom facilities are available.

How to Get There   Take U.S. 1 or SR 874 south to 152nd Street. Turn left onto Zoo Road. At the end of the road, turn right and look for signs to the museum.

Hours   Open weekends, 11:00 A.M. to 4:00 P.M. Train rides leave hourly beginning at noon.

Fares   Adults, $4; children (under 12), $1.

Contact   Gold Coast Railroad Museum, 12450 SW 152nd Street, Miami, FL 33177. Telephone (305) 253-0063 or (305) 253-4675; fax (305) 233-4641.

NAPLES

NAPLES DEPOT

The Naples Depot was built in 1927 for Seaboard Air Line. Train service ended in 1971; in 1974, the depot was included on the National Register of Historic Places.

Fully restored in 1978, the depot now serves as a civic and cultural center, but has a number of railroad relics on display nearby. Among them are a Southern Railway caboose, a 1940s Pullman car, and a 1940s Hirschhorn Club Car that houses the Memorabilia Museum, including railroad mementos from around the country. A train whistle blows at 12 noon Monday through Saturday. Future plans include establishing a full-scale railway museum. The depot also has a gift shop.

How to Get There   From Fort Myers take I-75 south to the Naples exit (16). Turn right onto Pine Ridge, then turn left onto Goodlett-Frank Road. When the road ends turn right; the depot is two blocks down.

Hours   Open weekdays, 9:00 A.M. to 5:00 P.M.

Fares   Admission is free.

Contact   Naples Depot, 1051 Fifth Avenue South, Naples, FL
33940. Telephone (941) 262-1776.

P A L A T K A

DAVID BROWNING RAILROAD MUSEUM

Named after a veteran railroad station master, this museum is
operated by the Palatka Railroad Preservation Society and focuses on preservation of local railroad history. The museum is
housed in the Historic Union Depot, a brick and wood turn-of-
the-century station that once serviced several rail lines. The
collection includes a variety of railroad memorabilia, photos,
railroad documents, and displays.

The highlight of the museum is Railrodeo, an operating
HO-gauge model train layout—one of the world's largest mobile model railroads. Created by the late Irvin P. Saylor, a train
enthusiast and professional photographer, Railrodeo is a
6,750-pound mobile railroad featuring 16 trains that operate
on 600 feet of track. It depicts some of the sights captured during Saylor's experience as a photographer.

Future plans include construction of a model train layout
of Palatka and Putnam County railroading, a static display, and
a complete restoration of a 1969 caboose.

How to Get There   From Jacksonville take Highway 17 south
to Palatka. In Palatka, the museum is on the corner of 11th and
Reid. Look for the Red Caboose.

Hours   Open the first Sunday of each month, 1:00 P.M. to
4:00 P.M. The museum is also open on other occasions; call for
updates.

Fares   Admission is free (donations are welcome).

Contact   Palatka Railroad Preservation Society, P.O. Box 206, East Palatka, FL 32131-0206. Telephone (904) 328-7103 (Jerry Iser); (904) 325-7425 (Howard Blasczyk); or (904) 329-5538 (Louise Woolever).

PANAMA CITY

JUNIOR MUSEUM OF BAY COUNTY

The Junior Museum of Bay County was designed primarily for children ages 2 to 12, and features elements of the American pioneer period. Among the museum exhibits are model railroad displays created and maintained by the Panhandle Model Railroad Club. From September to mid-November each year, a Club train layout is displayed in the **Junior Museum Annex.** A larger Club display (30 square feet), composed of 25 to 30 lines all operating together, is exhibited in the main hall from mid-November through December. Both 19th- and 20th-century period trains are represented. To help the youngest children view the exhibit, the museum provides stools.

Behind the museum, children will especially enjoy climbing aboard and ringing the bell of Engine 904, a 1943 road-switcher train that originally transported freight and passengers from Florida to Alabama.

How to Get There   From north Florida, take I-10 to Route 231 south to Panama City. Take a right on 15th Street (Highway 98), then turn right onto Jenks Avenue. Pass the first traffic light at the intersection of 19th Street. The museum is on the left.

From east or west, take Route 98 to Jenks Avenue. Go north on Jenks Avenue through the 19th Street intersection. The museum is on the left.

Hours   The Junior Museum Annex Display is open September to mid-November: Saturday, 9:00 A.M. to 4:00 P.M.; Sunday, 1:00 to 4:00 P.M.

The main exhibit hall is open mid-November through December 30: Monday to Friday, 9:00 A.M. to 4:30 P.M.; Saturday, 10:00 A.M. to 4:00 P.M.

Fares   Admission is free.

Contact   Junior Museum of Bay County, 1731 Jenks Avenue, Panama City, FL 32405. Telephone (904) 769-6128; fax (904) 769-6129.

P A R R I S H

FLORIDA GULF COAST RAILROAD MUSEUM

The Florida Gulf Coast Railroad Museum is a volunteer organization involved in railroad preservation and operation. It pays tribute to the American railroad with a diesel ride originating at its depot. Visitors can take a 1-hour, 15-minute journey on diesel-powered locomotives that pull open window coaches and air-conditioned lounge cars. The museum's collection of rolling stock and equipment is on display outdoors. The train operates rain or shine.

How to Get There   From I-75, take exit 45 (Moccasin Wallow Road) to U.S. 301. Go south for a quarter of a mile to the Parrish Post Office. The train is due east.

Hours   Train departures: Saturday, 11 A.M., 1 P.M., and 3 P.M.; Sunday, 1 P.M. and 3 P.M.

Fares   Adults, $8; children, $5.

Contact   Florida Gulf Coast Railroad Museum, P.O. Box 355, Parrish, FL 34219. Telephone (941) 377-4016.

WINTER HAVEN

CYPRESS JUNCTION

Cypress Gardens, created in 1936, is a 200-acre tropical garden theme park known for thousands of plant and flower varieties and for waterskiing performances. In its own building on the grounds is Cypress Junction, an HO-gauge model railroad exhibit depicting the four seasons and the terrain of different parts of the United States, from Miami to Maine. Up to 20 trains operate at one time over more than 1,100 feet of track. Four hundred buildings, 4,800 miniature human and animal figures, and 4,500 trees comprise the landscape. Highlights of the display include a replica of Mount Rushmore, a logging camp, oil field, haunted house, Bavarian castle, train wreck, thunderstorm, circus, and an operating drive-in theater.

Maintenance for the exhibit is handled by the volunteers of the Cypress Model Railroad Society.

Special Events   Various floral festivals.

How to Get There   From Orlando or Tampa, take I-4 to U.S. Highway 27 south to SR 540 west, toward Winter Haven. Follow the highway signs to Cypress Gardens.

Hours   Open daily, 9:30 A.M. to 5:30 P.M.

Fares   Adults, $27.95 plus tax; seniors (55 and over), $22.50; children (ages 6 to 12), $17.95 plus tax. Children under six years of age are free of charge.

Contact   Cypress Junction, P.O. Box 1, Cypress Gardens, FL 33884. Telephone (800) 282-2123 or (941) 324-2111; fax (941) 324-7946.

GEORGIA

D U L U T H

SOUTHEASTERN RAILWAY MUSEUM

The Southeastern Railway Museum is an open-air museum on 12 acres of land. It has steam locomotives, Pullman cars, antique wooden freight cars, and cabooses. One of the museum's most interesting attractions is a Pullman private car, the *Superb,* which was unveiled in 1995 after a 20-month renovation effort. Built in 1911, the steel railcar carried President Warren Harding on a cross-country trip to Alaska and then became his funeral train when he died in August 1923. The *Superb* featured every possible appointment: kitchen, bathroom (including a shower), observation lounge, and a public address system that enabled Harding to transmit whistle-stop speeches coast to coast—a railroad first.

The museum offers diesel train rides on the museum's track, aboard cabooses or open-air freight cars.

How to Get There   The museum is located on Buford Highway, a quarter of a mile south of Pleasantville Road.

Hours   April to November: open Saturday, 9:00 A.M. to
5:30 P.M. Also open the third Sunday of each month, 12:00
to 5:30 P.M.

Fares   Adults, $4; seniors and children under 12 years, $2.

Contact   Southeastern Railway Museum, Atlanta Chapter
NRHS, 3966 Buford Highway, P.O. Box 1267, Duluth, GA
30136. Telephone (770) 476-2013.

K E N N E S A W

KENNESAW CIVIL WAR MUSEUM

The best reason to visit this attraction (formerly the Big Shanty
Museum) is to see the *General,* a steam locomotive made famous when it was stolen by Union troops in the 1862 Andrews
Railroad Raid. According to legend, Confederate soldiers were
taking a 20-minute breakfast break in Big Shanty (Kennesaw's
name at the time) when Union raiders uncoupled the cars and
stole the 1855 locomotive. Union efforts were thwarted within
eight hours of the attempt when the train ran out of fuel.

Originally an antique cotton gin, the museum houses the
engine and tender of the *General* and includes historical
exhibits and a video depicting the raid. Outside the museum is
the *Little Red Caboose,* a renovated car once part of Norfolk &
Southern Railroad, a train depot, and Kennesaw Mountain
Battlefield Park.

How to Get There   Kennesaw Civil War Museum is 25 miles
north of Atlanta off I-75. Take exit 118 into Kennesaw.

Hours   Open Monday through Saturday, 9:30 A.M. to 5:30
P.M.; Sunday, 12:00 noon to 5:30 P.M. Weekday winter hours
(December, January, and February): 10:00 A.M. to 4:00 P.M.

Fares   Adults, $3; seniors, $2.50; children, $1.50.

Contact   Kennesaw Civil War Museum, 2829 Cherokee Street, Kennesaw, GA 30144. Telephone (800) 742-6897 or (770) 427-2117.

STONE MOUNTAIN

STONE MOUNTAIN RAILROAD

The Stone Mountain Railroad offers a diesel train ride that began operation in 1962 through Stone Mountain Memorial Park. The 5-mile, 25-minute trip around Stone Mountain includes a trip narrative and two station stops. Those stops are at Walk Up Trail Station, where a 1.3-mile trail leads visitors up the mountain, and at Wildlife Trails Station, featuring animals once indigenous to Georgia and a petting zoo with domesticated animals.

Special Events   Ghost Mountain Hayrides (flat cars pulled by a diesel); Christmas Train.

How to Get There   From Atlanta, take U.S. 78 east to the interior of Stone Mountain Park. Enter the park, follow the road to a fork and turn right at the fork. The parking lot is on the left.

Hours   Operates year-round: Monday to Thursday, 10:00 A.M. to 5:20 P.M.; Friday to Sunday, 10:00 A.M. to 7:20 P.M. (longer hours May to December and during the 1996 Olympics).

Fares   Adults (ages 12 to 55), $3.50; children (ages 3 to 11), $2.50.

Contact   Stone Mountain Railroad, P.O. Box 778, Stone Mountain, GA 30086. Telephone (404) 498-5600.

W A Y C R O S S

OKEFENOKEE HERITAGE CENTER

The Okefenokee Heritage Center is a nonprofit local-history and art museum dedicated to the heritage of southeast Georgia. Two 19th-century homes, an early-20th-century print shop, a turn-of-the-century communal settlement, Native American relics, and an African American heritage exhibit are among the displays presented. Train fans will especially enjoy exploring the fully restored 1912 Baldwin 100-ton locomotive and former Atlantic Coast Line depot (circa 1900) outside on the site. The center offers a shaded picnic area and gift shop.

How to Get There   The center is located 2 miles west of downtown Waycross, between U.S. 1 and U.S. 82, on Augusta Avenue.

Hours   Open Monday through Saturday, 10:00 A.M. to 5:00 P.M.; Sunday, 1:00 P.M. to 5:00 P.M. Closed major holidays.

Fares   Adults, $2; youth (ages 4 to 18), $1; children under three years of age are free of charge.

Contact   Okefenokee Heritage Center, Inc., 1460 North Augusta Avenue, Waycross, GA 31503-4954. Telephone (912) 285-4260.

HAWAII

OAHU RAILWAY AND LAND COMPANY

Run by the Hawaiian Railway Society on the island of Oahu, this narrow gauge train takes a scenic round-trip ride with a view of the ocean, ghost towns, and cane fields. Special features of the ride include a choice of open-air or enclosed cars and an informative narrative on board describing the history of the OR & L. The train began in 1890, carrying items like raw sugar and molasses to Honolulu Harbor, and continued through World War II, adding ammunition, soldiers, and military supplies from Pearl Harbor. The last train ran in 1947.

The Sunday ride travels past Fort Barrette (circa 1930), two ghost town sites (Gilbert and Sisal), Makaha mountain range, and the old Ewa Plantation, begun in 1890.

Sunday rides are on a first come, first served basis, at 1:00 P.M. and 3:00 P.M. Special weekday rides are available for groups by reservation only.

How to Get There   From Honolulu, take H-1 Freeway west to exit 5A (Fort Weaver Road), which leads in one direction only. Turn right onto Renton Road. Look for the railroad sign; the station is on the left.

Hours   Weekends: departures at 12:30 P.M. and 2:30 P.M.

Fares   Sundays: Adults, $8; seniors (ages 62 and over), $5; children (ages 2 to 12), $5. Children under two years of age are free.

Contact   Hawaiian Railway Society, P.O. Box 1208 Ewa Station, Ewa Beach, HI 96706. Telephone (808) 681-5461; fax (808) 681-4860.

LAHAINA

LAHAINA-KAANAPALI & PACIFIC RAILROAD

This Maui railroad, nicknamed the *Sugar Cane Train,* takes visitors on a one-hour, round-trip steam train ride through sugar cane fields. Each trip features a conductor who sings and narrates the ride as passengers enjoy ocean and mountain views. The train ride is also offered in combination with other attractions, such as local museums, movies, and land-sea packages.

A railroad double-decker bus and the Kaanapali Trolley provide free transportation to and from the area. Free parking and souvenir shops are located at Lahaina Station.

How to Get There   The station is on Highway 30, north of the center of Lahaina. Exit west at the Pizza Hut signal light. Then turn right onto Limahana; the station is at 957 Limahana Place.

Hours   Open 9:45 A.M. to 5:30 P.M.; train leaves at regular intervals.

Fares   One-way: adults, $9.50; children (ages 3 to 12), $5. Round-trip: adults, $13.50; children (ages 3 to 12), $7. Infants not occupying a seat are free of charge.

Contact   Lahaina-Kaanapali & Pacific Railroad, P.O. Box 816, Lahaina, Maui, HI 96767-0816. Telephone (808) 661-0089.

IDAHO

A T H O L

SILVERWOOD

Silverwood is a family-oriented theme park, including more than 15 carnival rides, daily air shows, biplane rides, and an indoor ice show. Special features include an authentic 19th-century steam train ride on the Silverwood Central Railway, which travels through rustic northern Idaho countryside. Restaurants and eateries are scattered throughout the park.

How to Get There   Silverwood can be reached north of Coeur d'Alene on Highway 95. Look for signs.

Hours   Mid-June to early September: open daily.
Mid-May to early June and early September to early October: open weekends, 11:00 A.M. to 8:00 P.M.

Fares   General (ages 8 to 64), $18.99 plus tax; young/young at heart (ages 3 to 7 or under 48 inches; 65 and over), $9.99

plus tax. After 5:00 P.M., all tickets $8.99 plus tax. Season passes are available.

Contact   Silverwood, North 25255 Highway 95, Athol, ID 83801. Telephone (208) 683-3400.

W A L L A C E

NORTHERN PACIFIC
DEPOT RAILROAD MUSEUM

Silver, lead, and zinc attracted the railroads to the Coeur d'Alene Mining District of Idaho in the late 1800s. The Northern Pacific Depot Railroad Museum captures that history. The depot (relocated in 1986) is an elegant, castle-like structure made of bricks imported from China.

Ticket windows, a waiting room, and a telegrapher's desk are on display on the first floor; on the second floor, visitors can see how a station agent's family lived in a space now featuring a pictorial history and railroad memorabilia.

How to Get There   The museum is located in downtown Wallace at 6th and Pine streets. Take I-90 to Coeur d'Alene (exit 61). Turn left off the freeway and follow the road into town.

Hours   Summer: open daily, 9:00 A.M. to 7:00 P.M.
Spring and fall: open daily, 9:00 A.M. to 5:00 P.M.
Winter: open Tuesday to Saturday, 10:00 A.M. to 3:00 P.M.

Fares   Adults, $2; seniors (65 and above), $1.50; children (ages 6 to 16), $1; family rate, $6; children under six years of age are free of charge.

Contact   Northern Pacific Depot Museum. 6th and Pine, Wallace, ID 83873. Telephone (208) 752-0111.

ILLINOIS

CHICAGO

MUSEUM OF SCIENCE AND INDUSTRY

This hands-on museum is dedicated to helping visitors of all ages explore science and technology through interactive displays and exhibits. It features a five-story, Omnimax theater with six-channel digital sound; a 16-foot walk-through replica of the human heart; a baby chick hatchery; "Colleen Moore's Fairy Castle;" a space center featuring practice modules used by Apollo 8 astronauts; and a coal mine tour to explore a typical Illinois mine shaft.

Train fans will particularly enjoy the Transportation Zone, a combination of exhibits, including historic artifacts like the United Airline 727 airplane, the *Spirit of America* automobile, Buchanan's Number 999 Locomotive (restored), and the Museum and Santa Fe Model Railroad.

The museum has three stores and five restaurants, including an ice cream parlor, and it is accessible to disabled visitors.

MUSEUM OF SCIENCE AND INDUSTRY, CHICAGO

The Museum and Santa Fe Model Railroad can be found in the Transportation Zone, featuring great vehicles of sea, land, and air.

How to Get There   The museum is located at 57th Street and Lake Shore Drive in Chicago.

Hours   Open daily (except Christmas): weekdays, 9:30 A.M. to 4:00 P.M.; weekends, 9:30 A.M. to 5:30 P.M.

Fares   Museum: adults, $6; seniors (65 and over), $5; children (ages 5 to 12), $2.50; children under five years of age are free of charge. (Additional charges for Omnimax theater showings.) On Thursdays, admission is free.

Contact   Museum of Science and Industry, 57th Street and Lake Shore Drive, Chicago, IL 60637-2093. Telephone (312) 684-1414.

FREEPORT

SILVER CREEK & STEPHENSON RAILROAD

The Silver Creek & Stephenson Railroad, operated by the Stephenson County Antique Engine Club, began offering steam train excursions in 1986 along the right-of-way once owned by the Chicago, Milwaukee, St. Paul & Pacific Railroad. A 1912 Heisler locomotive provides the power.

The railroad also features the Silver Creek Depot (where visitors can watch the stationmaster agent operate telephone, telegraph, and semaphore controls); a railroad shed; and a museum. Rolling stock includes three cabooses (one a wooden caboose dating back to 1889) and a flat car. The railroad also has a novelty booth and lunch stand.

How to Get There   From Chicago, take I-90 west to Rockford. At Rockford, take Highway 20 west to Freeport. Take Business 20 into Freeport and exit South Street (Walnut); turn left onto Walnut. The museum and train are at the intersection of Walnut and Lamm streets.

Hours   Open 11:00 A.M. to 5:00 P.M. Excursions are offered on a limited number of days between Memorial Day and late October; call for exact dates.

Fares   Adults, $4; children (under 12), $1.50.

Contact   Stephenson County Antique Club, Inc., Silver Creek & Stephenson Railroad, P.O. Box 255, Freeport, IL 61032. Telephone (815) 232-2306 or (815) 232-2198 (on the days the train is operating); or Stephenson County Convention and Visitors Bureau at (800) 369-2955.

M O N T I C E L L O

MONTICELLO RAILWAY MUSEUM

The nonprofit Monticello Railway Museum was founded in 1966 and is dedicated to the preservation of railway history and artifacts. In addition to museum exhibits and rolling stock on the building site, visitors can take a one-hour narrated and scenic ride in a vintage train. Departures are offered at two stations: the Illinois Central and Wabash Depots. The museum has a gift shop and a snack car.

Special Events   Throttle Time; School Days; Throw Momma on the Train; Caboose Trains; Railroad Days; Depot Day; Father's Day Bluegrass and More; Fireworks Train; Ghost Train and Haunted Car; Lunch with Santa on the Train.

How to Get There   The museum is at exit 166 (Market Street) off I-72, between Champaign and Decatur, Illinois.

Hours   May through October: open weekends and holidays. From Illinois Central Depot (at museum): departures at 1:00 P.M., 2:00 P.M., 3:00 P.M., and 4:00 P.M.
  From Wabash Depot (downtown): departures at 1:30 P.M., 2:30 P.M., and 3:30 P.M.

Fares   Adults, $5; seniors (62 and over), $3; children (ages 4 to 12), $3; children three years and under are free of charge.

Contact   Monticello Railway Museum. P.O. Box 401, Monticello, IL 61856. Telephone (800) 952-3396 or (217) 762-9011.

U N I O N

ILLINOIS RAILWAY MUSEUM

The Illinois Railway Museum encourages visitors to explore its wealth of train exhibits and displays. Housing one of the largest collections of historic railway equipment in the United States, six buildings contain over 2 miles of displays. Passenger service began in 1966 at the museum, and today, visitors can choose a variety of train ride choices, including steam and diesel rides, interurban trains, and streetcars. A Burlington Zephyr and other diesels operate during special events. The main departure station is at an 1851 depot.

The museum has provided train, streetcar, and scene support to a host of motion picture productions, including the recent movies *A League of Their Own* and *The Babe*.

A gift shop, bookstore, refreshment area, and picnic facilities are on the museum grounds.

Special Events   Railway Day; Annual Trolley Pageant; Diesel Weekend; Vintage Transport Extravaganza; Railfan Weekend.

How to Get There   From Chicago, take I-90 to U.S. Route 20 (Marengo exit). Drive northwest on Route 20 to Union Road (about 4.5 miles). Go north on Union Road and follow signs to the museum.

From Rockford, take I-90 to U.S. Route 20, then take the Cherry Valley Belvidere exit. Drive east on Route 20 through Marengo to Union Road. Turn left on Union Road to Olson Road. Go right (south) on Olson to the museum.

Hours   Steam trains run at about one-and-a-half-hour intervals; electric cars run half-hourly. Call ahead for specific times.

April: Museum open; trains run Sundays only.

May, September, and October: Museum open; trains run weekends only.

Memorial Day to Labor Day: Trains run daily.

Fares   Adults, $6 to $8; children, $3.50 to $7; families, $20 to $30.

Contact   Illinois Railway Museum, P.O. Box 427, Union, IL 60180. Telephone (800) BIG RAIL (recorded info) or (815) 923-4321 or (815) 923-4000.

VALLEY VIEW MODEL RAILROAD

The Valley View Model Railroad, created by model railroad enthusiast Ted Voss, is a miniature operating railroad complete with real and imaginary scenes from the past and present. The "Little Northwestern Railroad" includes carefully detailed cities and towns, animation, sound effects, and more than 16 trains and 8 miles of track in operation. (Note: The exhibit is not under glass.)

A new addition on the site of the collection is the "Kiddie Cart Train Ride." The railroad also has a gift shop.

How to Get There   Follow directions to the Illinois Railway Museum (previous entry). The railroad is three-quarters of a mile north of the museum.

Hours   Memorial Day through Labor Day: open Wednesday, Saturday, and Sunday, 1:00 P.M. to 6:00 P.M.

Fares   Adults, $4; seniors, $3.50; children, $2; children under five years of age are free of charge.

Contact   Ted Voss, Valley View Model Railroad, 17108 High-bridge Road, Union, IL. Telephone (815) 923-4135.

INDIANA

CONNERSVILLE

WHITEWATER VALLEY RAILROAD

The Whitewater Valley Railroad has been in operation for over 22 years and offers a scenic 16-mile journey along the path of the Whitewater Canal and Laurel Feeder Dam. A two-hour layover in the 19th-century town of Metamora gives visitors an opportunity to stroll walkways, explore over 100 shops, and observe wheat being ground into flour at a water-powered grist mill.

The railroad has refreshments and a gift shop at the station. Visitors are free to bring along a picnic lunch to eat on the train. Dinner trains also are offered twice a month.

NOTE: Connersville does not observe daylight savings time.

Special Events Memorial Day; Labor Day; 4th of July; Spring Adventure Trains; Canal Days; Fall Foliage Trips; Metamora Christmas Walk.

How to Get There   From Indianapolis, take I-70 east to the Connersville exit (State Road 1) south into Connersville. Follow the railroad tracks (approximately 33 blocks) and turn south on State Road 121. The depot is four-and-a-half blocks south on State Road 121.

From Cincinnati, take I-74 west to the Brookville exit. Drive west on U.S. 52 through Brookville. Then take State Road 1 north to Connersville. Turn left at the first stop light. Turn left again at the next stop light. The street ends in four blocks and the entrance is just ahead.

Hours   May through October: 12:01 P.M. departure from Connersville on weekends and holidays.

May: 10:00 A.M. departure from Connersville, Wednesday through Friday.

October: 10:00 A.M. departure from Connersville, Thursday and Friday.

The dinner train is available on the first and third Friday of each month, April to November, by prepaid reservations only. It departs at 6:00 P.M. for Laurel, Indiana.

Fares   Round-trip: adults (over 12), $11; children (ages 2 to 12), $5; children under two years of age are free of charge.

One-way (to Metamora or to Connersville): adults (over 12), $9; children (ages 2 to 12), $4; children under two years of age are free of charge.

Dinner train: $18 per person.

Contact   Whitewater Valley Railroad, P.O. Box 406, Connersville, IN 47331. Telephone (317) 825-2054. The street address is 300 South Eastern Avenue, Connersville, IN 47331.

C O R Y D O N

CORYDON 1883 SCENIC RAILROAD

The Corydon 1883 Scenic Railroad travels along tracks first owned by one of the oldest short lines in the United States—

the Louisville, New Albany & Corydon Railroad. Excursions feature a diesel engine built in 1951. Visitors are offered a narrated, 16-mile (one-and-a-half hours) round-trip through southern Indiana, departing from a depot in Indiana's first capital, Corydon. In 1995, new features to the line were added: rail diesel cars, passenger cars with large windows, air conditioning and heating, and restrooms.

Special Events   Civil War Weekend (reenactment) in September.

How to Get There   Corydon, 30 minutes west of Louisville, Kentucky, is located on I-64. Take exit 105, turn right, and then turn left at the fourth stop light. Continue for 1.5 miles to railroad.

Hours   May through October: open Friday, Saturday, and Sunday.

NOTE: Schedule could be expanded for the 1996 season after completion of track work. Check for updates.

Fares   Adults, $8; seniors, $7; children, $5.

Contact   Corydon 1883 Scenic Railroad, Walnut and Water Streets, P.O. Box 10, Corydon, IN 47112. Telephone (812) 738-8000.

E L K H A R T

NATIONAL NEW YORK CENTRAL RAILROAD MUSEUM

Elkhart may seem an unlikely site for the National New York Central Railroad Museum, which is dedicated to the New York Central Railroad. But the town was once an important New York Central Railroad.

A 1915 rail coach and an adjoining freight house complex comprise the museum. An equipment yard includes a collection of New York Central rolling stock: a rare Mohawk steam loco-motive, a diesel-electric built in 1953, a 1915 wooden caboose, a bay window caboose built in 1963, and a steam wrecker. Currently, the museum is undergoing a major renovation that will add interactive exhibits, including a fiber-optic steam loco-motive, *Living Blueprint*, which simulates the experience of operating a steam engine.

Rail fans will especially enjoy standing on an observation platform to watch the trains operating along Conrail's main line in Elkhart.

How to Get There   From Indianapolis take U.S. 31 north to South Bend. Then take the U.S. 20 bypass. Go right (east) on U.S. 20, and exit U.S. 33 for Elkhart. Turn left off the exit; the museum is straight ahead.

Hours   Tuesday through Friday: 10:00 A.M. to 2:00 P.M.; Sat-urday and Sunday, 10:00 A.M. to 3:00 P.M. Closed on Monday and on major holidays.

Fares   Adults, $2; seniors, $1; students (ages 6 to 14), $1; children under six years of age are free of charge.

Contact   National New York Central Railroad Museum, 721 South Main Street, P.O. Box 1043, Elkhart, IN 46515. Tele-phone (219) 294-3001.

FORT WAYNE

FORT WAYNE RAILROAD HISTORICAL SOCIETY

Like so many railroad societies and organizations, the Fort Wayne Railroad Historical Society was formed to complete a special project. Members spent five years restoring a badly neglected engine. Thanks to their years of effort, the *Nickel*

Plate 765, a steam locomotive, began operating again in 1979—the first time since 1958. The Society expects to operate it at the Logansport Festival in July 1996.

Currently, the 765 is undergoing repairs, but the Society expects to complete restoration of another engine, C & O 2716. Two passenger coaches, two steam engines, and a 44-ton diesel also make up the collection.

How to Get There   From Indianapolis, take I-69 north to I-469 to Route 30. Go east on route 30 to Ryan Road and then North on Ryan Road to Edgerton Road. Go east on Edgerton Road 1 mile and the Society is on the right.

Hours   Saturdays: 9:00 A.M. to 3:00 P.M. Sundays: 10:00 A.M. to 3:00 P.M. Call for additional times.

Fares   Free. Donations are welcome.

Contact   Fort Wayne Railroad Historical Society, P.O. Box 11017, Fort Wayne, IN 46855. Telephone (219) 493-0765.

F R E N C H   L I C K

INDIANA RAILWAY MUSEUM

The Indiana Railway Museum, a nonprofit organization dedicated to railway preservation and restoration, houses over 90 pieces of railroad equipment at its site. Train equipment includes steam and diesel locomotives, passenger and freight cars, and electric cars.

The museum also features two kinds of railway excursions that depart from the former Monon Passenger Station, a 1907 limestone structure. The **Springs Valley Electric Railway,** with a 1930s trolley, travels between French Lick and West Baden, reminiscent of streetcar travel between 1903 and

1919. The **French Lick, West Baden & Southern,** built in the 1970s to resemble a 1920s branch line, runs a diesel locomotive on a 20-mile trip (1 hour, 45 minutes) through the Hoosier National Forest and the 2,200-foot Burton tunnel.

The museum operates a gift shop, and a refreshment car accompanies all train trips.

Special Events   Train Robberies.

How to Get There   From Indianapolis, take I-65 south to Scottsburg. Then take Highway 56 west. Stay on Highway 56 (towards Jaspar) to the French Lick exit. Turn right and look for the railroad tracks. The museum entrance is located on Monon Street.

Hours   Trolley ride: open weekends in April, May, and November, 10:00 A.M. to 4:00 P.M.; open daily, June through October, 10:00 A.M. to 4:00 P.M.

Locomotive ride: open weekends and holidays, April through November, with departures at 10:00 A.M., 1:00 P.M., and 4:00 P.M. Call for select days of departures.

Fares   Adults, $8; children (ages 3 to 11), $4; children under three years of age are free of charge.

Contact   Indiana Railway Museum, P.O. Box 150, French Lick, IN 47432. Telephone (800) 74-TRAIN or (812) 936-2405.

K N I G H T S T O W N

CARTHAGE, KNIGHTSTOWN & SHIRLEY RAILROAD

The Carthage, Knightstown & Shirley Railroad (CK&S) offers a one-hour, 10-mile round-trip excursion on tracks once belonging to the Cleveland, Cincinnati, Chicago & St. Louis Railroad. Departing from a former New York Central freight and passenger station, passengers ride in a locomotive with antique coach, covered open platform car, and caboose through scenic landscape, under a railroad bridge, and to the Carthage railway yard, where they can examine railway equipment on display.

The railroad depot has a gift shop, memorabilia and refreshments, and an outdoor picnic area. The platform car can accommodate wheelchair patrons.

Special Events   Knightstown Jubilee Days; Knightstown Festival; Pumpkin Patch.

How to Get There   From I-70, take exit 115. Pick up State Road 109 south to Knightstown. Look for the signs.

Hours   May through October: departure on Friday at 11:00 A.M.; departures on Saturday and Sunday at 11:00 A.M., 1:00 P.M., and 3:00 P.M. Also open summer holidays.

Fares   Adults, $6; children (ages 3 to 11), $4; children under three years of age are free of charge.

Contact   Carthage, Knightstown & Shirley Railroad, 112 West Carey Street, Knightstown, IN 46148. Telephone (317) 345-5561 or (800) 345-2704 (Indiana only).

M A D I S O N

MADISON RAILROAD STATION

Madison was an important railroad center in the 1800s, and the Jefferson County Historical Society opened a museum in the Madison Railroad to commemorate that in 1988. Built in

1895, the building served as a passenger station until the 1930s and later was used for freight. The station celebrated its 100th anniversary in 1995; it is currently under restoration.

One of its special features is a two-story waiting room. Adjacent to the station is an antique caboose, which is also available for viewing.

The Society is creating a permanent exhibit of a working model railroad depicting Madison.

How to Get There   From Cincinnati, take I-71 south. The museum is north of U.S. Highway 421 in Madison.

Hours   April to Thanksgiving: open Monday to Saturday, 10:00 A.M. to 4:30 P.M.; Sunday, 1:00 P.M. to 4:00 P.M. All other months: open Monday to Friday, 10.00 A.M. to 4:30 P.M.

Fares $2 per person.

Contact   Madison Railroad Station, 615 West First Street, Madison, IN 47250. Telephone (812) 265-2335.

MICHIGAN CITY

HESSTON STEAM MUSEUM

The Hesston Steam Museum encourages visitors to discover the delights of an outdoor operating museum featuring a host of steam-driven vintage equipment. Rail enthusiasts will enjoy a short ride through 155 acres of lush meadows and forests on large and small coal-fired steam locomotives. Visitors can also tour a display of steam-operated machinery or hike through parts of rural Indiana.

The museum offers a special Labor Day Weekend event: a steam show, where visitors can see demonstrations of how vintage steam-powered machines operate. The museum and rides are sponsored by the La Porte Historical Steam Society.

Special Events   North-South Skirmish Group Musket and Cannon Competition; Hesston Steam and Power Show; Cider Fest.

How to Get There   From Indianapolis, take I-94 to exit 1 (New Buffalo/La Porte). Pick up U.S. 39 south. You will see a locomotive on the corner at 1000 North. Turn left there and go 2.5 miles to Hesston Steam Museum.

Hours   Memorial Day to Labor Day: open Saturday, Sunday, and holidays, 12:00 noon to 5:00 P.M.
    Labor Day to October: open Sunday only, 12:00 noon to 5:00 P.M.

Fares   Big trains: adults, $3; children (under 12), $2.
    Fourteen-inch railway: adults, $2; children (under 12), $2.
    Little trains: adults, $2; children (under 12), $2.
    Infants not occupying a seat are free of charge.

Contact   Hesston Steam Museum, County Road 1000 North, La Porte, IN 46350. Telephone (219) 872-7405.

NOBLESVILLE

INDIANA TRANSPORTATION MUSEUM

The Indiana Transportation Museum offers visitors a chance to examine vintage steam, diesel, and electric rail equipment; railroad artifacts; operating scale models on a garden railway; and to ride an electric trolley car. Throughout the year, the museum also sponsors locomotive train trips.
    Every August, the museum presents "Fairtrain," a special train celebration featuring rides and exhibits.

Departures are from Hobbs Station, which also has a gift shop. Situated in Forest Park, museum visitors have access to playgrounds and picnic areas.

Special Events   Fairtrain; Hobo Days; I've Been Working on the Railroad; Spencer Antique Train and Car Festival; Fall Foliage; Ghost Train.

How to Get There   Noblesville is 20 miles north of downtown Indianapolis. From U.S. Highway 31/Meridian Street, go to State Road 32/Westfield. Go east to Noblesville, then north on State Road 19 to Forest Park.

From I-69 north, take State Road 37. Go north to State Road 32, west to State Road 19, then north to Forest Park.

Hours   Museum: open 10:00 A.M. to 5:00 P.M., Tuesday through Sunday, from Memorial Day to Labor Day; also open on weekends in April, May, September, and October.

Trains: open Saturday and Sunday, with departures at 12:30 P.M. and 2:30 P.M.

Fares   Adults, $3 to $7; children (ages 4 to 12), $2 to $5; children three years of age and under are free of charge.

Contact   Indiana Transportation Museum, P.O. Box 83, Noblesville, IN 46060-0083. Telephone (800) 234-TRAIN or (317) 773-6000.

NORTH JUDSON

HOOSIER VALLEY RAILROAD MUSEUM, INC.

The creation of the Hoosier Valley Railroad Museum (formerly the Miami County Steam Locomotive Association) began in

BRUCE EMMONS, HOOSIER VALLEY RAILROAD MUSEUM, INC.

C&O K-4 Class Locomotive.

1961, when the organization received a gift from the Chesapeake & Ohio Railway Company: steam locomotive 2789. The main attraction now at the museum (and currently under restoration), the 2789 has since been joined by five train buildings and over 20 pieces of train equipment that include steam and diesel engines, passenger, Pullman and parlor cars, freight cars, and cabooses. A helpful walking tour of the museum is also offered.

Like other railroad museums, the Hoosier Valley Railroad Museum is a nonprofit organization dedicated to preserving railroad history, restoring antique rail equipment, and educating visitors on aspects of railroad life.

How to Get There   From Indianapolis, take Highway 421 north to Highway 10. Turn east on Highway 10 to North Judson. At Main Street turn right. Go three blocks through downtown and turn right to the entrance of the museum.

OLD WAKARUSA RAILROAD

At the end of the run, homestyle Amish cooking awaits riders of the Old Wakarusa.

Hours   Open Saturdays year-round, 8:00 A.M. to 5:00 P.M.

Fares   Free. Donations are welcome.

Contact   Hoosier Valley Railroad Museum, Inc., P.O. Box 75, North Judson, IN 46366. Telephone (219) 223-3834.

WAKARUSA

OLD WAKARUSA RAILROAD

The Old Wakarusa Railroad (15-inch gauge, one-third semi-scale) was built by rail enthusiasts in 1989. It offers a 1.5-mile ride through a 100-foot tunnel and over two bridges, making a stop to visit farm animals. A 1957 replica of the 1862 *General* locomotive serves as the main locomotive engine.

The railroad also operates a restaurant next door featuring Amish-style cooking.

Special Events   Pumpkin Trains; Winter Wonderland Trains.

How to Get There   The railroad and restaurant are located on State Road 19 in Wakarusa. From Gary or South Bend, take the Indiana Tollroad to exit 92 (State Road 19). Take the road south for 13 miles. The railroad is half a mile south of the traffic light in Wakarusa.

Hours   April through October: open Monday to Saturday, 11:00 A.M. to dark (train departs every 30 minutes).

Fares   Adults, $3; children, $3; children under four years of age accompanied by paying adult are free of charge.

Contact   Old Wakarusa Railroad, State Road 19, Wakarusa, IN 46573. Telephone (219) 862-2714.

IOWA

B O O N E

BOONE & SCENIC VALLEY RAILROAD

The Boone & Scenic Valley Railroad takes visitors on a 14-mile excursion from Boone to Fraser. A diesel train operates on weekdays; steam train rides are offered on weekends. Led by a JS #8419 engine built in Datong, China, the steam train travels (1 hour, 45 minutes) through the Des Moines River Valley, crossing a 156-foot-high trestle and a river bridge.

A new depot houses the **Iowa Railroad Museum,** where visitors can view antique rail equipment and visit a gift shop and snack bar. Trolley rides are also offered on weekends.

How to Get There   From Des Moines, take I-35 to Ames, then U.S. 30 West to Boone. Go north on Story Street to 10th. Go west six blocks to 225 10th Street.

Hours   Memorial Day weekend to October 31: open weekdays, with train departure at 1:30 P.M.; Saturday, Sunday, and holidays, with train departures at 11:00 A.M., 1:30 P.M., and 4:00 P.M.

Fares   Diesel train: adults, $8; children (ages 5 to 12), $4.
Steam train: adults, $10, children (ages 5 to 12), $4.
Children under five years of age carried by an adult are free of charge.

Contact   Boone & Scenic Valley Railroad, P.O. Box 603, Boone, IA 50036. Telephone (800) 626-0319 or (515) 432-4249.

C O L F A X

TRAINLAND USA

Created by toy train enthusiast Red Atwood with help from friends and neighbors, Trainland USA is one of the world's largest operating toy train museums. Featuring Lionel trains and accessories, the exhibit depicts railroad development throughout the United States during three periods: frontier, steam, and diesel. Complete with an automated train control system, a display area the size of two ranch homes, and 4,000 feet of track, the exhibits include animated displays that visitors can operate and hand-painted scenery.

How to Get There   Trainland USA is on Highway 117, 2.5 miles north of the intersection with I-80.

Hours   Memorial Day through Labor Day: open daily, 9:00 A.M. to 7:00 P.M.
In September: open weekends only, 12:00 noon to 6:00 P.M.
On the weekend after Thanksgiving: open Friday, Saturday, and Sunday, 12:00 noon to 6:00 P.M.

Fares   Adults, $3.50; seniors (55 or over), $3; children (ages 3 to 12), $1.50; children under three years of age are free of charge.

Contact   Trainland USA, R.R. 2, Colfax, IA 50054. Telephone (515) 674-3813.

COUNCIL BLUFFS

RAILSWEST RAILROAD MUSEUM

The Rock Island Railroad was important in bridging the Mississippi River in the mid-1800s. The former 1899 Rock Island
Railroad depot, listed on the National Register of Historic
Places, is the site of the Railswest Railroad Museum. On display
are a Burlington handcar, dining car memorabilia, vintage
photos, and other items.

A special feature of the museum is its operating HO
model railroad layout. Approximately 22 by 34 feet, the
display depicts railroading in its heyday and the dominant role
it played in the region.

Special Events   Depot Days; Christmas at the Depot.

How to Get There   The museum is 1 mile north of I-80 off exit 3.

Hours   Memorial Day through Labor Day: open Monday,
Tuesday, Thursday, Friday, and Saturday, 10:00 A.M. to 4:00
P.M.; Sunday, 1:00 P.M. to 5:00 P.M. Closed on Wednesday.

Fares   Adults, $2.50; seniors (60 or over), $2; children (ages
6 to 12), $1.25; children under six years of age are free of
charge.

Contact   Railswest Railroad Museum, 16th Avenue and South
Main Street, Council Bluffs, IA 51503. Telephone (712) 323-
5182 or (712) 322-0612.

DONNELLSON

FORT MADISON, FARMINGTON
& WESTERN RAILROAD

The Fort Madison, Farmington & Western Railroad takes passengers for a 2-mile trip through the woods led by an engine called a

Doodlebug, which can pull one train car. The restored *Doodlebug* (used as a house for half a century) departs from the Minerville Depot. The train passes through Iowa countryside and the Mississippi River Valley, and climbs a steep incline before returning to the station. The railroad grounds house old railcars, locomotives, an engine house, and a handcar that visitors can pump. Photos and railroad artifacts are also available for viewing.

Special Events   Santa Train.

How to Get There   The railroad is off Iowa Highway 2 between U.S. 61 and U.S. 218, near Wilson Lake Park.

Hours   Memorial Day to October: open weekends and holidays. Grounds are open from 12 noon to 5:00 P.M. Train rides operate from 12:30 to 4:30 P.M. (departure every hour on the half-hour).

Fares   Adults, $4; students (ages 5 to 18), $3; children under five years of age are free of charge.

Contact   Fort Madison, Farmington & Western Railroad, Minerville Station, 2209 220th Street, Donnellson, IA 52625. Telephone (319) 837-6689.

M A S O N   C I T Y

IOWA TROLLEY PARK

The Mason City & Clear Lake Electric Railway Historical Society was founded in 1987 to preserve trolley car heritage. It established Iowa Trolley Park and offers weekend trolley car rides between Mason City and Clear Lake on a rail line rebuilt in 1989 by the Iowa Traction Railroad, a freight company. Equipment used are an open-bench trolley car and an interurban.

How to Get There   From Des Moines, take I-35 north. Exit at Clear Lake (the first exit) and look for signs to the trolley park.

Hours   Memorial Day weekend to Labor Day weekend: departures from Clear Lake at 12:30 P.M., 2:30 P.M., and 4:30 P.M.; departures from Mason City at 1:30 P.M. and 3:30 P.M.

Fares   Call for information.

Contact   Mason City & Clear Lake Electric Railway Historical Society, P.O. Box 956, Mason City, IA 50401-0956. Telephone (515) 357-RIDE.

MOUNT PLEASANT

MIDWEST ELECTRIC RAILWAY

The Midwest Old Settlers and Threshers, an organization dedicated to preserving the Midwestern agricultural heritage, operates heritage museums, the Midwest Electric Railway, and the Midwest Old Threshers Reunion. The railway operates seven streetcars for the public on Sundays in the summer.

The reunion is an agricultural heritage celebration held annually since 1950. A five-day festival ending on Labor Day, the Threshers features over 100 operating steam engines, craft shows, educational programs, electric trolleys and steam trains, agricultural and theater museums, food, and music on a 60-acre campground.

Special Events   Midwest Old Threshers Reunion.

How to Get There   Midwest Electric Railway and Midwest Old Threshers are located 50 miles south of Iowa City and I-80, at the intersections of U.S. Highways 218 and 34.

Electric trolleys offer the perfect leisurely Sunday ride.

Hours   In June, July, and August: open Sunday, 1:00 P.M. to 5:00 P.M. Also operates throughout the Midwest Old Threshers Reunion/Labor Day weekend.

Fares   Admission is $1.

Contact   Midwest Old Settlers and Threshers, Threshers Road, Mount Pleasant, IA 52641. Telephone (319) 385-8937.

KANSAS

ABILENE & SMOKY VALLEY RAILROAD

The Abilene & Smoky Valley Railroad, established in 1993, features a 6-mile ride through Kansas farm country. The line pulls a 100-year-old wooden coach/diner and other vintage equipment on a track first laid in 1887. The scenic ride makes a river crossing that was once used by cowboys to water cattle. The depot, also built in 1887, is available for touring.

Special Events   Lilac Days; Old Settlers Days; Chisholm Trail Days.

How to Get There   From I-70 to the Buckeye exit south. The railroad is at the third set of tracks.

Hours   Memorial Day to Labor Day: Tuesday to Friday, 10:00 A.M. and 2:00 P.M.; Saturday, 10:00 A.M., 2:00 P.M., and 4:00 P.M.; Sunday, 2:00 P.M. and 4:00 P.M.

On weekends, the depot closes when the final train returns.

Fares   Adults (12 and above), $7.50; children (ages 3 to 11), $5.50.

Contact   Abilene & Smoky Valley Railroad, P.O. Box 744, Abilene, KS 67410. Telephone (913) 263-1077 or (913) 263-0118.

L E N E X A

LENEXA HISTORICAL SOCIETY

The Lenexa Historical Society operates a historical complex at Sar-Ko-Par Trails Park, a 53-acre city park designed to preserve Lenexa's history. Settlement of Lenexa increased with the arrival of the railroad, and the park features the Lenexa Railroad Depot, a restored station containing railroad memorabilia; a retired Northern Pacific caboose; a Conestoga wagon; and the Legler Barn Museum, an 1864 rebuilt barn.

The Society's future plans for the museum include restoration of the Strang Line (Interurban) waiting station and a Frisco Railroad work car, the upgrading of the caboose, and the creation of a railroad video.

How to Get There   From Kansas City, Missouri, take I-35 southwest to 87th Street. Turn right (west) to Lackman Road. On the south side of 87th Street and Lackman Road is Legler Barn.

Hours   Tuesday to Saturday, 10:00 A.M. to 4:00 P.M.; Sundays, 1:00 P.M. to 4:00 P.M.

Fares   Admission is free.

Contact   Lenexa Historical Society, 14907 West 87th Street Parkway, Lenexa, KS 66215-4135. Telephone (913) 492-0038.

LENEXA HISTORICAL SOCIETY

The Lenexa Railroad Depot is a restored station filled with railroad memorabilia.

KENTUCKY

HARDIN

HARDIN SOUTHERN RAILROAD

The *Nostalgia Train,* operated by the Hardin Southern Railroad since 1993, offers two-hour, 18-mile diesel excursions through Clarks River Valley over the 100-year-old route of the Nashville Chattanooga & St. Louis Railway. Along the way, passengers can view a variety of wildlife, including birds, deer, fox, and rabbit, and enjoy beautiful forests and farmland.

The railroad cars were built for transcontinental operation and feature picture windows and reclining seats. Refreshments are sold at the station and in Hardin.

NOTE: Passengers board in the center of Hardin, on SR 905, across from the library, half a mile east of SR 641.

Special Events Easter Bunny Special; Quilter's Special; Mother's Day; Santa Special; Father's Day; Nostalgia Train Anniversary; Halloween.

How to Get There   Hardin is two hours from Nashville. From Nashville, take I-24 north to the Purchase Parkway, then south on the Parkway to the Hardin/Murray exit. Hardin is 6 miles south on SR 641. Look for signs to the railroad.

Hours   May 25 to October 27: open weekends, with departures at 1:00 P.M. and 3:30 P.M. (This schedule is tentative. Call for information.)

Fares   Adults, $9.75; children (ages 3 to 12), $6.

Contact   Hardin Southern Railroad, P.O. Box 20, Hardin, KY 42048. Telephone (502) 437-4555.

N E W   H A V E N

KENTUCKY RAILWAY MUSEUM

The Kentucky Railway Museum began operations in 1958 with the display of the unrestored 1905 steam locomotive #152, a wood combine coach, and a caboose. Since then, the museum has acquired many more pieces of equipment.

Located in a replica of a New Haven depot, the museum also offers a scenic train excursion ride between New Haven and Boston, Kentucky; it's a one-and-a-half-hour, 22-mile trip. Diesels provide the train's power during the regular season; on major holidays and special weekends, passenger cars are powered by the now-restored locomotive #152.

The museum has a gift shop.

Special Events   Santa Trains.

How to Get There   From Louisville, take I-65 to exit 105; then take KY 61 to Boston. Pick up KY 52 and make a left into New Haven. Take exit 31 and turn right. The museum is three blocks from the last turn at 136 S. Main Street.

Hours   April to November: open Saturdays, Sundays, and most major holidays. June to Labor Day: open Tuesday through Friday.

Fares   Adults, $12.50; children (ages 2 to 12), $8; children under two years of age are free of charge.

Contact   Kentucky Railway Museum, 136 South Main Street, New Haven, KY 40051-0240. Telephone (800) 272-0152 or (502) 549-5470.

S T E A R N S

BIG SOUTH FORK SCENIC RAILWAY

The Big South Fork Scenic Railway provides a 7-mile, 45-minute excursion through the coal country of southeastern Kentucky. The journey, which includes canopied open side excursion cars pulled by diesel-electric locomotives, runs from Stearns to Blue Heron and travels into the Big South Fork National River and Recreation Area. The landscape includes beautiful mountain views, boulders, a hand-cut granite rock tunnel, creeks and rivers, and wildlife.

Blue Heron is the site of a restored coal mining community administered by the National Park Service. Passengers disembark there for a one-and-a-half-hour layover, and park rangers offer talks on the various exhibits. Featured nearby are an original coal tipple, which once separated and loaded hundreds of tons of coal an hour, and a wood trestle.

Special Events   Season Opening; Easter Bunny and Egg Hunt; Mother's Day; Spring Flora Interpretive; Spring Fling Night Run; Pioneer Day; Father's Day; Carnival; July 4th and 6th; Gospel Music Celebration; Country Night Out; Clogging Night Out; Country Music Celebration; Haunted Train Rides.

How to Get There   From Lexington, take I-75 south to exit 11 at Williamsburg. Head west on Highway 92 to Stearns. The depot is on the right.

Hours   April, May, and September: open Wednesday through Sunday; June, July, August, and October: open daily.
Weekdays: departure at 11:00 A.M.; Saturday and Sunday: departures at 11:00 A.M. and 3:00 P.M.

Fares   Round-trip: adults, $9.50; seniors (60 and over), $9; children (ages 4 to 12), $4.95; children under three years of age are free of charge.

Contact   Big South Fork Scenic Railway, P.O. Box 368, Stearns, KY 42647. Telephone (606) 376 5330.

V E R S A I L L E S

BLUEGRASS SCENIC RAILROAD

The Bluegrass Scenic Railroad is sponsored by the nonprofit Bluegrass Railroad Museum, a group dedicated to preserving railroad history and restoring railroad artifacts. Built in 1889 by the Louisville Southern Railroad, the 5.5 miles of track used by the line takes passengers on a 90-minute scenic excursion ride from Versailles through Kentucky's Bluegrass region. A highlight of the trip is the view from a railroad trestle 1,658 feet long and 280 high that overlooks the Kentucky River.
Among the items owned by the museum are two steam and five diesel locomotives, a bay window caboose, a post office car, and a baggage car.

Special Events   Hobo Days; Wild West Train Robbery; Lady Gangster Train Robbery; Civil War Drama and Train Robbery; Clown Daze; Halloween Ghost Train; Santa Claus Special.

How to Get There   From Lexington (I-64 or I-75), take route 922 south (exit 115) to New Circle Road. Take New Circle Road west to U.S. 60 west to downtown Versailles. Turn left on Main Street, then right on U.S. 62 west. The museum and railroad are 1.5 miles from downtown on Beasley Road in the Woodford County Park.

From Elizabethtown (I-65), take the Bluegrass Parkway to U.S. 60. Take U.S. 60 west to downtown Versailles. Turn left on Main Street, then right on U.S. 62 west.

From Frankfort (I-64), take U.S. 60 east (exit 58) to U.S. 62 west.

Hours   Last weekend in May through third weekend in October: Saturdays, 10:30 A.M., 1:30 P.M., and 3:30 P.M.; Sundays, 1:30 P.M. and 3:30 P.M.

Fares   Adults, $7; seniors (62 and above), $6; children (ages 2 to 12), $4; children under two years of age are admitted free of charge. Museum admission is free.

Contact   Bluegrass Scenic Railroad, P.O. Box 27, Versailles, KY 40383. Telephone (800) 755-2476 or (606) 873-2476.

LOUISIANA

DeQuincy Railroad Museum

Founded in 1895, DeQuincy was once a thriving railroad town at the intersection of two major railroads. Vestiges of the town's railroad past can be found in the DeQuincy Railroad Museum, where a 1913 steam locomotive, caboose, coach, and railroad memorabilia are on display. The museum, housed in a former Kansas City Southern depot, was built in 1923 and is on the National Register of Historic Places. DeQuincy hosts the annual Louisiana Railroad Days Festival, which is held the second weekend in April.

The museum is handicapped accessible and has a playground and park.

Special Events   Louisiana Railroad Days Festival.

How to Get There   From Lake Charles, drive west across the river to Sulphur. Take Highway 27 north into DeQuincy.

Hours   Monday through Friday, 9:00 A.M. to 5:00 P.M.; Saturday and Sunday, 12:00 noon to 4:00 P.M.

Fares   Admission is free, but donations are accepted.

Contact   DeQuincy Railroad Museum, P.O. Box 997, DeQuincy, LA 70633. Telephone (318) 786-2823.

G R E T N A

LOUISIANA STATE RAILROAD MUSEUM

Following completion of a two-year project to restore a former Texas-Pacific Railroad Station to its 1905 appearance, the Louisiana State Railroad Museum is expected to open in the summer of 1996.

Currently on display are a Porter Locomotive, which formerly hauled cars of river silt, and a Box Cab Electric. Visitors may view these at Mel Ott Park, 1 mile away.

Future plans include restoration of a 1921 Audubon Park locomotive and steam excursions around New Orleans. Classes are available on operating locomotive equipment.

How to Get There   The museum is 20 minutes from Vieux Carre in New Orleans. Take Business 90 west across the river bridge. Take the second exit at Lafayette Street. Turn right and follow LA 18 signs. Turn left at 5th Street, then right at Huey P. Long Avenue. The museum is at 3rd Street and Huey P. Long Avenue.

Hours   The museum is expected to open in June 1996 (call ahead).Weekdays only, 10:00 A.M. to 4:00 P.M. Closed Saturday, Sunday, and holidays, except by special appointment.

Fares   Donations are requested.

Contact   Louisiana State Railroad Museum, P.O. Box 8412, New Orleans, LA 70182. For taped information and appointments call (504) 283-8091.

N E W   O R L E A N S

St. Charles Streetcar and Riverfront Streetcar

New Orleans can claim a long streetcar history, as the first city west of the Allegheny Mountains to establish passenger rail service. Today, visitors have the chance to learn about that history while riding vintage streetcars along two routes.

The St. Charles Streetcar takes a 13.2-mile scenic route of antebellum mansions, two universities, historic monuments, and a tunnel of live oaks.

The Riverfront Streetcar operates six renovated cars, built in the 1920s by American and Australian companies, along a beautiful 1.9-mile route with scheduled stops at parks, hotels, shops, aquarium, art galleries, walkways, and restaurants.

Streetcars equipped with handicapped ramps are available.

How to Get There   The streetcars can be boarded along St. Charles Avenue and along the Mississippi River.

Hours   The St. Charles Streetcar operates 24 hours a day. The Riverfront Streetcar operates from 7:00 A.M. to 11:00 P.M.

Fares   Basic fare is $1 for the St. Charles Streetcar and $1.25 for the Riverfront Streetcar.

Contact   Regional Transit Authority, 6700 Plaza Drive, New Orleans, LA 70127-2677. Telephone (504) 248-3900.

MAINE

BOOTHBAY

BOOTHBAY RAILWAY VILLAGE

Boothbay Railway Village presents a collection of exhibits depicting turn-of-the-century Maine and New England life, spread over eight acres and contained in 27 buildings. Included are a one-room schoolhouse, an exhibit of early toys, a bank, hotel, hat shop, and antique cars and trucks. The village also features steam train rides on the **Boothbay Central Railroad,** a narrow gauge steam train built in 1938 that takes passengers on a 1.5-mile, 20-minute ride over a bridge, past a duck pond, and along a roadbed dating back to 1894. The trains depart from the Freeport Station, which contains railroad memorabilia and artifacts.

Special Events   Father's Day; Children's Day; Maine Narrow Gauge Railroad Day; Fall Foliage Festival; Halloween at the Village.

How to Get There   From Portland, take I-95 north to Route 1 (Brunswick exit). Follow Route 1 to Wiscasset, then turn onto Route 27 south. The Village is 8 miles from the turn.

Hours   Open 9:30 A.M. to 5:00 P.M., mid-June to mid-October. Train runs on the half hour.

Fares   Adults, $6; children (ages 2 to 12), $3. Children under the age of two are free of charge.

Contact   Boothbay Railway Village, Route 27, Boothbay, ME 04537. Telephone (207) 633-4727.

KENNEBUNKPORT

SEASHORE TROLLEY MUSEUM

From the late 1800s to the 1930s, streetcars were the dominant mode of city transportation. Their history has been preserved at the Seashore Trolley Museum, in operation since 1939. One of the oldest and largest of its kind, the museum offers visitors

SEASHORE TROLLEY MUSEUM

City of Manchester car, once part of the Manchester Street Railway.

SEASHORE TROLLEY MUSEUM

Car 1391, one of the *Yale Bowl Fleet* trolleys that transported college foot-
ball fans to bowl games through the 1940s.

displays of more than 200 transit vehicles from around the
world. A large touring area, a guided walking tour, and a 1.5-
mile ride in restored trolley cars await visitors. Other features
are two barns with displays of trolleys and restored cars, a
restoration shop, and a library.

The museum has a visitor center, with a museum store,
exhibits, restrooms, and a snack bar. It also serves as the departure point for trolley rides and guided tours.

Special Events   Kids' Day Free; USA Trolley Parade; Independence Day; Moxie Congress; Maine Antique Power Days;
Cajun Fest; Vidbel's Olde Tyme Circus; Canadian Weekend;
Labor Day Weekend; Member's Day Open House; Ghost Trolley Haunted Rides; Christmas Prelude by the Sea.

How to Get There   From Boston, take I-95 north to the Maine
Turnpike. Take exit 3, Route 35 to Kennebunkport. Turn onto

Route 1 north for 2.8 miles, and turn right at the yellow blinking light.

From Kennebunkport, go to the west end of Maine Street, and turn right on North Street, which becomes Log Cabin Road.

Hours   May to December: open daily Memorial Day to mid-October 10:00 A.M. to 5:30 P.M. Open on weekends only during the rest of the year.

Call for exact days and times for both the museum and the trolley rides. Museum store and grounds are open one hour after the last trolley ride.

Fares   Adults, $7; seniors (60 or over), $5; children (ages 6 to 16), $4.

Contact   Seashore Trolley Museum, Log Cabin Road, P.O. Box A, Kennebunkport, ME 04046-1690. Telephone (207) 967-2712.

P H I L L I P S

SANDY RIVER & RANGELEY LAKES RAILROAD

The Sandy River & Rangeley Lakes Railroad is a successor to the old Sandy River and Phillips & Rangeley Railroads. The narrow gauge lines provided transportation for passengers traveling to the resort area of Rangeley, while the timber industry used the line for carrying freight south.

Today a replica steam locomotive pulls an 1884 antique passenger car on a short scenic journey along the route of the Phillips and Rangeley Railroad. On the site of the railroad is a museum with artifacts and souvenirs, boxcars and railroad equipment, and new and vintage railroad buildings.

Special Events   Old Home Days (third weekend in August).

How to Get There   Take Route 4 north, through Farmington, to Phillips (about 18 miles from Farmington). In Phillips there's an airstrip and a building supply company. On left, gas tanks are visible. Make a right from there. Go half a mile to railroad on Bridge Hill Road.

Hours   June through October: open the first and third Sundays in the month. Call ahead for specific hours.

Fares   Adults, $3; children (ages 6 to 18), $2. Children under the age of six are free of charge.

Contact   Sandy River & Rangeley Lakes Railroad, P.O. Box B, Phillips, ME 04966. Telephone (207) 639-3352.

PORTLAND

MAINE NARROW GAUGE RAILROAD COMPANY AND MUSEUM

The Maine Narrow Gauge Railroad Company and Museum is a nonprofit organization preserving the narrow gauge railroad collection of the late Ellis D. Atwood. The collection, once part of the Edaville Railroad in South Carver, Massachusetts, arrived in Maine in 1993. The Atwood equipment includes passenger cars, boxcars, cabooses, track vehicles, and steam locomotives, which are on display at the Portland Company buildings, the site of the railroad and museum.

The railroad offers steam or diesel train rides from mid-May to mid-October and welcomes passengers to sit in the engineer's cab. The museum has a souvenir shop.

NOTE: A playground with jungle gym, swings, and large play area is located a few blocks from the museum.

Special Events   Open House; Santa Visit; Rail Fair; Fireworks Special.

How to Get There   From Portland, take I-295 to exit 7, Franklin Arterial and Fore Street. Make a left, cross India Street, and climb the hill toward Eastern Promenade. The site is located at 58 Fore Street.

Hours   The museum is open daily, 10:00 A.M. to 4:00 P.M., from mid-May to mid-October; train rides operate from 11:00 A.M. to 4:00 P.M. (on the hour). Open weekends from mid-October to mid-May.

Fares   Train rides: adults, $3; children (ages 4 to 12), $2. Children under four years of age are free of charge. Admission to the museum is free.

Contact   Maine Narrow Gauge Railroad Company and Museum, 58 Fore Street, Portland, ME 04101. Telephone (207) 828-0814.

U N I T Y

BELFAST & MOOSEHEAD LAKE RAILROAD

The Belfast & Moosehead Lake Railroad was first chartered in 1870 and runs both a freight and tourist line. Departing from one of two depots (the circa-1940 Thorndike Station in Unity and the 1890 Belfast Station), passengers can climb aboard a steam locomotive (Unity) or a diesel-powered train (Belfast) for a one-and-a-half-hour excursion ride that includes quiet fields, beautiful waterfront, and an occasional moose sighting. Early arrivals for the steam locomotive will enjoy watching the train out on the turntable as part of a pre-ride show.

Both diesel and steam trains, which run twice a day from either location, include refreshments, entertainment, and a train robbery show on board. Combination train rides with meals, riverboat cruises, and overnight stays are also offered.

BELFAST & MOOSEHEAD LAKE RAILROAD

A turn-of-the-century steam locomotive pulls into the depot in the station's heyday.

How to Get There   From Portland, take I-95 to Augusta, Maine. Exit at Route 3. Go toward the coast to reach Belfast. Once in Belfast, follow signs for the waterfront until reaching the Belfast Station.

To reach the Unity Station, take I-95 to Fairfield, exit 35. Take Route 139 east to Unity. Stay on 139 to reach Unity.

Hours   May through October 20: departures at 11:00 A.M. and 1:00 P.M. (Belfast) and 12:00 noon (Unity). Call for schedule of exact days.

Fares   Train only: adults, $8; children (ages 3 to 16), $4. Train and breakfast or lunch: adults, $15; children (ages 3 to 16), $7.50.

Rail & Sail: adults, $15; children (ages 3 to 16), $7.50. Rail & Sail (with breakfast or lunch): adults, $18; children

(ages 3 to 16), $9. Rail & Sail (with meal and motel): adults, $49; children (ages 3 to 16), $24.50.
Children under three years of age are free of charge.

Contact   Belfast & Moosehead Lake Company, One Depot Square, Unity, ME 04988. Telephone (800) 392-5500 or (207) 948-5500.

W I S C A S S E T

MAINE COAST RAILROAD

The charming village of Wiscasset is home to the Maine Coast Railroad. A diesel-powered locomotive takes passengers from Wiscasset to Newcastle, over tidal rivers and wildlife marshes, and past eagle, osprey, and heron habitats.
The railroad also offers a "rail and sail" tour package, which includes a train ride and narrated trip on a lobster boat through Sheepscot River. The engineer welcomes visitors to tour the cab.

How to Get There   From Boston, take I-95 north to Portland to 295 north. Continue to Route 1 to Wiscasset.
From the north, take Route 1 south to Wiscasset; or I-95 south to Route 27 in Augusta, south to Wiscasset. The railroad station is on Water Street.

Hours   Open daily from the end of June through Labor Day.

Fares   Adults, $10; children (ages 4 to 12), $5. Children under the age of four are free of charge.

Contact   Maine Coast Railroad, P.O. Box 614, Wiscasset, ME 04578. Telephone (207) 882-8000 or (207) 882-7499; fax (207) 882-7699.

MARYLAND

B & O RAILROAD MUSEUM

The B & O Railroad Museum at Mt. Clare Station, built in 1930, is the site of America's first passenger train departure. A replica of that train, Peter Cooper's *Tom Thumb,* is a museum display.

Located on a 37-acre site, the museum contains over 120 pieces of full-sized railroad equipment, a large collection of railroad artifacts, and a majestic, 22-sided 1884 roundhouse, which until 1953 served as a repair shop for passenger cars operating on the B & O Railroad. The roundhouse features a wooden turntable and over 20 restored historic steam, diesel, and electric locomotives. Front and back yards offer visitors the opportunity to view other railcars and locomotives on exhibit. Model train enthusiasts will especially enjoy the museum's 12-foot-by-40-foot HO model layout built in 1956.

Throughout the year, the B & O Railroad Museum offers a 3-mile, 25-minute round-trip train ride on the Mt. Clare Express from Mt. Clare Station to the Carrolton Viaduct.

The museum has a gift shop, a snack bar, picnic tables, and free parking.

How to Get There   The museum is 10 blocks from Baltimore's Inner Harbor. Take I-95 north to exit 53 to I-395 north. Follow signs to Martin Luther King, Jr. Boulevard. Turn left onto Lombard Street. Then turn left onto Poppelton, which leads to the museum entrance.

Hours   Open daily (except Thanksgiving and Christmas Day), 10:00 A.M. to 5:00 P.M. Train rides: departures at 11:30 A.M., 12:30 P.M., 2:00 P.M., and 3:00 P.M.

Fares   Adults (13 and over), $6; seniors (60 and over), $5; children (ages 5 to 12), $3. Train rides are $2 for visitors with paid admission to the museum. Children four years of age and under are free of charge.

Contact   B & O Railroad Museum, 901 West Pratt Street, Baltimore, MD 21223-2699. Telephone (410) 752-2490; fax (410) 752-2499.

BALTIMORE STREETCAR MUSEUM

The city of Baltimore acquired its first streetcar tracks in 1859, and the important role of streetcars in the development of Baltimore is captured at this museum. The museum is a nonprofit organization dedicated to the preservation of streetcars and their history. Highlights include an audiovisual presentation on Baltimore's streetcar history, a tour of the museum's rich streetcar collection, including cars built between 1898 and 1944, and a streetcar ride that takes visitors on a tour past the former roundhouse and freight station of the Maryland and Pennsylvania Railroad. The museum has a gift shop.

Special Events   Grandparents' Day; Antique Automobile Show; Holly Trolley.

How to Get There   Take I-95 north to Baltimore Beltway. Then take I-83 towards Baltimore. Exit at North Avenue and turn left. Turn right at Maryland Avenue. Go to next signal, Lafayette, and turn right. Go a quarter of a mile on right hand side to the museum on Falls Road.

Hours   June through October: open Saturday and Sunday, 12:00 noon to 5:00 P.M.; rest of the year: open Sunday (except Christmas), 12:00 noon to 5:00 P.M.

Fares   Adults, $4; children (ages 4 to 11), $2. Children under the age of four are free of charge.

Contact   Baltimore Streetcar Museum, 1901 Falls Road, P.O. Box 4881, Baltimore, MD 21211. Telephone (410) 547-0264.

CHESAPEAKE BEACH

CHESAPEAKE BEACH RAILWAY MUSEUM

Listed on the National Register of Historic Places, the Chesapeake Beach Railway Museum presents the history of both Chesapeake Beach, a bayside resort built at the turn of the century, and the Chesapeake Beach Railway. The railroad line operated between 1900 and 1935, providing daily rail service to resort patrons on the "Honeysuckle Route," a one-hour excursion through southern Maryland. The same line also carried freight. The museum contains artifacts, an audiovisual presentation, photos, and displays related to the resort and to transportation of the period.
    The museum is handicapped accessible.

How to Get There   From Washington, D.C., take I-95 to Route 4 south to Calvert County. From Baltimore, take I-695 to Route 301 south to Route 4 south. Across Calvert County line, take a left on Route 260. Go 5 miles to Chesapeake Beach and turn right on Route 261 to the museum.

Hours May through September: open daily, 1:00 P.M. to 4:00 P.M.; in April and October: open weekends, 1:00 P.M. to 4:00 P.M. Open by appointment at other times.

Fares Admission is free.

Contact Chesapeake Beach Railway Museum, P.O. Box 783, Chesapeake Beach, MD 20732. Street address: 4155 Mears Avenue, Chesapeake Beach, MD 20732. Telephone (410) 257-3892.

CUMBERLAND

WESTERN MARYLAND SCENIC RAILROAD

A three-hour, 32-mile round-trip excursion ride from picturesque Cumberland to Frostburg in western Maryland on *Mountain Thunder* offers riders a great opportunity to explore a variety of terrain. The line goes through the Allegheny Mountains, over a bridge, around a horseshoe curve, through a 1,000-foot mountain tunnel, and up a 2.8-percent grade. Visitors have a one-and-a-half-hour stop in Frostburg, where they can enjoy a picnic or restaurant lunch and watch the train crew use the turntable to reposition the engine for the return trip.

The departure point in Cumberland (now the Western Maryland Station Center) was built in 1913 and now houses a museum, visitors bureau, ticket office, and gift shop. The Old Depot in Frostburg, built in 1891, once served as a freight station for the former Cumberland and Pennsylvania Railroad. Today, it offers mountain views from its restaurant, gift shop, and bakery. A carriage museum, with displays of every kind of horse-drawn transport imaginable from sleighs to town cars, is open to the public.

The engine, built in 1916, once served as a switching engine and coal hauler.

Special Events   Mother's Day; Cumberland Heritage Days and Train Raid; Father's Day; Frostburg Derby Day Special; Drumfest Express; Halloween Train; Santa's Express; Hip Hop Trains; Fall Foliage.

How to Get There   From Washington, D.C., take I-70 west (toward Frederick). In Hancock, exit onto I-68 at the left exit, and drive to downtown Cumberland (exit 43C). Turn left off the highway and cross a traffic light to the parking area.

Hours   April to September: departs 11:30 A.M., Tuesday through Sunday.
October: departs 11:00 A.M. and 4 P.M.
November and December: departs 11:30 A.M., weekends only.

Fares   Regular season: adults, $14.75; seniors (60 or over), $13.25; children (ages 2 to 12), $9.50; one-way, $12.75.
In October: adults, $16.75; seniors (60 or over), $16.25; children (ages 2 to 12), $10.50; one-way, $15.75.
Children under two years of age (not occupying a seat) are free of charge.

Contact   Western Maryland Scenic Railroad, 13 Canal Street, Cumberland, MD 21502. Telephone (800) TRAIN-50 or (301) 759-4400.

SILVER SPRING

NATIONAL CAPITAL TROLLEY MUSEUM

The National Capital Trolley Museum, an operating museum, offers visitors the opportunity to view and ride trolleys from the museum's rich collection of American and European street-cars (all built between 1899 to the 1940s) and to learn about the historic Washington, D.C., streetcars that operated for 100 years. Artifacts, photo displays, and an operating miniature trolley line all help to tell the story.

Special Events   Cabin Fever Day in February (includes a family scavenger hunt); Snow Sweeper Day in March (a demonstration of snow removal in the trolley era); Fall Open House (visitors can see all trolleys in operation or on display); Holly Trolleyfest (celebration with lights, toy trains, and Santa on a streetcar).

How to Get There   From downtown Washington, D.C., take 16th Street north to Georgia Avenue to Layhill Road. Go up Layhill to Bonifant, make a right on Bonifant. Museum is 1 mile down on the left.

Hours   January to November: open weekends and holidays, 12:00 noon to 5:00 P.M.
    July and August: also open on Wednesday, 11:00 A.M. to 3:00 P.M.
    December (Holly Trolleyfest): open Saturday and Sunday, 5:00 P.M. to 9 P.M. Closed Christmas Eve, Christmas Day, New Year's Eve, and New Year's Day.

Fares   Museum: Admission is free. Trolley ride: adults, $2; children (ages 2 to 18), $1.50; children under two years of age are free of charge.

Contact   National Capital Trolley Museum, P.O. Box 4007, Silver Spring, MD 20914. Street address: 1313 Bonifant Road, Silver Spring, MD 20904. Telephone (301) 384-6088.

MASSACHUSETTS

BEVERLY

BEVERLY HISTORICAL SOCIETY AND MUSEUM

The core of the Walker Transportation Collection at the Beverly Historical Society and Museum was created and donated by Laurence Breed Walker, a railroad enthusiast. The exhibit has been expanded since its arrival at the museum in 1969 and now includes thousands of photographs, film and video, recordings of steam train sounds, railroad models, and a variety of train memorabilia. The museum also has an extensive library on transportation history.

How to Get There   From Boston, take I-95 or I-93 to 128 east (Glocester). Exit at Beverly, and follow road 1A or 62 to downtown. The historical society is at 117 Cabot Street.

Hours   Open Wednesday, 7:00 P.M. to 10:00 P.M., and by appointment.

Fares   Admission is free.

Contact   Walker Transportation Collection at the Beverly Historical Society and Museum, 117 Cabot Street, Beverly, MA 01915. Telephone (508) 922-1186.

H Y A N N I S

CAPE COD RAILROAD

The Cape Cod Railroad runs two-hour round-trip diesel excursion trains along tracks first created in the late 1800s, when rail travel was the primary form of transportation in the area. The narrated journey makes a stop in Sandwich Village, where passengers may take a Sandwich Glass Museum tour or visit a beach boardwalk, and then continues to Cape Cod Canal, the widest man-made canal in the world and a popular fishing, hiking, and camping area. Along the way, visitors may catch a glimpse of osprey, hawks, and blue heron. Ecology Discovery tours take visitors to a conservation preserve for a guided marsh walk. Dinner trains are also offered.

Rolling stock includes a 1950s dome car, a Budd car, and locomotives built in the 1940s and 1950s. Refreshments are available on all trains.

Special Events   Christmas trains.

How to Get There   From Route 6, take exit 7 (it becomes Willow Street). Head toward Hyannis, go across Route 28 and turn onto Yarmouth Road (follow signs to Hyannis). Follow Yarmouth until it ends. Make a right onto Main Street. The depot is on the right.

Hours   May: open weekends and holidays; June to October: open daily except Mondays, unless a holiday.

Departures at 10:00 A.M., 12:30 P.M., and 3:00 P.M.

Fares $41.86 per person, plus tax.

Contact   Cape Cod Railroad, 252 Main Street, Hyannis, MA 02601. Telephone (508) 771-3788.

L E N O X

BERKSHIRE SCENIC RAILWAY MUSEUM

The Berkshire Scenic Railway Museum was founded in 1984 as a nonprofit organization committed to preserving and presenting the history of Berkshire railroading through a collection of artifacts and a tourist train ride. Located in a restored 1902 Lenox railroad station, the museum collection includes several locomotives, a former New Jersey Transit coach, a coach from the Pennsylvania Railroad, two cabooses and a boxcar, baggage trucks, area railroading exhibits, and operating model railroads.

The museum currently offers "Short Shuttle" narrated trips along track in the railway yard. Every child who visits the engineer's cab receives an engineer's cap. Future plans are to resume long-distance excursions on track between Lee and Great Barrington, Massachusetts. The museum also has a gift shop.

Special Events   Santa Special; Halloween Specials; Operation Lifesaver; Band Day; Fire Apparatus Day; Restoration Party.

How to Get There   From Route 20 (Pittsfield), take exit 2. Drive through Lenox and look for Berkshire Scenic Railway signs. The museum is 2 miles from the exit on Willow Creek Road.

Hours   Memorial Day through October: open 10:00 A.M. to 4:00 P.M., Saturday, Sunday, and holidays. Train rides operate every half hour.

Fares Museum admission is free. Train rides: adults, $1.50; seniors, $1; children (ages 2 to 12), $1.

Contact Berkshire Scenic Railway Museum, P.O. Box 2195, Lenox, MA 01240. Telephone (413) 637-2210.

L O W E L L

LOWELL NATIONAL HISTORICAL PARK

The city of Lowell, Massachusetts, was once a booming industrial center. Lowell National Historical Park, established in 1978 and operated by the National Park Service, commemorates the

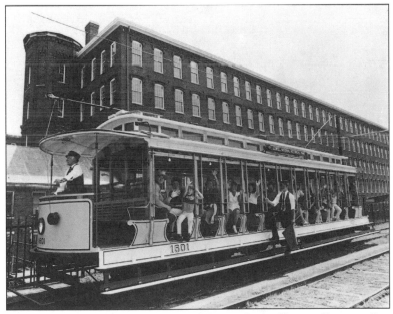

JAMES HIGGINS, LOWELL NATIONAL HISTORICAL PARK

Trolley passengers travel past the Boott Cotton Mills Museum, a former textile mill.

town's importance to the American Industrial Revolution. The park contains a variety of displays, including historic cotton textile mills; the Boott Cotton Mills Museum, with operating looms and exhibits; a "Working People Exhibit" on worker housing; the "Suffolk Mill Turbine Exhibit" on waterpower; and more than 5.5 miles of canals in operation. Guided walking tours of the park are offered throughout the year.

Train fans will enjoy taking a ride on a turn-of-the-century, closed or open-air trolley that runs along 1 mile of Boston and Maine Railroad track. The journey takes visitors from the downtown mill area to the canal barge system in the park. Boat tours are offered along the canals in the summer.

NOTE: Reservations are recommended for all guided tours.

How to Get There   Take the Lowell Connector from Route 495 (exit 36) or Route 3 (exit 30N) to Thorndike Street (exit 5N). Follow signs for Lowell National and State Park.

Hours   Open daily, except Thanksgiving, Christmas, and New Year's Day.

Fares   Museum tours vary. Call ahead.

Contact   Lowell National Historical Park, 169 Merrimack Street, Lowell, MA 01852-1796. Telephone (508) 970-5000.

MICHIGAN

ANN ARBOR

ARTRAIN

Three refurbished passenger cars, a baggage car, and a caboose converted into galleries, studio, and office space comprise the Artrain, a nonprofit mobile art museum that takes visual arts exhibits to communities throughout the country. Begun in 1971, the Artrain has traveled to over 500 communities in 38 states.

The Artrain creates new exhibits by borrowing from other sources and each year gives shows in different regions of the country. Themes are changed every two to three years.

The 1996, 1997, and 1998 touring seasons will feature "Art in Celebration," with exhibits from the Smithsonian Associates Collection. The grand opening took place at Union Station in Washington, D.C., the weekend of March 23–25, 1996.

Fares   Fares depend on the site. The average charge is $3.

Contact   Artrain, 1100 North Main Street, Suite 102, Ann Arbor, MI 48104. Telephone: (313) 747-8300 or (800) ART-1971.

BRIDGEPORT

JUNCTION VALLEY RAILROAD

A quarter-sized railroad display, a scenic 2-mile ride through wooded valleys and along waterways, a 100-foot tunnel, and more than 865 feet of bridges and trestles are featured at the Junction Valley Railroad. Created by train enthusiast William A. Stenger, Jr., the railroad also includes over 30 buildings and stations, a 10-stall roundhouse, up to 5-percent grades, and more than 60 operating track switches.

A picnic area, playground, pavilions, hobby shop, and concession stands are also on the site.

Special Events Opening Day; Halloween Spook Train; Christmas Fantasyland Train; Railroad Days; Carnival Days; Valley of Flags; Father's Day; Mother's Day; Popsicle Thursday.

JUNCTION VALLEY RAILROAD
Visitors take a scenic 2-mile ride aboard the Junction Valley Railroad.

How to Get There   Take I-75 to Bridgeport (exit 144). Turn south off the exit, pass the flashing yellow light at the corner of Dixie Highway and Junction Road, and look for a train replica on top of the building.

Hours   Mid-May through Labor Day: open Monday to Saturday, 10:00 A.M. to 6:00 P.M.; Sunday, 1:00 P.M. to 6:00 P.M.
     September through the first week of October: open Saturday and Sunday only, 1:00 P.M. to 5:00 P.M.

Fares   Adults, $4.25; seniors, $4; children, $3.50.

Contact   Junction Valley Railroad, 7065 Dixie Highway at Junction Road, Bridgeport, MI 48722. Telephone (517) 777-3480.

C O O P E R S V I L L E

COOPERSVILLE & MARNE RAILWAY

The Coopersville & Marne Railway offers a one-hour trip on a historic diesel passenger train. The train departs from downtown Coopersville A gift shop is located in the depot.

Special Events   Summerfest; Great Train Robbery; Murder Mystery Dinner Train; Pumpkin Train; Santa Train.

How to Get There   From Grand Rapids, take I-96 west to Coopersville. Take exit 16 or 19 and follow signs that say "Ride the Train" to the depot.

Hours   July to September: open Saturday, with departures at 1:00 and 3:00 P.M.

Fares   Adults (ages 14 and above), $7.50; seniors, $6.50; children (ages 4 to 13), $4.50; children three years of age and under are free of charge.

Contact   Coopersville & Marne Railway, Danforth Street, P.O. Box 55, Coopersville, MI 49404. Telephone (616) 837-7000.

DETROIT

DETROIT TROLLEY

Turn-of-the-century trolleys can be hailed along the streets of downtown Detroit. Operating since 1976, the nine cars move along Washington Boulevard and Jefferson Avenue between Grand Circus Park and the Renaissance Center. Visitors can board at designated trolley stops or hail one between stops.

The trolleys feature two open-air cars (including a one-of-a-kind double-decker) and seven closed cars built in England, Portugal, Germany, and the United States between 1895 and the 1920s.

How to Get There   The trolleys are located in downtown Detroit, along Washington Boulevard and Jefferson Avenue.

Hours   Trolleys operate from 8:30 A.M. to 5:30 P.M. (hours are extended during special events).

Fares   The fare is $.50.

Contact   Detroit Department of Transportation, 1301 East Warren, Detroit, MI 48207. Telephone (313) 933-1300 or 935-4910; fax (313) 833-5523.

FLINT

HUCKLEBERRY RAILROAD

The Huckleberry Railroad is part of the offerings at Crossroads Village, a re-creation of Genesee County, Michigan, life in the

GENESEE COUNTY PARKS & RECREATION COMMISSION

The Huckleberry Railroad is just one of the historic rides for visitors at Crossroads Village.

1800s. The village, a facility of the Genesee County Parks and Recreation Commission, opened in 1976. It includes 30 historic buildings, with craftspeople in period costumes working at a variety of tasks common to the era, including live demonstrations at the gristmill, cidermill, and sawmill.

Today's narrow gauge track, two-thirds the size of the original standard gauge track, is pulled by a historic Baldwin steam locomotive departing from the Crossroads Depot. The *Huckleberry* carries up to 500 passengers on a 35-minute ride. The village also offers rides on a paddle wheel riverboat for a 45-minute scenic cruise and on an antique Ferris wheel and a carousel.

Special Events Huckleberry Ghost Train; Christmas at Crossroads.

How to Get There From Detroit, take I-75 to I-475 south and exit 13 (Saginaw Street). Go north on Saginaw to Stanley

Road. Go east on Stanley to Bray Road and south on Bray. The village is located on the east side of the road.

Hours   Crossroads Village: from mid-May to Labor Day, open daily, 10:00 A.M. to 5:30 P.M.; in September, open Saturday, Sunday, and holidays, 11:00 A.M. to 6:30 P.M.

Train rides: operate weekdays, 11:00 A.M. to 4:00 P.M. (train departs hourly); Saturday, Sunday, and holidays, 12:00 noon to 5:00 P.M.

Fares   Adults, $8.25; seniors age 60 and over, $7.25; children (ages 4 to 12), $5.50; children three and under are free of charge.

Contact   Huckleberry Railroad, Genesee County Parks and Recreation Commission, 5045 Stanley Road, Flint, MI 48506. Telephone (810) 736-7100.

IRON MOUNTAIN

IRON MOUNTAIN IRON MINE

The Iron Mountain Iron Mine provides mine visitors with raincoats and hard hats to wear before presenting a one-hour guided mining operations tour through 2,600 feet of underground drifts and tunnels. Designated a Michigan State Historical Site, the mine was discovered in 1870.

The gift shop includes a display of mining equipment and sells an array of rocks and minerals, antique ironware, and a variety of other souvenirs.

NOTE: Be sure to wear comfortable walking shoes and warm clothing to accommodate the mine temperature of 43°F.

How to Get There   The site is 12 miles east of Iron Mountain in Vulcan, MI. Take U.S. 2 and look for signs to the mine.

Hours   Memorial Day to October 15: open 9:00 A.M. to 5 P.M. Tours last one hour.

Fares   Adults, $5.50; children (ages 6 to 12), $4.50; children under six years of age are admitted free of charge.

Contact   Iron Mountain Iron Mine, P.O. Box 177, Iron Mountain, MI 49801. Telephone (906) 563-8077.

OWOSSO

MICHIGAN STATE TRUST FOR RAILWAY PRESERVATION

Also known as Project 1225, this nonprofit organization offers visitors a great opportunity to visit a mobile, one-exhibit museum and learn about steam locomotive operations first-hand. With an emphasis on preserving the heritage of steam railroading, Project 1225 involves the running of a 1941 steam

MICHIGAN STATE TRUST FOR RAILWAY PRESERVATION

Project 1225 offers visitors the chance to learn how steam trains operate.

locomotive built for the Pere Marquette Railway. Although it is not an excursion train, locomotive #1225 is operated several times during the summer, and visitors may run the train over a portion of track during the Preservation's "Engineer for an Hour" programs.

First on exhibit at Michigan State University in 1957, the locomotive was restored and relocated to Owosso. In 1988, locomotive #1225 returned to the tracks, where visitors can now see how steam trains operate. Its covered quarters are located in a portion of a railroad backshop once used by the Ann Arbor Railroad (now owned by the Tuscola & Saginaw Bay Railway Company).

How to Get There   The museum is in southeast Owosso, off Highway M-71 (Corunna Avenue). From the exit, turn north onto Oakwood Street and left at the abandoned bridge, into the yard of the Tuscola & Saginaw Bay Railway Company. Drive to the end of the path, cross the tracks, and turn left to the brick machine shop.

NOTE: Trains may move in the yard at any time.

Hours   Open Saturdays (except major holidays), 10:00 A.M. to 6:00 P.M.

Fares   Call for information.

Contact   Michigan State Trust for Railway Preservation, Inc., P.O. Box 665, Owosso, MI 48867-0665. Telephone (517) 725-9464.

SOO JUNCTION

TOONERVILLE TROLLEY

Toonerville Trolley is named after a 1930s and 1940s cartoon series by the company's trolley passengers. Tahquamenon Boat

Service, Inc. operates a combination train and riverboat excursion in Michigan's Upper Peninsula. Departing from Soo Junction, a 24-inch narrow gauge Plymouth locomotive pulls open or enclosed cars (depending on the season) along 6 miles of track through the forested habitat of bear, deer, birds, and other wildlife. On the two-hour riverboat ride, passengers take a narrated tour of the Tahquamenon River on a 21-mile cruise to upper Tahquamenon Falls. At the falls, visitors enjoy a layover of 1 hour and 15 minutes, during which they can walk a 3600-foot wooded nature trail.

A coffee and gift shop and depot are located in Soo Junction.

NOTE: An enclosed boat and trolley operate after Labor Day. Warm clothing is recommended.

How to Get There   Soo Junction is 16 miles east of Newberry and a few miles off Highway M-28.

Hours   Open June 15 through October 6: departure at 10:30 A.M.; return at 5:00 P.M.

Fares   Adult, $16; children (ages 6 to 15), $8; children under six years of age are admitted free of charge.

Contact   Tahquamenon Boat Service, Inc., Rural Route 2, P.O. Box 938, Newberry, MI 49868. Telephone 888-77-TRAIN or (906) 876-2311 (depot) or (906) 876-2313 (dock) or (906) 293-3806 (if no answer at the other numbers).

TRAVERSE CITY

SPIRIT OF TRAVERSE CITY

A one-quarter-scale steam locomotive, the *Spirit of Traverse City* (locomotive #400) travels on almost half a mile of track through the Clinch Park Zoo and marina. The train ride provides visitors a beautiful view, overlooking the breathtaking landscape of northern Michigan. The *Spirit of Traverse City* offers up to 40 trips a day.

Special Events Family Fun Day.

How to Get There The site is on West Traverse Bay at Clinch Park Zoo. From Detroit take I-75 north to Graling. Then take 72 west to Acme. Turn left onto U.S. 31 (south) and follow it into Traverse City. Park in the lot and take the zoo tunnel to the plaza.

Hours Memorial Day weekend to Labor Day: open daily, 10:00 A.M. to 4:30 P.M.

Fares Adults, $1; children (ages 5 to 12), $.50; children under five years of age are admitted free of charge.

Contact Spirit of Traverse City, 625 Woodmere Avenue, Traverse City, MI 49686. Telephone (616) 922-4910.

WALLED LAKE

MICHIGAN STAR CLIPPER DINNER TRAIN AND COE RAIL SCENIC TRAIN

The Michigan Star Clipper Dinner Train features an elegant five-course meal, live entertainment, and a cash bar; the Coe Rail Scenic Train offers a beautiful one-hour excursion through the West Bloomfield Sanctuary and Wetlands—the perfect spot to help kids explore nature.

Sponsors recommend the Coe Rail Scenic Train for educational school trips, children's birthday parties, fall foliage tours, and other special events.

Special Events   Hobo Halloween.

How to Get There   From Detroit, take I-696 to I-96 west, exit 162 (Novi Walled Lake exit). Go north on Novi Road to 13 Mile Road. Turn right (east) onto 13 Mile Road to Decker Road. Drive 2 miles and then turn left (west) onto Maple. Maple Road ends at Pontiac Trail; turn right, about 300 yards to the depot.

Hours   April to October: open 1:00 P.M. to 2:30 P.M.

Fares   Adults, $7; seniors (65 and above), $6; children (ages 2 to 10), $6; infants not occupying a seat are admitted free of charge.

Contact   Michigan Star Clipper/Coe Rail Scenic Train, 840 North Pontiac Trail, Walled Lake, MI 48390. Telephone (810) 960-9440.

MINNESOTA

CURRIE

END-O-LINE RAILROAD PARK AND MUSEUM

The End-O-Line Railroad Park and Museum has a rich variety of offerings. Created by the early efforts of 4-H volunteers, the End-O-Line began with the restoration of a manually operated train turntable in 1972.

Today, the End-O-Line, which is on the National Register of Historic Sites, has an extensive collection of exhibits depicting railroading in southwestern Minnesota. Among the displays are the recently acquired Georgia Pacific train engine and tender, a caboose, motorcar, an HO scale model train display (featuring complete landscaping, mural, and sound effects), and railroad memorabilia. Visitors can also view a section foreman's house built by the Chicago & Northwestern line, a general store from 1873, a schoolhouse, and the Currie Depot and Engine House.

A special attraction is the full-sized outdoor model train created by Henry Hilfers, a train enthusiast. His collection now

END-O-LINE RAILROAD PARK AND MUSEUM

Vintage section foreman's tools are on display in the engine house.

includes steam and diesel engines and seven cars along a track with a water tower, crossing signals, and a depot.

The End-O-Line offers a one-and-a-half-hour tour to visitors. All buildings are handicapped accessible.

How to Get There   Currie is located on State Highway 30 and County Road 38 in southwestern Minnesota. From Worthington, take Highway 59 to Avoca. Then take County Road 38 north to Currie for 6 miles. Pick up Highway 30 west, then County Road 38 north. The site is located on the north edge of Currie at 440 North Mill Street.

Hours   Memorial Day to Labor Day: open Monday to Friday, 10:00 A.M. to 12:00 noon and 1:00 P.M. to 5:00 P.M.; Saturday and Sunday, 1:00 P.M. to 5:00 P.M.

END-O-LINE RAILROAD PARK AND MUSEUM

This general store was built in 1873 by the founders of Currie, Minnesota.

Fares   Donations are requested.

Contact   End-O-Line Railroad Park and Museum, P.O. Box 42, Currie, MN 56123. Telephone (507) 763-3113 (Louise Gervais, curator) or (507) 763-3409 (Dorothy Ruppert, assistant director).

DASSEL

THE OLD DEPOT MUSEUM

The Old Depot Museum is housed in the former Cokato Depot, a 1913 Great Northern rail station. The museum presents a variety of railroad memorabilia. Inside the museum are a picture gallery with illustrations of railroad history and advertisements; baggage carts and a track inspector's bicycle; railroad equipment, including flashing signals, brass bells, and a large collection of antique lanterns; and numerous miniature trains on display. Outside the museum are two other special attractions: a wooden caboose with a potbellied stove and other original equipment (children are welcome to climb aboard and to sit in the brakeman's seat); and a half-scale stationary train on the grounds of the museum—also accessible to climbing children.

How to Get There   From Minneapolis, take U.S. 12 west to Dassel (about 50 miles). Enter Dassel and the depot is on the right, off the highway.

Hours   Memorial Day to October 1: open daily, 10:00 A.M. to 4:30 P.M.

Fares   Adults, $2; children (under 12), $1; infants are admitted free of charge.

Contact   The Old Depot Museum, 651 West Highway 12, Dassel, MN 55325. Telephone (612) 275-3876.

D U L U T H

THE DEPOT (ST. LOUIS COUNTY HERITAGE AND ARTS CENTER)

Formerly the Duluth Union Depot, the Depot began its rail operations in 1892 and is listed in the National Register of Historic Places. An elegant structure, it was designed in the château architectural style and resembles a European castle. During its peak years the depot served as a station stop for up to 55 daily train connections to both coasts.

Rail traffic operations ended in 1969 and the depot was renovated. It currently houses the St. Louis County Heritage and Arts Center on four levels and includes eight cultural agencies, among them a world culture and children's museum, the Duluth Children's Museum, and the Lake Superior Museum of Transportation (see next entry). **Depot Square** re-creates downtown Duluth at the turn of the century, with 22 storefronts.

Strollers and wheelchairs are available at no charge.

How to Get There   Take I-35 to the Fifth Avenue west exit. Turn left onto Superior Street. Then turn left onto Sixth Avenue west. This road runs into the parking lot of the depot.

Hours   From May to mid-October: open daily, 10:00 A.M. to 5 P.M.

From mid-October to April: open Monday to Saturday, 10:00 A.M. to 5:00 P.M.; Sunday, 1:00 P.M. to 5:00 P.M.

Closed New Year's Day, Easter Sunday, Thanksgiving Day, Christmas Eve, and Christmas Day.

Fares   Adults (ages 12 and older), $5; children (ages 3 to 11), $3; family (parents and children through age 11), $15.

Contact   The Depot, 506 West Michigan Street, Duluth, MN 55802. Telephone (218) 727-8025.

LAKE SUPERIOR MUSEUM OF TRANSPORTATION

The Lake Superior Museum of Transportation presents railroad history through a vast collection of train exhibits and displays. The enclosed main museum exhibit gallery (on the spot of the former Duluth Union Depot train shed, see previous entry), is especially appealing to children, because visitors are free to climb aboard many of the trains on display. Other features at the museum are Minnesota's first locomotive (the *William*

LAKE SUPERIOR MUSEUM OF TRANSPORTATION

Minnesota's first locomotive, the 1861 *Williams Crooks,* is on display at the museum.

Crooks), a model train exhibit, railroad dining car china, and miscellaneous train tools.

A 10-minute streetcar ride is offered to visitors during the summer, and the **North Shore Scenic Railroad,** which is adjacent to the museum, provides scenic excursions (from one-and-a-half hours to six hours in length) along Lake Superior.

NOTE: 19th-century "Belgian Block" flooring in the museum may limit mobility for strollers and wheelchairs. Stairways provide the only interior access to some of the railroad exhibits.

How to Get There   See the previous entry for directions.

Hours   Museum: open daily, year-round. Train ride: late spring through October (call for schedule information). Trolley hours are 10:00 A.M. to 4:30 P.M. Memorial Day through Labor Day.

Fares   Adults, $5; children (under 12), $3; family (two adults and children under 12), $15.
Trolley: free. Train ride: call for fare information.

Contact   Lake Superior Museum of Transportation, 506 West Michigan Street, Duluth, MN 55802; telephone (218) 727-0687. Or, North Shore Scenic Railroad (same address as above); telephone (218) 722-1273.

R O L L A G

WESTERN MINNESOTA STEAM THRESHERS REUNION

The Western Minnesota Steam Threshers Reunion is an operating museum that highlights early machines and crafts on 230 acres of land. Held every Labor Day weekend, the four-day event features steam-powered machinery and technology and pioneer crafts. Among the offerings are a ride on the Ortner Railroad, a line with 600 feet of track, passenger cars, a water tower, and a bridge; an 85-foot diner/sleeper car; railroad depots; antique cars and trucks; gas- and steam-powered grain threshing machines; a pioneer farm; daily parades; steam train and vintage merry-go-round rides; and Miniatureland, one of the world's largest collections of scale and model equipment.

Meals are served daily, and primitive camping is available. Live music plays throughout the weekend.

How to Get There   Rollag is a 45-minute drive from Fargo, Detroit Lakes, and Fergus Falls. From the Fargo/Moorhead area, drive east on Highway 10 for approximately 20 miles. Turn right onto Highway 32 for 10 miles. The Western Minnesota Steam Threshers Reunion showgrounds are on the left.

Hours   Open Labor Day weekend only.

Fares   Season pass, $10 per person for a total of four days; daily pass, $7 per person; children under 15 years of age are free of charge.

Contact   Western Minnesota Steam Threshers Reunion, Lynette Briden, 2610 1st Avenue, North Fargo, ND 58102. Telephone (701) 235-9311 or (701) 232-4484.

S T .   P A U L

TWIN CITY MODEL RAILROAD CLUB

The Twin City Model Railroad Club, a nonprofit organization, displays "Trains at Bandana," a quarter-inch-scale model of United States railroading from the 1930s to the 1950s, with special focus on the Twin Cities area. The panoramic presentation

BARB GAWTRY, TWIN CITY MODEL RAILROAD CLUB

"Trains at Bandana" is a quarter-inch scale model of U.S. railroading from the 1930s to 1950s.

of the Twin City Terminal Railway features scenic river views, bridges, a trolley system, locomotive, passenger and freight train models, a working turntable, and roundhouse. The exhibit is 3,000 square feet and up to five trains can operate simultaneously on four main lines and one branchline. (Saturdays and Sundays are "full operation" days, when the four main-line trains are running.)

The exhibit is located at Bandana Square, a restored complex and former home of the century-old Northern Pacific Railway facility. Steam and diesel locomotives and other rail equipment are on display there.

Special Events   Northern Pacific Day; Circus Trains and Displays; North Coast Limited Day; Soo Line Day; CBQ Day.

How to Get There   Bandana Square is between downtown Minneapolis and St. Paul. Take Highway 94 towards Snelling to Bandana Boulevard east. Go east one block until a steam locomotive on a pedestal is in view. The club is on the north side of the street.

Hours   Monday to Friday: open 10:00 A.M. to 8:00 P.M.; Saturday: open 10:00 A.M. to 6:00 P.M.; Sunday: open 12:00 noon to 5:00 P.M.

Fares   Suggested donations: $1 or $2 per family.

Contact   Twin City Model Railroad Club, Bandana Square, Box 261021, Bandana Boulevard East, St. Paul, MN 55108. Telephone (612) 647-9628.

STILLWATER

STILLWATER DEPOT LOGGING AND RAILROAD MUSEUM

The Stillwater Depot Logging and Railroad Museum with its 28-foot-high atrium is a place where visitors can learn about the history of Stillwater. The importance of logging and the railroad to the community is presented through photographs, artifacts, and other displays.

The museum is the departure point for the sophisticated *Minnesota Zephyr Limited,* which provides a beautiful 15-mile scenic ride through woodlands and along the St. Croix River and Brown's Creek. It climbs more than 250 feet upward on its trek. The ride is designed for sophisticated, adults-only dining. The three-and-a-half-hour journey, spent in five beautifully restored dining cars (including an 80-foot glass dome car built in 1938), offers a five-course meal and a romantic atmosphere.

How to Get There   From Minneapolis, take Highway 36. It merges with Highway 95 north. On Highway 95 (Main Street), is the entrance to the depot.

Hours   Museum: open every day from Memorial Day through Christmas, 10 A.M. to 5:00 P.M.

All other months: open Friday 4:00 P.M. to 7:00 P.M.; Saturday 12:00 P.M. to 7:00 P.M.; Sunday 10:00 A.M. to 4:00 P.M.

Fares   Admission is free.

Contact   Minnesota Zephyr, 601 North Main, P.O. Box 573, Stillwater, MN 55082. Telephone (800) 992-6100 or (612) 430-3000.

MISSISSIPPI

N E W T O N

NEWTON STATION

Newton Station, a railway depot listed on the National Register of Historic Places, was first built in 1860. It burned down in 1863 in Grierson's raid during the Civil War. It was rebuilt in 1905 and served various rail lines, including the Illinois Central, for many years. The station was restored and reopened in 1992, and it now houses a coffee shop, meeting rooms, and a chamber of commerce.

Alongside the station are operating rail tracks that today serve the Kansas City Southern, a freight line. Up to eight trains run past the station every day.

How to Get There From Jackson take I-20 east to exit 109. Turn right off the exit and continue to the Highway 80 and Highway 15 intersection. Look for signs with a picture of a train. Follow the signs to the railroad.

Hours   No special tours are offered, but the station is open most days. Call for information.

Fares   Admission is free.

Contact   Newton Station, Chamber of Commerce, 128 South Main Street, P.O. Box 301, Newton, MS 39345. Telephone (601) 683-2201.

S H E L B Y

SHELBY PUBLIC LIBRARY

The Shelby Public Library is a Mississippi landmark with the look and feel of a train station. That's because the library is the former Shelby Depot, built at the beginning of the 20th century, now repainted and restored. It was the site of the first Delta railroad line connecting towns such as Memphis, Vicksburg, and New Orleans. During its heyday in the 1920s, eight passenger and four freight trains made daily stops at the station. Although it closed in 1968, care has been taken to preserve the depot's originality and artifacts for viewing.

How to Get There   From Jackson, take I-55 north to Granada. Exit at the Cleveland exit and follow the road to Ruleville. Take Highway 61 north to Shelby.

Hours   Open Monday, Tuesday, Thursday, and Friday, 9:00 A.M. to 5:00 P.M. (closed for lunch from 12:00 noon to 1:00 P.M.); Saturday, 9:00 A.M. to 12:00 noon.

Fares   Admission is free.

Contact   Shelby Public Library, P.O. Box 789, Shelby, MS 38774. Telephone (601) 398-7748.

V A U G H A N

CASEY JONES RAILROAD MUSEUM AND STATE PARK

Like the **Casey Jones Village** in Jackson, Tennessee, the Casey Jones Railroad Museum and State Park is a tribute to Jonathan Luther Jones, an engineer whose heroic efforts saved the lives of his crew in a train crash, but cost him his own. (See the entry for the Casey Jones Home and Railroad Museum in Jackson, Tennessee.) The museum, which is housed in a railroad depot near the site of the train crash, includes exhibits on railroads and their influence on the development of Mississippi, as well as train memorabilia. A static steam locomotive display is also on view next to the museum.

How to Get There   From Jackson, take I-55 north to exit 133. The museum is 1 mile from the exit. Signs for the museum can be seen along the Interstate.

Hours   Open Monday, Tuesday, Thursday, and Friday, 8:00 A.M. to 4:00 P.M.; Wednesday and Saturday, 8:00 A.M. to 12:00 noon.
   Closed Sundays, Thanksgiving, Christmas, and New Year's Day.

Fares   Adults, $1; children, $.50.

Contact   Casey Jones Railroad Museum State Park, 10901 Vaughan Road #1, Vaughan, MS 39179. Telephone (601) 673-9864.

MISSOURI

B R A N S O N

BRANSON SCENIC RAILWAY

The Branson Scenic Railway takes 40-mile round-trip (1 hour, 45 minutes) narrated diesel excursions through the beautiful Ozark hills and valleys. Operating on an active freight line of the Missouri and Northern Arkansas Railway, the railway departs from the recently restored 1906 depot. Climate-controlled vista dome cars, a club car, and coaches built in the 1940s and 1950s are offered. The journey includes travel through tunnels and across trestles, and entertainment on board. Sandwiches, snacks, and soft drinks can be purchased on the train.

The railway is equipped with handicapped accessible cars and ramps. A gift shop is also on the premises.

Special Events   Easter Bunny Train; Santa Claus Trains; Dinner Trains.

How to Get There   Take I-44 south to Springfield, then take Highway 65 south to Branson. Exit at Highway 76 and turn east; the railway is at the foot of downtown Branson, five blocks from the exit.

Hours   March, November, and December: open Wednesday through Saturday; in April: open Monday through Saturday; May through October: open daily.
    Departures at 8:30 A.M., 11:00 A.M., 2:00 P.M., and 4:30 P.M. (hours vary according to month of operation).

Fares   Adults, $20.21; seniors (55 or above), $19.11; students (ages 13 to 18), $14.75; children (ages 4 to 12), $9.56; children three years of age and under are admitted free of charge.

Contact   Branson Scenic Railway, 206 East Main Street, Branson, MO 65616-2716. Telephone (800) 2-TRAIN-2 or (417) 334-6110.

E U R E K A

SIX FLAGS OVER MID-AMERICA

Six Flags Over Mid-America is one of several Six Flags theme parks across the United States. Features and attractions include family entertainment, action spectaculars, music revues, and thrilling rides.
    Train attractions at Six Flags include a narrow gauge steam train ride that makes five trips per hour along a 1.25-mile track through the park, with open-air coaches and a caboose; the Old Chicago Depot; and the Run-Away-Mine Train Ride (one of the Mid-America's original rides), which goes through the largest coal mine in the Midwest.

How to Get There   From St. Louis, take I-44 west to exit 261. The park is adjacent.

Hours April through October: opens at 10:00 A.M. Closing hours vary. Call ahead.

Fares Adults, $30.82; seniors (55 and older), $15.44; children, $25.50. Two-day and season passes are also available.

Contact Six Flags Over Mid-America, P.O. Box 60, Eureka, MO 63025. Telephone (314) 938-5300; fax (314) 587-3617.

G L E N C O E

WABASH, FRISCO & PACIFIC RAILWAY

The Wabash, Frisco & Pacific Railway, operating in Glencoe since 1969, was named after three railroads based in St. Louis in the late thirties. The railway runs a 12-inch narrow gauge steam locomotive Sunday afternoons, May to October (weather permitting), in open-air wooden benched cars. The 2-mile, 30-minute round-trip scenic excursion passes through forest and crosses several bridges.

Train enthusiasts of all ages will enjoy watching the crew turn the engine around after arriving halfway; the locomotive travels along the same track on the return trip to Glencoe.

The railway has 27 railroad cars, including passenger, gondola, caboose, hopper, tanker, box, and wooden benched flat cars in its stock.

How to Get There From St. Louis, take I-44 west to the Eureka exit. Turn right onto Highway 109, follow it into Glencoe (about 4 miles), and turn right onto Washington Avenue. The depot is at the end of the street, 199 Grand Avenue.

Hours May to October: open Sunday, 12:00 noon to 4:20 P.M. (weather permitting).

Fares Admission is $2; children three years of age and under are admitted free of charge.

Contact   Wabash, Frisco & Pacific Association, 1569 Ville Angela Lane, Hazelwood, MO 63042-1630. Telephone (314) 587-3538 or (314) 351-9385.

J A C K S O N

ST. LOUIS IRON MOUNTAIN & SOUTHERN RAILWAY

The St. Louis Iron Mountain & Southern Railway operates two steam locomotive excursion trips of varying lengths. Departing from Jackson, the journeys include a 10-mile round-trip to Gordonville (1 hour, 20 minute), and a two-hour, 16-mile round-trip dinner train to Dutchtown.

Steam locomotive #5 was built in 1946 and first operated as a switch engine for an Illinois company; the 1926 coaches used were formerly electric cars. Other rolling stock include a bay window caboose and a 1920s cupola caboose.

The railway operates a diesel engine during the winter months.

Special Events   Magic Express; Halloween Express; Santa Express; Murder Mystery; Train Robberies; Easter Egg Hunts; Fall Foliage; Chocoholic Express; "Elvis" Weekend; Civil War Reenactment; Native American Days.

How to Get There   From St. Louis, take I-55 south to exit 99 (Jackson). Turn right onto Highway 61 and follow it for 4 miles to Highway 25. The railroad is at the intersection of the two highways.

Hours   April to October (steam season): Gordonville train departs at 11 A.M. and 2 P.M. on Saturday; 1 P.M. on Sunday, Wednesday, and Friday. Dutchtown dinner train departs on Sunday at 5:00 P.M.

November to March (diesel season): Gordonville train departs at 12:30 P.M. on Saturday.

Fares   Gordonville: adults, $10; children (ages 3 to 12), $5; children under three years of age are free of charge.

Dutchtown (with dinner): adults, $22; children (ages 3 to 12), $16; children under three years of age are free of charge (if sharing meal).

Dutchtown (no dinner): adults, $12, children (ages 3 to 12), $6; children (under 3), free.

Contact   St. Louis Iron Mountain & Southern Railway, P.O. Box 244, Jackson, MO 63755. Telephone (800) 455-RAIL or (314) 243-1688.

SPRINGFIELD

FRISCO RAILROAD MUSEUM

An educational resource center and historic memorabilia display facility, the Frisco Railroad Museum opened in 1986. Dedicated exclusively to the St. Louis–San Francisco Railway (or Frisco) line, the museum has more than 5,000 memorabilia items from caboose operations to telegraph service. Over 2,000 of these items are on display at a former Frisco traffic control command center.

Other exhibits at the museum are a wooden passenger coach with part-Pullman car, part-Frisco dining car interior, and a depot agent's office. Children will especially enjoy ringing an authentic Frisco locomotive bell.

Restoration of a Frisco diner-lounge car, two cabooses, and a boxcar are currently underway.

The museum operates a gift shop with a wide variety of Frisco and railroad souvenirs.

How to Get There   From Springfield, take I-44 west to exit 77. Turn left onto Highway 13 (the Kansas Expressway) and another left at Commercial Street.

Hours   Open year-round, Tuesday to Saturday, 10:00 A.M. to 5:00 P.M. Closed Sundays and Mondays.

Fares   Adults, $2; children (under 12), $1.

Contact   Frisco Railroad Museum, 543 E. Commercial Street, Springfield, MO 65803. Telephone (417) 866-7573.

S T .   J O S E P H

PATEE HOUSE MUSEUM

Built in 1858, the Patee House Museum building was originally a hotel. Four stories tall, it served as Pony Express headquarters in 1860 and is now a National Historic Landmark.

The museum offers a variety of displays, including the last Hannibal & St. Joseph Railroad train, a wood-burning steam locomotive that carried Pony Express mail to St. Joseph, a Baldwin locomotive, an 1877 railroad depot, and a railway mail car invented by a St. Joseph postmaster. A toy carousel shop features electric trains. The museum cosponsors an annual June Pony Express rerun, where riders travel the original trail between St. Joseph and Sacramento in 10 days.

Special Events   Annual Pony Express Rerun.

How to Get There   From I-29, take U.S. 36 west to the 10th Street exit, drive six blocks north and turn right onto Mitchell Avenue. The museum is two blocks down.

Hours   April to October: Monday through Saturday, 10:00 A.M. to 5:00 P.M.; Sunday, 1:00 P.M. to 5:00 P.M.

November, January, February, and March: Saturday, 10:00 A.M. to 5:00 P.M.; Sunday 1:00 P.M. to 5:00 P.M.

Fares   Adults, $3; children, $1.50; children under six years of age are free of charge.

Contact   Patee House Museum, Pony Express Historical Association, 12th and Penn Streets, Box 1022, St. Joseph, MO 64502. Telephone (816) 232-8206.

S T .   L O U I S

MUSEUM OF TRANSPORTATION

The Museum of Transportation originated in 1944 as the National Museum of Transport. Since its first acquisition 50 years ago (an 1880 mule-drawn streetcar), the number of acquisitions has grown to a rich and extensive collection of transportation pieces. Ninety percent of the exhibits are outdoors.

The museum has been owned and operated by the St. Louis County Parks and Recreation Department since 1984. Situated on more than 39 acres of land and between two 19th-century limestone tunnels, the museum has autos, buses, aircraft, boats, trains, and other exhibits that vividly reflect more than 150 years of transportation history.

Train enthusiasts will particularly enjoy the large and diverse collection of 65 locomotives, including the world's largest steam locomotive, the Union Pacific "Big Boy"; the elegantly appointed Vanderbilt private railcar, built in 1905 with dining room, kitchen, bedroom, and bath; restored streetcars; and a ride on the Abbott Railroad, a miniature train that operates on the museum grounds from April through October. Children also have an opportunity to ring a locomotive bell during their visit.

Visitors may choose a guided or self-guided tour of the museum. Also, souvenirs and refreshments are available at the museum.

NOTE: Because 90 percent of the museum collection is outdoors, comfortable shoes and appropriate seasonal clothing are recommended.

MUSEUM OF TRANSPORTATION, ST. LOUIS, MISSOURI

Union Pacific's *Big Boy,* the world's largest steam locomotive, is one of the highlights at the Museum of Transportation.

How to Get There   From I-270, take the Dougherty Ferry Road exit and travel west to Barrett Station Road. Turn left. The museum is on the right.

Hours   Museum: open daily, 9:00 A.M. to 5:00 P.M. Closed Thanksgiving, Christmas, and New Year's Day. Abbott Railroad: open April through October.

Fares   Ages 13 to 64, $4; ages 5 to 12, and 65 and over, $1.50.

Contact   Museum of Transportation, St. Louis County Department of Parks and Recreation, 3015 Barrett Station Road, St. Louis, MO 63122-3398. Telephone (314) 965-7998 (info and reservations) or (314) 965-6885 (museum association).

MONTANA

E S S E X

IZAAK WALTON INN

For train enthusiasts heading to **Glacier National Park** and **Bob Marshall Wilderness,** the Izaak Walton Inn provides breathtaking scenery and railroad attractions. The inn was built in 1939 to serve Great Northern Railway train employees, and now also offers accommodations in converted cabooses that are fully heated and insulated. Overlooking a scenic hill, the cabooses offer patrons a great view of the former rail yard and the mountains.

Summer and ski packages are available.

How to Get There   The inn is just off Highway 2 near mile marker 180, on Izaak Walton Inn Road (at the southern end of Glacier National Park in northwestern Montana). Look for railroad signs.

Hours   Open year-round. Call for availability.

Fares   Caboose cottages (three-night minimum stay): $425 per three-night stay.

Contact   Izaak Walton Inn, P.O. Box 653, Essex, MT 59916. Telephone (406) 888-5700.

NEBRASKA

FREMONT

FREMONT & ELKHORN VALLEY RAILROAD

The Fremont & Elkhorn Valley Railroad, the longest and largest tourist railroad in Nebraska, offers a 3-hour, 30-mile round-trip excursion ride in vintage open-window or air-conditioned coaches. The train takes passengers from Fremont to Hooper, a town with a 19th-century main street listed in the National Register of Historic Places. A museum and souvenir shop are open to visitors in the train depot.

The Fremont Dinner Train, which runs along the same track, is independently operated. Call (800) 942-7245 for more information.

How to Get There From Omaha, take Highway 275 to Business 30 west into Fremont. Take Business 30 through Fremont to Somers Avenue (last stop light) and turn left. The train is four-and-a-half blocks south on the west side of the street.

Hours   April, November, and December: departures Sunday only, 1:30 P.M.

May through October: departures at 12:00 noon Saturday, at 2:00 P.M. Sunday.

Additional Saturday runs may be available from June through August. Call ahead for specifics.

Fares   Adults, $11; children (ages 4 to 12), $6. Children three years of age and under are admitted free of charge.

Contact   Fremont & Elkhorn Valley Railroad, 1835 North Somers Avenue, Fremont, NE 68025. Telephone (402) 727-0615.

NORTH PLATTE

WESTERN HERITAGE MUSEUM

The Lincoln County Historical Society presents the rich history of Lincoln County, Nebraska, through the Western Heritage Museum, which is housed in several historic buildings on nine acres of land. Train enthusiasts will especially enjoy exploring the Brady Island Depot, a furnished 1866 station (built by the Union Pacific Railroad), a caboose, an HO-scale model display featuring Union Pacific trains, and the Fredericksen House, the 1899 furnished home of a former Union Pacific engineer.

Other exhibits include a tribute to local citizens who helped with the World War II canteen (a hospitality effort for American soldiers passing through North Platte); a 1903 country school; a Pony Express building; the county's first homestead, built in 1869; and a Lutheran church.

A large gazebo provides a picnic area.

NOTE: The museum is not wheelchair accessible, but efforts will be made to assist disabled visitors.

How to Get There   From Lincoln, take I-80 west to North Platte (about four hours). Take exit 177; the museum is on North Buffalo Bill Avenue.

Hours   Saturday before Memorial Day to Labor Day: open daily, 9:00 A.M. to 8:00 P.M. After Labor Day through September 30: open daily, 9:00 A.M. to 5:00 P.M.

Fares   Donations are accepted.

Contact   Lincoln County Historical Society, 2403 North Buffalo Bill Avenue, North Platte, NE 69101. Telephone (308) 534-5640.

UNION PACIFIC MUSEUM
AND DEPOT DISPLAY

Union Pacific Railroad headquarters and the largest railroad classification yard in the world are located in North Platte. It's also the site of the Union Pacific Museum and Depot Display, which contains a former Hershey, Nebraska, train depot (complete with real operating signaling equipment that visitors may use); railroad memorabilia; and depot furnishings. Three train exhibits are also on display: the *Challenger* engine #3977 (once the largest engine in the world), unit 6922 (a freight engine), and a baggage car.

   The museum and depot display are located in a small section of Cody Park, a 100-acre city recreational site with a children's park and playground, swimming pool, an enclosed wildlife area with donkeys, peacocks, deer, and geese, a carnival with an antique carousel and kiddie rides, tennis courts, and a picnic area.

How to Get There   From Lincoln, take I-80 west to North Platte (about four hours). Take exit 177 and get onto Highway 83; take it through town. Cody Park is on north Highway 83, at the north edge of town.

Hours   Open Memorial Day through Labor Day, 8:00 A.M. to 9:00 P.M.

Fares   Museum admission is free. A fee is charged for swimming and carnival rides.

Contact   Union Pacific Museum and Depot Display, Cody Park, 1402 North Jeffers, North Platte, NE 69101. Telephone (308) 534-7611.

OMAHA

OMAHA ZOO RAILROAD

The Omaha Zoo Railroad is a narrow gauge line that runs on the grounds of the Henry Doorly Zoo. Built in 1968, the railroad operates steam locomotives with four to five open-air coaches on an oval-shaped track past animal displays. The zoo

WILLIAM KRATVILLE, OMAHA ZOO RAILROAD

Locomotive #119 steams eastbound from the depot.

OMAHA ZOO RAILROAD

Locomotive #395-104 tours the garden at Bailey Wye.

also features one of the largest indoor rain forests, the Lied Jungle, the Kingdom of the Seas Aquarium, and a soon-to-be-completed IMAX theater.

The steam locomotives include #395-104, an Austrian engine originally built in 1890 and restored in the 1970s, and #119, a 5/8-scale replica of a Union Pacific locomotive built in 1968.

Special Events   Membership Days; Halloween Terror Train.

How to Get There   In Omaha, take I-80 (either direction) to the 13th Street exit. Turn south; zoo entrance is adjacent.

Hours   April through Memorial Day, and Labor Day through October: open weekends only; Memorial Day through Labor Day: open daily.

Zoo hours are 11:00 A.M. to 4:00 P.M.

Fares   Zoo: adults, $7; children (ages 5 to 11), $3.50; children four years of age and under are admitted free of charge. Train ride: adults, $2.50; children (ages 3 to 11), $1.50; children under three years of age are admitted free of charge.

Prices are subject to change every spring. Call or write ahead for updates.

Contact   Omaha Zoo Railroad, Henry Doorly Zoo, 3701 South 10th Street, Omaha, NE 68107-2200. Telephone (402) 733-8401; fax (402) 733-4415.

NEVADA

CARSON CITY

NEVADA STATE RAILROAD MUSEUM

The Nevada State Railroad Museum presents over 50 pieces of railroad equipment, including five steam locomotives, restored coaches, and freight cars. Most of the equipment originated with the short line Virginia & Truckee Railroad (V&T). A special feature is the *Virginia & Truckee #25*, built in 1905 and used in Hollywood movies after it was purchased by RKO Studios in 1947. Excursion rides are available on steam trains or motorcars.

Special Events   Father's Day; Fourth of July; Santa Train.

How to Get There   Take U.S. 395 to Carson City. The museum is visible from the highway (look for a train car and yellow depot building on the right).

Hours   Museum: open year-round, Wednesday to Sunday, 8:30 A.M. to 4:30 P.M.

Motor car: open Memorial Day to Labor Day, 10:00 A.M. to 4:00 P.M.; departures every 30 minutes.

Steam trains: run selected summer weekends and holidays, 10:00 A.M. to 4:00 P.M.; departures every 40 minutes. Call ahead for availability.

Fares   Museum: adults, $2; children under 18 years of age are admitted free of charge.

Motor car: adults, $1; children (ages 6 to 11), $.50; children five years of age and under are admitted free of charge.

Steam train: adults, $2.50; children (ages 6 to 11), $1; children five years of age and under are admitted free of charge.

Contact   Nevada State Railroad Museum, Capitol Complex, Carson City, NV 89710. Telephone (702) 687-6953; fax (702) 687-8294.

EAST ELY

NEVADA NORTHERN RAILWAY MUSEUM

The Nevada Northern Railway Museum has a rich collection of railway exhibits that reflect the importance of railway and copper mining to the development of 20th-century White Pine County. The museum offers a guided tour of its property. Among the displays are nearly 30 buildings and structures, including a depot, roundhouse, and machine and blacksmith shops. Historic steam, diesel, and electric locomotives and passenger and freight cars are also featured.

The original Nevada Northern Railway operated between 1906 and 1983, with both freight and passenger service. The railroad complex was donated by its owner, the Kennecott Copper Corporation, to the city of Ely.

NEVADA NORTHERN RAILWAY

Steam locomotive #40 rests in front of the East Ely depot.

Since 1987, the White Pine Historical Railroad Foundation, which administers the museum, has offered tourist railroad excursions 14 to 22 miles in length and one-and-a-half
hours to one-and-three-quarter hours in duration. The journey
on the "Ghost Train of Old Ely" takes passengers on one of two
routes: on a steam locomotive through a curved tunnel and up
a canyon, or on a diesel train through a valley.

The museum offers engineer instruction classes on both
steam and diesel locomotives.

Special Events   Nevada Northern Raildays; Fireworks, Trains,
and Barbecue.

How to Get There   From Las Vegas, take I-15 north, 22 miles
to Hiko; turn left. Turn onto Highway 318 toward Lund; from
Lund drive 20 miles to the junction of Highways 93 and 50
(stop sign). Turn right and drive 20 miles to Ely.

Locomotive #40 in action as it takes passengers on the Keystone excursion.

Hours   Museum: Memorial Day to Labor Day, open weekends only. Train rides: Memorial Day to Labor Day, open weekends only; departures at 1:30 P.M. and 3:30 P.M. (steam) and at 5:30 P.M. (diesel).

Fares   Museum tour: admission is $2.50; children under 10 years of age are admitted free of charge. Trains: adults, $10 to $18; seniors (65 or above), $8 to $12; juniors (ages 12 to 18), $8 to $16; children (ages 5 to 11), $4 to $8; children under five years of age accompanied by an adult are admitted free of charge.

Contact   Nevada Northern Railway Museum, Avenue A at 11th Street, P.O. Box 150040, East Ely, NV 89315. Telephone (702) 289-2085.

VIRGINIA   CITY

VIRGINIA & TRUCKEE RAILROAD

An operating shortline, the Virginia & Truckee Railroad has a long and rich history. Built in 1869 to serve gold and silver ore mining interests, the line ran up to 45 trains a day, at its peak, from Virginia City on to Gold Hill.

Today, the railroad runs 35-minute conductor-narrated and steam-powered excursion rides in open cars or a caboose over the original right-of-way between Virginia City and Gold Hill, past mine ruins. The original 19th-century Virginia & Truckee depot still stands and is the railroad departure point. Passengers can make the round-trip visit on the same train or disembark at the Gold Hill depot, visit the mining town, and return on the next train back to Virginia City.

How to Get There   Take highway 341 into Virginia City to the C Street exit. Turn downhill at Taylor Street and then turn right onto F Street to the depot.

Hours   Late May to early October: open daily, 10:30 A.M. to 5:45 P.M.

Fares   Adults, $4.50; children (ages 5 and above), $2.25; children under five years of age are admitted free of charge. All Day Pass: $9.00.

Contact   Virginia & Truckee Railroad Company, P.O. Box 467, Virginia City, NV 89440. Telephone (702) 847-0380.

NEW
HAMPSHIRE

BRETTON WOODS

MOUNT WASHINGTON COG RAILWAY

On a clear day, this excursion offers visitors a glimpse of four
New England states from a beautiful mountain setting. That's
what's in store for riders of the Mount Washington Cog Railway, the world's first mountain-climbing cog railway. Created in
1869 by retired businessman Sylvester Marsh, the railway
climbs the highest peak in the Northeast, full of breathtaking
scenery and a dramatic 30- to 40-degree temperature change
from ground level to mountain top. The train travels 3 miles
each way on its tracks, the second steepest in the world, including a crossing of "Jacob's Ladder"—a trestle with a 37-percent
grade. The narrated journey includes a brief stop to replenish
the coal and water supply (it uses a ton of coal and a thousand
gallons of water each trip to the mountain) and a 20-minute
stop on the summit of the mountain, where visitors may explore the state park and observation center, or stay longer and
take a later train.

The railway has a museum, gift shop, and restaurant.

NOTE: Be sure to bring a sweater or jacket and to make advance reservations.

How to Get There   From Concord, take I-93 north to exit 35 to Route 3 north. Drive 10 miles to a stop light (Twin Mountains) and turn right. Drive 6 miles to Route 302 west. Look for signs to the station, which is about another 6 miles.

Hours   In May: open weekends, departures at 11:00 A.M. and 2:00 P.M.; late May through late June: open daily, with departures at 11:00 A.M. and 2:00 P.M.
      In summer months, open daily with hourly departures (call ahead for specific times).
      After October 14, call ahead for schedule.

Fares   Adults, $35; children (ages 6 to 12), $24; children under six years of age not occupying a seat are free of charge.
      Museum admission is free.

Contact   Mount Washington Cog Railway, Route 302, Bretton Woods, NH 03589. Telephone (800) 922-8825 or (603) 278-5404, ext. 6 (in New Hampshire).

I N T E R V A L E

HARTMANN MODEL RAILROAD AND TOY MUSEUM

The Hartmann Model Railroad and Toy Museum was created by lifelong train enthusiasts Roger and Nelly Hartmann, originally from Switzerland. The museum features elaborately detailed American and European train layouts, from G- to Z-scale, and train collectibles and memorabilia. The museum relocated and was newly expanded in 1995.
      The **Brass Caboose Hobby Shop,** adjacent to the museum, carries railroad hobby supplies.

How to Get There   The museum is 4 miles north of North Conway, at the corner of Route 302/16 and Town Hall Road.

Hours   Open year-round (except Mother's Day, Easter, Thanksgiving, and Christmas), Monday through Saturday, 9:00 A.M. to 5:00 P.M.; Sunday, 10:00 A.M. to 5:00 P.M.

Fares   Adults, $5; seniors, $4; children (ages 6 to 12), $3; children five years of age and under accompanied by an adult are admitted free of charge.

Contact   Hartmann Model Railroad and Toy Museum, P.O. Box 165, Intervale, NH 03845. Telephone (603) 356-9922.

LINCOLN

HOBO RAILROAD

A turn-of-the-century train station in Lincoln provides the departure point for this railroad line. Two scenic train rides are offered: a 15-mile journey between Lincoln and the Lower Woodstock region, and a longer 55-mile journey from the White Mountains along the Pemigewasset River. Passengers can ride in a variety of vintage enclosed cars.

Special Events   HoBOO Halloween Train; Ho-Ho-HOBO Santa Train; Fall Foliage Train Rides; Caboose Train; Gold Panning Demo Train.

How to Get There   From I-93, take exit 32, across the Kancamagus Highway to Lincoln. This will take you right to the railroad.

Hours   Memorial Day weekend through fall foliage: open daily, with departures at 11:00 A.M., 1:00 P.M., 3:00 P.M., 5:00 P.M., and 7:00 P.M. Call for spring, fall, and winter schedules.

Fares   Adults, $7; children (ages 4 to 11), $4.50; children under four years of age are admitted free of charge.

Contact   Hobo Railroad, P.O. Box 9, Lincoln, NH 03251. Telephone (603) 745-2135.

White Mountain Central Railroad, Inc.

The White Mountain Central Railroad's (WMCR) wood-burning steam locomotives take visitors on 30-minute, 2.5-mile round-trip excursion rides in the summer. The train passes through the last remaining railroad covered bridge of its kind along the scenic Pemigewasset River. The vintage locomotives date back to the twenties and thirties.

WMCR operates in conjunction with a family vacation attraction called **Clark's Trading Post,** a multifaceted playground in North Woodstock, New Hampshire, that includes a half-hour performance with trained black bears, "Merlin's Mystical Mansion," a visit to an 1884 replica of a firehouse (with horse-drawn fire equipment), the Americana Building, Clark Museum (with antique cameras and children's toys, among others), and Avery's Garage, which has antique autos, car memorabilia, water bumper boat rides, and a host of other activities fun for children and adults.

How to Get There   Take Interstate 93 in New Hampshire to exit 33. Go south 1 mile on Route 3. Follow signs to Clark's Trading Post.

Hours   Memorial Day through June: open weekends; July to Labor Day: open daily; Labor Day to mid-October: open weekends.

Departures are every hour on the half hour, 11:30 A.M. to 4:30 P.M.

Fares Clarks Trading Post (includes train rides): adults, $7; children (ages 6 to 11), $5; children (ages 3 to 5), $1; children under three years of age are free of charge.

Contact White Mountain Central Railroad, P.O. Box 1, Lincoln, NH 03251. Telephone (603) 745-8913 or (603) 745-2262.

M E R E D I T H

WINNIPESAUKEE SCENIC RAILROAD

The Winnipesaukee Scenic Railroad departs from two locations (Meredith or Weirs Beach) and takes a one-hour or two-hour 55-mile journey from the White Mountains to the Lakes region, along the largest lake in New Hampshire, Lake Winnipesaukee. Special features on the train ride are a "Hobo Picnic Lunch," and a "Make Your Own Ice Cream Sundae." A combination boat and train excursion with the M/S Mt. Washington (connecting with the train at Weirs Beach) is also available. The Winnipesaukee Scenic Railroad and the Lincoln-based **Hobo Railroad** are both owned and operated by the Clark family.

Special Events Easter Bunny Train; Mother's Day Dinner Train; Weirs Fun Trains; Fireworks Train; Fall Foliage; Ho-Ho-Hobos Santa Train.

How to Get There From I-93, take exit 23 east on Route 104 to Route 3. For Meredith, turn left onto Route 3 north. For Weirs Beach, turn right onto Route 3 south. Look for the sign that reads "Where the Boats Meet the Train."

Hours Memorial weekend through June: open weekends; late June through Labor Day weekend: open daily; Labor Day through fall foliage: open weekends. Call ahead for specific departure times.

Fares One-hour ride (Weirs Beach): adults, $6.50; children (ages 4 to 11), $4.50.

Two-hour ride (Meredith and Weirs Beach): adults, $7.50; children (ages 4 to 11), $5.50. Children under four years of age are admitted free of charge.

Contact Winnipesaukee Scenic Railroad, P.O. Box 9, Lincoln, NH 03251. Telephone (603) 279-5253 (summer) or (603) 745-2135 (year-round).

NORTH CONWAY

CONWAY SCENIC RAILROAD

Since 1974, the Conway Scenic Railroad has operated along a rail line built in the 1870s by the Portsmouth, Great Falls and Conway Railroad, and makes a wonderful scenic railroad visit.

Departing from a beautifully restored 1874 Victorian depot in North Conway, passengers have the option of three train ride choices: two valley routes and a trip to Crawford Notch, pulled by coal-burning steam locomotives or diesel trains.

One valley route covers the breathtaking landscape of Mount Washington Valley and the White Mountains on a 55-minute round-trip ride from North Conway to Conway (steam or diesel); the second valley route is a two-hour round-trip to Bartlett (diesel only). In open air or enclosed antique cars, the excursions cross rivers and a 225-foot wooden trestle while rolling through fields and woodlands.

The Crawford Notch trip, inaugurated in 1995, is a five-hour, 50-mile round-trip diesel-electric excursion. It features the Frankenstein Trestle and Willey Brook Bridge (great engineering achievements of the early 20th century), beautiful mountain scenery, and flowing streams.

In addition to the rides, visitors can tour a beautifully maintained railroad terminal area, listed on the National Register of Historic Places. The grounds include a freight house, fuel handling facility, bunk and car house, and a four-stall roundhouse and 85-foot turntable, where visitors can watch a locomotive brought in after a run. Other restored stationary locomotives and cars on the grounds are also on display.

Well-informed staff and crew are available to answer questions about the trains and provide information sheets on the most commonly asked questions about the railroad. The station includes a museum, gift shop, and snack bar. First-class and dining cars are also available on select trains. Future plans include extension of the train run to Fabyan's Station, a northern terminus.

Special Events   Easter Bunny Express; North Conway Model Railroad Club Annual Show and Open House; Birthday Celebration; Boston & Maine Railroad Historical Society Day; Annual Railfan's Day; Inaugural Run (Fabyan Station); Halloween "Spooky Express"; Thanksgiving "Turkey Trotter"; Santa Claus Express; Polar Express.

How to Get There   From Boston, take I-95 north to Portsmouth to Route 16 (Spaulding Turnpike) north. North Conway Village is about two hours north on the turnpike; the station is in the center of the village.

Hours   Open April to December: North Conway to Conway begins in April; North Conway to Bartlett begins in May; North Conway to Crawford Notch begins in June.

Schedules vary for the three train routes. Call ahead.

Fares   The higher rates reflect first-class and dining charges. Conway trip: adults, $8 to $19.95; children (ages 4 to 12), $5.50 to $13.95.

Bartlett trip: adults, $13 to $39.95; children (ages 4 to 12), $8.50 to $27.95.

Crawford Notch trip: adults, $31.95 to $36.95; children (ages 4 to 12), $16.95 to $21.95.

Children under four years of age accompanied by paying adult are admitted free of charge.

Contact   Conway Scenic Railroad, 38 Norcross Circle, P.O. Box 1947, North Conway, NH 03860. Telephone (800) 232-5251 or (603) 356-5251.

NEW JERSEY

RINGOES

BLACK RIVER & WESTERN RAILROAD

In 1965, Black River & Western Railroad began running steam excursions between Flemington and Ringoes, New Jersey, along tracks formerly operated by the Pennsylvania Railroad. Today, both freight and passenger trains run along a 16-mile short line between Ringoes and Flemington (north) and Lambertville and Ringoes (south).

How to Get There From Newark take I-78 west to I-287 south to Route 202 south. This takes you to Flemington Circle. Go around the circle to Route 12, and take 12 west for three-quarters of a mile. The entrance is across the railroad tracks, on the right.

Hours Trains depart Flemington daily at 11:30 A.M., 1:00 P.M., 2:30 P.M., 4:00 P.M., and 5:30 P.M. (last train one-way only).
Trains depart Ringoes daily at 10:45 A.M., 12:15 P.M., 1:45 P.M., 3:15 P.M., and 4:45 P.M. (last train one-way only).

211

Fares   Adults, $7; children (ages 3 to 12), $3.50; children under three years of age are free of charge.

Contact   Black River & Western Railroad, P.O. Box 200, Ringoes, NJ 08551. Telephone (908) 782-9600.

W H I P P A N Y

WHIPPANY RAILWAY MUSEUM

The Whippany Railway Museum is located on a short line, freight-carrying railway, the Morristown & Erie. Housed in a restored 1904 freight house, the Whippany is one of the only museums in New Jersey devoted entirely to railroading. Visitors will enjoy viewing the restored *Jersey Coast* (restored to the

WHIPPANY RAILWAY MUSEUM

Visitors tour the railway yard.

appearance of a New Jersey Central observation car), a collection of railroad memorabilia, a tour through a railway yard that includes a wooden water tank (once used by steam trains), a coal yard, and a variety of museum and privately owned rail equipment.

A special highlight for children and adults is the Whippanong Valley Railroad, which at 30 feet in length is one of the largest Lionel train layouts in New Jersey. The turn-of-the-century Morristown & Erie Railway, fieldstone passenger station, and a charming duck pond are adjacent to the museum. A gift shop is also available.

Special Events   Santa Claus Special; Easter Bunny Express. Check with the museum for other special events.

How to Get There   From Newark, take I-280 west to I-80 west to I-287 south to New Jersey Route 10 east. Take Route 10 east for 1.5 miles to the Whippany Diner. Go around it, west on Route 10, and at the next intersection, turn right. The railroad station will be in view.

Hours   April to October: open Sundays, 12:00 noon to 4:00 P.M.

Fares   Adults, $1; children (under 12), $.50.

Contact   Whippany Railway Museum, P.O. Box 16, Whippany, NJ 07981-0016. Telephone (201) 887-8177.

NEW MEXICO

A L A M O G O R D O

TOY TRAIN DEPOT

Although the town of Alamogordo once claimed its own railroad, the "cloud climbing" Alamogordo & Sacramento Railroad and the Southern Pacific's train service ended in the late 1940s. That history is captured in the exhibits at the Toy Train Depot. Created by train enthusiast John Koval, the Depot is a nonprofit museum with an extensive collection of model trains, memorabilia, and an outdoor train ride. Housed in an 1898 former train depot built in Torrance, New Mexico, the Depot features five full rooms of train displays, including a depiction of Alamogordo's railroading past, four rooms of model trains, and nine operating layouts, from the smallest scale to the largest. The HO-gauge layout alone includes more than 1,200 feet of track in a single room.

The miniature outdoor train ride on the *1865*, a 16 inch–gauge train, runs every 30 minutes through Alameda Park, which includes a zoo.

The Depot has a gift and model shop.

How to Get There   From Albuquerque, take I-25 south to San Antonio. Cross Highway 82 east to Carrizozo and pick up U.S. 5470 south to Alamogordo. The depot is at the corner of White Sands Boulevard and Indian Wells; a semaphore is on display in the front.

Hours   Museum: summer hours are Wednesday through Monday, 12:00 noon to 5:00 P.M.; winter hours are Wednesday through Sunday, 12:00 noon to 5:00 P.M. Train ride: open from 12:30 P.M. to 4:30 P.M., with departures every 30 minutes.

Fares   Museum: adults, $1.50; children, $1. Train ride: adults, $2; children, $1.

Contact   Toy Train Depot, 1991 North White Sands Boulevard, Alamogordo, NM 88310. Telephone (505) 437-2855.

SANTA FE

SANTA FE SOUTHERN RAILWAY AND DEPOT

Unlike scenic train rides designed solely to carry passengers, the Santa Fe Southern Railway invites visitors to "ride a working freight" in comfortable vintage coaches. Departing from the Santa Fe Depot three times a week, the Santa Fe Southern carries freight between Santa Fe and Lamy, through beautiful New Mexico, along tracks originally laid by the Atchison, Topeka & Santa Fe Railway in 1879.

The original Santa Fe Depot was built in 1905; the Lamy Depot was built in the late 19th century. Visitors make a stop in Lamy, where they can dine on their own picnic lunch or enjoy a meal at the historic Legal Tender restaurant.

NOTE: Reservations are required.

Special Events   Special Trains.

How to Get There   In Santa Fe, take I-25 (either direction) to exit 282 (St. Francis Drive). Drive north 2.5 miles and turn right onto Cerrillos Road. Then turn left onto Guadalupe Street. The depot is after the first light.

Hours   The Santa Fe Southern Railway runs year-round. Open Tuesday, Thursday, and Saturday, with departure at 10:30 A.M. (return by 4:00 P.M.).

Fares   Ages 60 and above, $16; ages 14 and above, $21; ages 7 to 13, $16; ages 3 to 6, $5; ages two and under are free of charge (up to two babies per adult).

Contact   Santa Fe Southern Railway, Inc., 410 South Guadalupe Street, Santa Fe, NM 87501. Telephone (505) 989-8600 (8:00 A.M. to 5:00 P.M.); fax (505) 983-7620.

NEW YORK

ARKVILLE

DELAWARE & ULSTER RAIL RIDE

The Delaware & Ulster Rail Ride is a one-hour diesel excursion trip that originates at the Arkville Depot and travels through scenic countryside. Passengers ride in vintage coaches that are either enclosed or open-air. Conductors provide a narrative along the route.

Picnic facilities, restrooms, parking, exhibits, gift shop, and a snack caboose are on the property.

Special Events Train Robberies; Teddy Bear Run; Fall Foliage; Halloween Train; Children's Fun Festival; Grandparents' Day.

How to Get There Arkville is halfway between Kingston and Oneonta on Route 28. From Kingston, take New York State Thruway to Route 28 west exit. Take the first right (Pine Hill) after the exit and go 45 miles to Arkville. The train station is on the left side of the highway.

Hours   End of May to end of October: open weekends and holidays; early July to early September: open Wednesday to Sunday.
Departures at 11:00 A.M., 1:00 P.M., and 3:00 P.M.

Fares   Adults, $7; seniors, $5.50; children (ages 5 to 11), $4; children under five years of age are admitted free of charge.

Contact   Delaware & Ulster Rail Ride, Route 28, Arkville, NY 12406. Telephone (800) 225-4132 or (914) 586-DURR (depot).

D U N K I R K

ALCO-BROOKS RAILROAD DISPLAY

Steam locomotive #444, the main feature of the Alco-Brooks Railroad Display, was built in 1916 for the Boston & Maine Railroad and sold for use in a Massachusetts granite quarry in 1952. By 1953, it was replaced by a diesel and was out of service for 30 years. In 1986, Fletcher Granite Company donated the locomotive to the Historical Society of Dunkirk, and it was put on display at the Chatauqua County Fairgrounds, where it is now under restoration.

Other exhibits on the grounds include a wood-sided box car built in 1907, a New York Central caboose built in 1905, a work car, railroad crossing sign, and blinkers.

Children visiting the display are free to ring the locomotive bell and sit in the caboose. Society staff also teaches them about track safety and dispenses train coloring books that emphasize train lifesaving tips.

How to Get There   From Buffalo, take the New York State Thruway (I-187) to exit 59. Drive straight off the exit on Vineyard Drive, and when the street ends, turn right. Drive under the Thruway to the fairgrounds, located on Central Avenue.

Hours   June, July, and August: open on Saturdays (weather permitting), 12:00 noon to 4:00 p.m. Open daily during Chatauqua County Fair, the last full week in July.

Fares   Admission is free.

Contact   Historical Society of Dunkirk, NY, 513 Washington Avenue, Dunkirk, NY 14048. Telephone (716) 366-3797.

G O W A N D A

NEW YORK & LAKE ERIE RAILROAD

The New York & Lake Erie Railroad operates both freight service and passenger excursions. On the 20-mile, two-and-a-half-hour tourist trips, riders can enjoy the rural splendor of western New York's countryside and spend the first part of their journey climbing one of the steepest grades east of the Mississippi. Traveling along track built in the mid-1800s for the former New York, Lake Erie & Western Railroad, the train goes through a stone tunnel built in 1865 and makes one station stop. The line carried many famous figures in its early history, including Daniel Webster and President Millard Fillmore. Today's line has been captured in two major film productions: *The Natural,* and *Planes, Trains & Automobiles.*

The railroad's collection includes a 1965 diesel locomotive and five cars originally built in the 1920s and 1930s. Souvenirs and refreshments are sold, and passengers may carry their own snacks on board.

Special Events   Peter Cottontail Express; Santa Claus Express; Teddy Bear's Picnic; Kids' Day; Ghost and Goblin Party; Fathers Are Special; Ice Cream Social; Dinner Trains; Murder Mystery Train.

How to Get There   From Buffalo, take Route 62 south to Gowanda. In the center of town, turn onto South Water Street. It's half a mile to the depot.

Hours   Memorial Day weekend to the last weekend in October: Saturday and Sunday departure at 1:00 P.M. (all season). In October, additional Saturday and Sunday departure at 3:45 P.M. In July and August: additional Wednesday and Friday departure at 12:00 noon.

Fares   Adults, $8.50; seniors, $7.50; children (ages 3 to 11), $4; children under three years of age not occupying a seat are free of charge.

Contact   New York & Lake Erie Railroad, 50 Commercial Street, P.O. Box 309, Gowanda, NY 14070. Telephone (716) 532-5716.

KINGSTON

TROLLEY MUSEUM OF NEW YORK

Founded in 1955, the Trolley Museum of New York is a non-profit organization dedicated to preserving the history of rail transportation and its importance to the Hudson Valley Region. Situated on the original site of the Ulster & Delaware Railroad, the museum offers a 1.5-mile trolley trip from downtown Kingston to the Hudson River, with a stop at museum grounds. There, visitors can view displays of trolley, subway, and rapid transit cars used in the U.S. and Europe, and through the windows of the visitor center, can see up to eight trolleys currently under restoration.

How to Get There   The museum is two hours from Manhattan and one hour from Albany. Take NY State Thruway (I-187) to exit 19 (Kingston).

Hours   Memorial Day to Columbus Day: open Saturday, Sunday, and holidays, 12:00 noon to 5:00 P.M.

Fares   Adults, $3; children, $1.

Contact   Trolley Museum of New York, 89 East Strand, P.O. Box 2291, Kingston, NY 12401. Telephone (914) 331-3399.

MOUNT PLEASANT

CATSKILL MOUNTAIN RAILROAD

A scenic creek, train depots, and a 6-mile round-trip excursion on the Esopus Creek Shuttle through the Catskill Mountains are offered by the Catskill Mountain Railroad. Visitors have the option of a one-way trip (which can be coordinated with a white-water tube trip on the return) or a 40-minute round-trip excursion with opportunities for stops at a campsite, creek, and the Ulster & Delaware Depot, circa 1900. (The depot is currently under restoration.)

The railroad also makes a stop at the **Empire State Railway Museum.**

How to Get There   Take New York State Thruway (I-187) to exit 19 (Kingston). Follow Route 28 west for 22 miles to Mount Pleasant.

Hours   Memorial Day weekend to mid-October: open weekends and holidays; departures hourly, 11:00 A.M. to 5:00 P.M.

Fares   Adults, $4 (one-way), $6 (round-trip); children (ages 4 to 11), $2. Children under four years of age are admitted free of charge.

Contact   Catskill Mountain Railroad, Inc., P.O. Box 46, Shokan, NY 12481. Telephone (914) 688-7400.

O L D   F O R G E

ADIRONDACK SCENIC RAILROAD

The Adirondack Scenic Railroad offers diesel rail excursions in open-window cars along a beautiful stretch of Adirondack Park that includes forests, lakes, ponds, and rivers, with camping and hiking nearby. Operated by the Adirondack Railway Preservation Society, the area is listed in the National Register of Historic Places.

Trains depart twice a day for Carter, New York from Thendara Station, 4.5 miles south along Moose River.

Special Events   Friday Flaming Fall Foliage; Halloween Express; Santa Claus Special.

How to Get There   From Syracuse, take the New York State Thruway to the Utica exit. Take Route 12 north to Route 28 toward Old Forge. Continue approximately 26 miles, and the station is on the highway.

Hours   May to October: open daily, 10:00 A.M. to 4:00 P.M. October to November: open Saturday and Sunday, with departures at 11:30 A.M. and 2:30 P.M.

Fares   Adults, $6; children (ages 2 to 12), $4.

Contact   Adirondack Scenic Railroad, P.O. Box 84, Thendara, NY 13472. Telephone (315) 369-6290.

O W E G O

TIOGA SCENIC RAILROAD

The Tioga Scenic Railroad offers excursion rides from Owego, New York, along track built for the Southern Central Railroad in 1869. By 1871, the completed rail line extended to upstate New York and the Great Lakes and ultimately transported both anthracite coal and passengers.

Today, the railroad departs from the restored 19th-century Owego Depot on a variety of excursions. A local tour to Newark Valley is offered, a 22-mile, two-hour round-trip journey. Other trips include a scenic ride with breakfast, lunch, dinner, or dinner theater.

The railroad operates a diesel locomotive with two 1922 vintage passenger coaches and a 19th-century, open-air car. On-board entertainment includes sing-alongs, stories, and puppets for children.

The depot houses a gift shop, ice cream shop, and a large HO-scale model railroad.

Special Events   Easter Bunny Express; Halloween Express; Santa Express; Special Owego to Harford Excursions.

How to Get There   From Ithaca, take Route 96B to Route 96 toward Owego. Turn right at the light after the bridge. Then turn right onto West Avenue. Cross over a set of tracks; the station will be on the right.

Hours   Memorial Day to late October: open Saturday, 9:00 A.M. to 10:00 P.M.; Sunday, 11:00 A.M. to 5:00 P.M.

Fares   Excursion only: adults, $7; seniors, $6.50; children (ages 4 to 11), $5; children three years of age and under are admitted free of charge.

With breakfast: $16.95 per person. With lunch: $19.95 per person. With dinner: $29.95 per person.

Contact   Tioga Scenic Railroad, 25 Delphine Street, Owego, NY 13827. Telephone (800) 42-TIOGA or (607) 687-6786.

P H O E N I C I A

EMPIRE STATE RAILWAY MUSEUM

From the late 19th century to the 1940s, several major railroad lines made stops in the Catskill Mountains, an important commercial area, and provided both freight and passenger service. To help preserve that history, the Empire State Railway Museum was established in 1960 to educate visitors about the important role of the railroad to people living in the Catskills and the Hudson Valley. The museum contains railway cars under restoration: a 1900 wooden baggage car, caboose, boxcar, and a 1910 steam locomotive.

The **Catskill Mountain Railroad** makes a stop at the museum (see earlier entry).

WEBB LEONARD, EMPIRE STATE RAILWAY MUSEUM
Visitors relax outside the Empire State Railway Museum.

How to Get There   Take the New York State Thruway to exit 19 (Kingston). Then take Route 28 west to Phoenicia. From the Phoenicia exit, look for signs to the museum.

Hours   Memorial Day to mid-September: open Saturday, Sunday, and holidays, 10:00 A.M. to 5:00 P.M.

Fares   Admission is free.

Contact   Empire State Railway Museum, P.O. Box 455, Phoenicia, NY 12464. Telephone (914) 688-7501.

RUSH

ROCHESTER & GENESEE VALLEY RAILROAD MUSEUM

The Rochester & Genesee Valley Railroad Museum preserves the rich history of Genesee Valley railroading with a collection of railway trains and tourist rides. Housed in a turn-of-the-century depot that once served the Erie Railroad, the museum is undergoing restoration to re-create the depot's mid-1930 appearance. The rail collection on display includes: a 1930 self-propelled car; a 1926 Erie Railroad coach; a 1958 refrigerator car, both wooden and steel cabooses; a 1910 Pennsylvania Railroad sleeper/lounge car; a 1941 diesel locomotive; and a 1935 Erie Railroad milk car. Other exhibits are photographic displays of the valley's transportation history and historic films.

A 20- to 30-minute track car ride is offered between the museum and the **New York Museum of Transportation** from May to October, weather permitting. Gift shops are available in both museums.

How to Get There   Take I-390 to exit 11, then follow Route 251 west to East River Road (flashing red light). Turn right; the museum parking area is about a mile down.

Special Events   Fall Foliage tours.

Hours   Mid-May through October: open Sundays, 11:00 A.M. to 5:00 P.M.

Fares   Adults, $5; seniors, $4; students (ages 5 to 15), $3; family (two adults and four or more children), $15. Preschoolers are free of charge.

Contact   Rochester & Genesee Valley Railroad Museum, 282 Rush-Scottsville Road, Rush, NY 14543. Telephone (716) 987-1305.

SALAMANCA

SALAMANCA RAIL MUSEUM

The Salamanca Rail Museum is housed in a fully restored depot built in 1912 for the Buffalo, Rochester & Pittsburgh Railway. The interior of the museum includes a ticket office, "Ladies' Retiring Room," baggage room, video presentations, photographs, and artifacts primarily reflecting the Erie, the Baltimore & Ohio, the Buffalo, Rochester & Pittsburgh, and the Pennsylvania Railroads—all important to the development of the region.

A permanent display of train cars is on museum grounds. The collection includes two cabooses that children may tour, a box car, coach, and a crew camp car. The museum has a gift shop.

NOTE: Track conditions prevented rail excursions in 1995. Call ahead for an update.

How to Get There   From Buffalo, take Route 219 south, which leads right into Salamanca (about 1 hour and 15 minutes). The depot is visible from the highway.

Hours   April to December: open Monday to Saturday, 10:00 A.M. to 5:00 P.M.; Sunday, 12:00 noon to 5:00 P.M. Closed January through March and Mondays in April, October, and December.

Fares   Free (donations are appreciated).

Contact   Salamanca Rail Museum, 170 Main Street, Salamanca, NY 14779. Telephone (716) 945-3133.

S A L E M

BATTEN KILL RAILROAD

The village of Salem, New York, was an important railroad town in the 19th century, when the Rutland & Washington Railroad dominated the area. Today, the Batten Kill Railroad offers tourist rides between Salem and Shushan (near the Vermont state line).

Trains depart from Salem Station, which was built in 1907 and is currently under restoration as a railroad museum. The diesel excursion (2 hours, 10 minutes) takes passengers past a trout stream, dairy farms, 200-year-old homes, and a historic covered bridge. A one-hour layover in Shushan enables passengers to tour the town (first settled during the Revolutionary War) and visit the Covered Bridge and Georgi Museums.

NOTE: Call for information on wheelchair access.

How to Get There   From Albany, take I-87 north to exit 14 north. Turn right onto Route 29 east (to Greenwich). Then turn left onto Route 22 north. This leads into Salem; the railroad is on the left side of the highway.

Hours   Mid-May to late June: Friday departure at 2:30 P.M.; Saturday and Sunday departures at 11:00 A.M. and 2:30 P.M.

Late June to early September: Thursday and Friday departures at 10:15 A.M. and 2:30 P.M.; Saturday and Sunday departures at 10:15 A.M., 1:15 P.M., and 4:00 P.M.

Early September to late October: Thursday and Friday departures at 11:00 A.M. and 2:30 P.M.; Saturday and Sunday departures at 10:00 A.M., 12:45 P.M., and 3:20 P.M.

Fares   Adults, $8; seniors (60 and above), $7; children (ages 3 to 12), $4; children under three not occupying a seat are admitted free of charge.

Contact   Batten Kill Railroad, Salem Station, Route 22, Salem, NY 12865. Telephone (518) 692-2191 or (518) 854-3787.

WEST HENRIETTA

NEW YORK MUSEUM OF TRANSPORTATION

The New York Museum of Transportation displays a variety of train exhibits, including several trolleys, a caboose, a wooden interurban car, a steam locomotive built in the 1920s, and a subway car display depicting Rochester area subway operations. A visitors center offers artifacts, pictures, models for viewing, and a gift shop. A hands-on museum, children will especially enjoy exploring the interior of the many cars, trains, and trolleys on display.

From May through October, the New York Museum of Transportation and the **Rochester & Genesee Valley Railroad Museum** offer a joint museum and railroad package. A 20-minute track car ride is given along a 1.75-mile route between the two points. Museum volunteers built the track over a 15-year period.

NOTE: The interior of the trolleys are reached by stairs or steps, and track car rides are not handicapped accessible.

Special Events   Gandy Dancer Day; Phoebe Snow Day.

How to Get There   Take I-390 to exit 11, then follow Route 251 west to East River Road (flashing red light). Turn right; the Rochester & Genesee Valley Railroad Museum is about a mile down. Then take the train over to the New York Museum of Transportation.

Hours   Museum only: open year-round, Sunday, 11:00 A.M. to 5:00 P.M. Museum and ride package: May through October, open Sunday, 11:00 A.M. to 5:00 P.M.

Fares   May through October (check with museum for reduced rate, November through April): adults, $4; seniors (65 and above), $3; students (ages 5 to 15), $2; family (two adults and four or more children), $15.

Contact   New York Museum of Transportation, P.O. Box 136, West Henrietta, NY 14586. Telephone (716) 533-1113.

NORTH CAROLINA

DILLSBORO

GREAT SMOKY MOUNTAINS RAILWAY

The Great Smoky Mountain Railway offers both steam and diesel train rides through western North Carolina in the beautiful Great Smoky Mountains, through forests, across lakes, rivers, and waterfalls. The steam locomotive was used by the Army in World War II and was featured in the movie *This Property Is Condemned*. More than 3,000 pieces of railroad artifacts are housed in the **Great Smoky Mountains Historic Railway Museum,** which is next door to the railway's Dillsboro Depot.

Several scenic excursions are offered from the Dillsboro Depot: the Red Marble Gap Excursion, a four-and-a-half-hour trip along America's second highest railroad grade; Tuckasegee River Excursion, a three-and-a-half-hour trip that includes travel through a 700-foot-long hand-dug tunnel; and Nantahala Gorge Excursion, a four-and-a-half-hour trip that includes a trip to a gorge, a visit to the Bryson City Depot (circa 1880), and a tour of a renovated caboose (now a visitor center). A six-

Great Smoky Mountains Railway's locomotive #1702 steams out of Cowee Tunnel.

hour trip combining all three excursions is also offered, along with a seven-hour trip from Bryson City to the gorge that includes a guide-assisted white-water raft trip.

The railway offers standard coaches and open-car seating. For an additional surcharge, club car and crown coaches with heat and air conditioning are available. Refreshments are available on trains.

NOTE: Restroom facilities are not available on all open cars.

Special Events   Cottontail Express; Dogwood Special; Halloween Ghost Train; Santa Express.

How to Get There   From Asheville take I-40 west to exit 27 (junction with U.S. 74). Take U.S. 74 west; depots are just off the highway at exit 81 (Dillsboro) and exit 67 (Bryson).

Hours   Train rides and museum: open April to December (call for departure times).

Fares   Diesel train rides: adults, $18 to $54; children (ages 3 to 12), $9 to $38. Steam train rides: adults, $23 to $54; children (ages 3 to 12), $9 to $38.
Museum: adults, $3; children (ages 3 to 12), $2.
Children two years of age and under are free of charge to all attractions.

Contact   Great Smoky Mountains Railway, P.O. Box 397, Dillsboro, NC 28725. Telephone (800) 872-4681 or (704) 586-8811; fax (704) 586-8806.

H A M L E T

NATIONAL RAILROAD MUSEUM AND HALL OF FAME

The National Railroad Museum and Hall of Fame opened in 1976 and is dedicated to preserving and promoting railroad history. It is housed in a 1900 Victorian structure, a building that served as the former depot of the Seaboard Air Line Railway. Exhibits in the museum include rolling stock, replicas of locomotives and a caboose, photographs, maps, and a model railroad layout. The museum also has a gift shop.

How to Get There   From Charlotte, take I-74 east to the Hamlet exit. Turn right off the exit onto Raleigh Street, then left onto Main Street. The museum is on Main.

NATIONAL RAILROAD MUSEUM AND HALL OF FAME

This Victorian depot is now home to railroad treasures of bygone days.

Hours   Open Saturday, 10:00 A.M. to 5:00 P.M.; Sunday, 1:00 P.M. to 5:00 P.M. Open weekdays by appointment for groups and out-of-town visitors.

Fares   Admission is free.

Contact   Julius Cromwell, President, National Railroad Museum and Hall of Fame, Inc., 2 Main Street, Hamlet, NC 28345. Telephone (910) 582-3117.

NEW HILL

NEW HOPE VALLEY RAILWAY/
NORTH CAROLINA RAILROAD MUSEUM

The East Carolina Chapter of the National Railway Historical Society (NRHS) operates the New Hope Valley Railway and the

North Carolina Railroad Museum. Its collection includes passenger cars, steam engines, locomotives, baggage, and boxcars. The museum is staffed only on Saturday and train ride days (including group rides) but is available for touring the rest of the week.

Trains operate along 6.5 miles of track in Wake County (formerly owned by the Southern Railway Company) from Bonsal, North Carolina.

NOTE: Sponsors recommend arriving at least 30 minutes before the train ride.

Special Events   Christmas Train Ride; Saturday work sessions.

How to Get There   From Raleigh, take U.S. 1 south and exit at New Hill. Turn right onto New Hill for about 2 miles. Then turn left onto old U.S. 1 for about 2.5 miles. Turn left onto Bonsal Road. The museum is on Daisey Street.

Hours   May to December: open first Sunday of each month; trains leave every hour from 12:00 noon to 4:00 P.M.

Fares   Adults, $5; children (ages 1 to 12), $3; children under one year of age are free of charge.

Contact   East Carolina Chapter, NRHS, North Carolina Railroad Museum, P.O. Box 40, New Hill, NC 27562. Telephone (919) 362-5416.

S P E N C E R

NORTH CAROLINA TRANSPORTATION MUSEUM AT HISTORIC SPENCER SHOPS

The North Carolina Transportation Museum at Historic Spencer Shops is located on what was once the largest steam locomotive servicing center for Southern Railway. When the Spencer Shops complex (which began construction in 1896) closed in 1960, an effort was launched to preserve the historic buildings and create a transportation museum. Successful efforts led to the creation of the North Carolina Transportation History Corporation and the opening of the first exhibit area in 1983.

Train enthusiasts will enjoy touring the variety of transportation exhibits and riding locomotive #4, the former Buffalo Creek and Gauley Railroad steam train, or a diesel locomotive. The trip takes 50 minutes and provides visitors with a look at the operations once performed at Spencer Shops.

An $8 million renovation is underway at the museum. The roundhouse will have a major face-lift and, upon completion, all of the locomotives and rolling stock will be on display. The grand re-opening is set for mid-September, 1996.

Special Events   Santa Train.

How to Get There   From Charlotte, take I-85 north to exit 79 (Spencer Shops). Turn left off the exit and left again at the second stoplight (Highway 29 and Main Street).

Hours   Museum: open November through March, Tuesday to Saturday, 10:00 A.M. to 4:00 P.M., and Sunday, 1:00 to 4:00 P.M.; April through October, Monday to Saturday, 9:00 A.M. to 5:00 P.M., and Sunday, 1:00 P.M. to 5:00 P.M. Closed some holidays; check ahead.

Train rides: open daily April through Labor Day; weekends September to mid-December. Call ahead for diesel and steam departure times.

Fares   Diesel train rides: adults, $3.50; seniors and children, $2.50. Steam train rides: adults, $4; seniors and children, $3. Museum admission is free.

Contact   North Carolina Transportation Museum at Historic Spencer Shops, P.O. Box 165, Spencer, NC 28159. Telephone (704) 636-2889.

WILMINGTON

WILMINGTON RAILROAD MUSEUM

Like so many other communities in the United States, beginning in the 1800s, the railroad was the largest industry in Wilmington. In 1840, when the Wilmington and Weldon Railroad was completed, it comprised 161 miles of track and was then the longest continuous rail line in the world. That railroad line later merged with another line and became the Atlantic Coast Line Railroad. The Wilmington Railroad Museum is dedicated to that history and to highlighting the importance of railroads to the southeastern part of the United States.

Among the museum's exhibits are a steam engine built in 1910, a boxcar, two cabooses, model railroad displays, photographs, and memorabilia from a period of over 100 years. It also has a gift shop.

How to Get There   The museum is located in downtown Wilmington, at the corner of Red Cross and Nutt Streets.

Hours   Open Monday to Saturday, 10:00 A.M. to 5:00 P.M.; Sunday, 1:00 P.M. to 5:00 P.M.

Fares   Adults, $2; children (ages 6 to 12), $1; children under six years of age are admitted free of charge.

Contact   Wilmington Railroad Museum, 501 Nutt Street, Wilmington, NC 28401. Telephone (910) 763-2634.

NORTH DAKOTA

M A N D A N

NORTH DAKOTA STATE RAILROAD MUSEUM

Visitors to the North Dakota State Railroad Museum can ride a mini-train and discover a variety of train-related exhibits. Among them: over 200 model reproductions of hopper cars (grain carrying cars) and an operating model train; a display of timetables from every railroad in the United States; and a large collection of train photographs and North Dakota scenes.

In addition to these artifacts, the museum also displays two wooden cabooses and other rolling stock.

How to Get There From Bismarck, take I-94 to the Sunset exit for Mandan. Turn right off the exit, follow the Old Red Trail, and look for railroad signs. Turn left on 34th Street, then right on 30th Avenue to the museum.

Hours Museum: May to September, open daily, 1:00 P.M. to 5:00 P.M.

Mini-train: May to September, open Sunday and holidays, with departures at 2:00 P.M., 3:00 P.M., and 4:00 P.M.

Fares   Admission is free.

Contact   North Dakota State Railroad Museum, P.O. Box 1001, Mandan, ND 58554-1001. Telephone (701) 663-9322.

WEST FARGO

BONANZAVILLE, USA

Bonanzaville, USA takes visitors back to the days of the early pioneers and contains over 40 attractions spread throughout the Red River Valley Fairgrounds. Included are museums, antique and reproduction houses and shops, and artifacts from the pioneer period.

Train fans will enjoy a visit to the **Emden Depot and Railroad Museum,** which houses an 1883 locomotive and caboose, a railroad snowplow, and a 1930 steel 80-passenger coach. The Spud Valley Railroad is an automated miniature railroad display built and operated by a railroad club and housed in an old depot. (Both depots were owned previously by the Northern Pacific Railway.) Each August, the automated display is run manually during Bonanzaville's Pioneer Days celebration.

Special Events   Fur Traders Invasion; Pioneer Days; Haunted Village; Country Christmas.

How to Get There   From I-94 east, take exit 343 into West Fargo. Bonanzaville is on the right.

Hours   Memorial Day weekend to late October: open daily. Call for hours.

Fares   Adults, $6; students (ages 6 to 16), $3; family rate, $16; children under six years of age are free of charge.

Contact   Bonanzaville, USA, P.O. Box 719, West Fargo, ND 58078. Telephone (701) 282-2822 or (800) 700-5317.

OHIO

AKRON

THE DEPOT RESTAURANT AT QUAKER SQUARE

Train enthusiasts will enjoy the experience of dining in a former Railway Express Agency. A freight terminal that once served the B & O, Pennsylvania, and Erie Railroads has been converted into a restaurant. Located at Quaker Square (of Quaker Oats fame), it's complete with a collection of railroad memorabilia. Near the loading dock in an outdoor display are a 100-ton Burlington Railroad switching locomotive, a narrow gauge steam train, Pennsylvania Railroad solarium cars, a caboose, and a baggage car.

The restaurant is part of the Akron Hilton Inn at Quaker Square, a complex with hotel rooms that were once grain silos built in 1932 for the Quaker Oats company. The silos are listed on the National Register of Historic Places.

How to Get There From Cleveland, take I-77 south to exit 22a (Main and Broadway). Turn left onto Broadway and follow it for about 1 mile to Quaker Square.

Hours   Open daily, 11:00 A.M. to 8:00 P.M.

Fares   Call for dining prices.

Contact   Akron Hilton Inn at Quaker Square, 135 South Broadway, Akron, OH 44308. Telephone (216) 253-5970; fax (216) 253-2574.

BELLEVUE

MAD RIVER & NKP RAILROAD MUSEUM

The Mad River & NKP Railroad Museum contains a rich collection of railroad artifacts, rolling stock, and historic structures that depict the influence of railroading in the area. The museum is named after two of the earliest railroad companies in Bellevue, the Mad River and Lake Erie and the Nickel Plate Railroads, which arrived on the scene in the 1800s.

The museum is operated by the Mad River & NKP Railroad Society, a nonprofit group formed in 1972 to preserve railroad history. Among the exhibits are the Curtice Ohio Depot, built in 1882, a 1939 dome car, a wood gondola car, a Pennsylvania Railroad mail car, cabooses, a hopper car; and diesel engines.

The museum has a gift shop, picnic shelter, parking, and Monument Station, which houses displays, cars, and a video-viewing area.

Note: The Norfolk & Western and the Norfolk Southern freight trains operate alongside the museum. Visitors are urged to use caution.

How to Get There   From Columbus, take State Road 23 north to State Road 4 north (at Marion). Then take State Road 20 west (left turn); this will take you into Bellevue.

Hours   Memorial Day through Labor Day: open daily, 1:00
P.M. to 5:00 P.M. May, September, and October: open weekends
only, 1:00 P.M. to 5:00 P.M.

Fares   Admission is free. Suggested donations: adults, $2;
seniors, $1; children, $1; families, $5.

Contact   Mad River & NKP Railroad Society, 233 York Street,
Bellevue, OH 44811-1377. Telephone (419) 483-2222.

C O N N E A U T

CONNEAUT RAILROAD MUSEUM

Located in the former New York Central depot (built in 1900),
the Conneaut Railroad Museum is operated by the Conneaut
Chapter of the National Railway Historical Society. Its exhibits
include rare train memorabilia and several large- and small-
scale locomotive models and equipment with mannequins
serving as train crew at various displays. Engine 755 from the
Nickel Plate Railroad and a hopper and caboose from the
Bessemer & Lake Erie Railroad are also on exhibit along a track
on museum grounds.
    The museum sells refreshments and souvenirs.

How to Get There   From Cleveland, take I-90 to Conneaut;
exit Route 7 north. Turn right onto Mill Street and look for the
depot (across the railroad tracks). Parking is on the right.

Hours   Memorial Day to Labor Day: open daily, 12:00 noon
to 5:00 P.M.

Fares   Admission is free (donations are accepted).

Contact   Conneaut Chapter, National Railway Historical Society, Conneaut Railroad Museum, P.O. Box 643, Conneaut, OH 44030. Telephone (216) 599-7878.

D A Y T O N

Carillon Historical Park

Carillon Historical Park is a 65-acre historical museum complex that features the development of Miami Valley. Named for the 151-foot bell tower that figures prominently in the park, Carillon includes hundreds of artifacts, 20 buildings on site, working exhibits, and interpreters to help visitors explore the various collections. The 1905 *Wright Flyer III,* an airplane built by Orville and Wilbur Wright and designated a National Historic Landmark, is displayed in Wright Hall.

Train-related exhibits include the Bowling Green Train Station, the *Baltimore & Ohio #1* (B&O's oldest American-made locomotive), a railroad watchtower, a 1903 coach and parlor car, a city railway trolley, and a fireless locomotive. An added attraction is the operation of model trains by live steam on selected weekends by the Carillon Park Rail and Steam Society.

Music from the 57 bells in the carillon can be heard every Sunday during the operating season and on special event days.

How to Get There   From Columbus, take I-70 east to I-675 south, then Route 35 west to I-75 south. Take I-75 to exit 51, and turn east onto Edwin C. Moses Boulevard. Turn right on Stewart Street, right again on Patterson Boulevard, and right on Carillon Boulevard.

Hours   May 1 to August 31: Tuesday to Saturday, 10:00 A.M. to 6:00 P.M.; Sunday, 1:00 P.M. to 6:00 P.M.

September and October: Tuesday to Saturday, 10:00 A.M. to 5:00 P.M.; Sunday 1:00 P.M. to 5:00 P.M.

Park is closed on Mondays, except holidays.

Fares   Adults, $2; children (ages 6 to 17), $1; children under six years of age are admitted free of charge.

Contact   Carillon Historical Park, 2001 South Patterson Boulevard, Dayton, OH 45409. Telephone (513) 293-2841.

D E N N I S O N

DENNISON RAILROAD DEPOT MUSEUM

Thanks to a successful five-year restoration effort, the Dennison Railroad Depot (an 1873 structure built for the Pennsylvania Railroad) now houses the original ticket booth, railway office, waiting room, and exhibits for the Dennison Railroad Depot Museum. Nicknamed "Dreamsville," the depot served as a servicemen's canteen during both World Wars. Volunteers worked around the clock, providing free food and magazines during locomotive service stops to soldiers heading overseas.

Among the exhibits is a 1940s Thermos Bottle Engine. Special steam train rides are given several times a year.

Special Events   Fall Foliage, Murder Mystery, Santa Train.

How to Get There   From northbound I-70, take I-77 north to State Road 36 east (Dennison exit). Turn right off the exit, and another right at the first stop sign (look for railroad tracks). The depot is about nine blocks down from the last turn.

Hours   Museum: Tuesday to Saturday, 10:00 A.M. to 5:00 P.M.; Sunday, 11:00 A.M. to 5:00 P.M.
Train rides: May to December, call ahead for schedule.

Fares   Adults, $3; seniors, $2.50; students (ages 7 to 18), $1.75; children under the age of seven are free of charge.

Contact   Dennison Railroad Depot Museum, P.O. Box 11, 400 Center Street, Dennison, OH 44621. Telephone: (614) 922-6776.

DOVER

WARTHER MUSEUM

The history of steam locomotives is depicted in the hand-carved working miniature trains created by the late Ernest Warther. Sixty-four working models and many famous trains are represented at the Warther Museum, including: the *Casey Jones*, the *General*, and *Texas* engines from the Civil War, the *John Bull*, the *Big Boy* of the Union Pacific, and the Lincoln Funeral Train. The extensive 73,000-button collection of Frieda Warther is also on display.

The museum has a two-acre parking area, which displays an antique steam engine, a caboose, and a reproduction railroad trestle. Picnic facilities are also available.

How to Get There   The museum is located half a mile east of I-77, at exit 83.

Hours   Open daily, 9:00 A.M. to 5:00 P.M. Closed Christmas, New Year's Day, Easter, and Thanksgiving.

Fares   Adults, $6; children (ages 7 to 17), $3; children six years of age and under are admitted free of charge.

Contact   Warther Museum, 311 Karl Avenue, Dover, OH 44622. Telephone (216) 343-7513.

JEFFERSON

ASTABULA, CARSON, JEFFERSON SCENIC LINE

The Astabula, Carson, Jefferson Scenic (ACJS) Line began operation in 1990 and shares track with a freight line. It features a one-hour, 12-mile round-trip scenic diesel excursion ride through woodsy backcountry and over bridges to Carson Yard. The train collection includes two ALCO diesel engines built in the 1950s, a 1922 passenger car, a Long Island Railroad commuter car, 1950 baggage car, and a 1956 red caboose.

The ACJS Line expects to complete the conversion of its baggage car into a rolling gift and refreshment shop by summer 1996.

NOTE: One passenger car is unheated, but it has a lavatory, air conditioning, and wide windows for great viewing. Another has windows that open, walkover seat backs, and ceiling fans.

Special Events   HoBo Car Rides.

How to Get There   From Cleveland take I-90 east to State Road 11 south. Exit at Route 46 to Jefferson. Turn left at the second stop light. Across the railroad tracks, make an immediate left into the Douglas Lumber parking lot. The platform is opposite.

Hours   Mid-June through late October: departures at 12:30 P.M., 2:00 P.M., and 3:30 P.M.

Fares   Adults, $6.50; seniors (ages 60 and over), $5.50; children (ages 3 to 12), $4.50; children under three years of age not occupying a seat are free of charge.

Contact   Astabula, Carson, Jefferson Scenic Line, P.O. Box 222, Jefferson, OH 44047-0222. Telephone (216) 576-6346.

JEFFERSON DEPOT

The Lake Shore and Michigan Southern Railroad Station, or Jefferson Depot, was built in 1872, has been restored, and was placed on the National Register of Historic Places in 1983. Trains steamed into Jefferson from August 1872 to August 1956, the time of the last scheduled stop. The building exhibits an authentic women-only waiting room, the original potbellied stove used at the station, and a 1918 caboose.

The depot is owned and operated by the Jefferson Depot, Inc., a nonprofit organization.

Special Events   Festival at the Depot; An Old Fashioned Williamsburg Christmas Party; Strawberry Festival-Craft Bazaar.

How to Get There   See the previous entry for directions to Jefferson.

Hours   Memorial Day through Labor Day: Sunday, 1:00 P.M. to 4:00 P.M.

Fares   Admission is free (donations are accepted).

Contact   Jefferson Depot, Inc., 147 East Jefferson Street, P.O. Box 22, Jefferson, OH 44047. Telephone (216) 293-5532 or (216) 576-1282.

L E B A N O N

I & O SCENIC RAILWAY

The I & O Scenic Railway takes passengers on a narrated, one-hour, 14-mile excursion along a former stage coach route. The landscape includes meadows, pastures, a creek, and wildflowers (in season). Powered by a former 1950s Chicago, Burlington and Quincy Railroad diesel electric locomotive, the line uses restored passenger coaches that once served as commuter cars for the Delaware, Lackawanna and Western Railroad. Visitors have the option of traveling in an open gondola car for a panoramic view of the area.

The station offers a gift shop.

0248   UNITED STATES

NOTE: The train has no heat or air conditioning or restrooms on board.

Special Events   Civil War Reenactment; Scout Saturdays; Sunday Dinner Tours; Mystery Dinner Tours; Train Rides with Santa.

How to Get There   The I & O Scenic Railway departs from South Broadway (U.S. Route 42), one block south of the Golden Lamb Inn.

Hours   In April and November: Saturday and Sunday only; May through October: Wednesday, Friday, Saturday, and Sunday. Departures at 10:30 A.M. and 12:00 P.M. (Wednesday and Friday); 10:30 A.M., 12:00 P.M., 1:30 P.M., and 3:00 P.M. (Saturday); 12:00 P.M., 1:30 P.M., and 3:00 P.M. (Sunday).

Fares   Adults, $9; seniors, $8; children (ages 3 to 12), $5.

Contact   I & O Scenic Railway, 198 South Broadway, Lebanon, OH 45036. Telephone (513) 398-8584.

LORAIN COUNTY

LORAIN & WEST VIRGINIA RAILWAY

The Lorain & West Virginia (L&WV) Railway, built in 1906, features 45-minute to 60-minute train excursions through scenic Lorain County along 2 miles of track. The 1950s diesel train carries *Mt. Baxter* (a Pullman lounge/sleeper car), and a wagon-top caboose. Portions of the train were captured in the film *The Natural*.

The L&WV Railway is operated by a foundation of the same name.

NOTE: The railway may not be operating in summer 1996; call ahead.

Special Events   Haunted Train Rides; Lorain County Fair.

How to Get There   From Cleveland, take I-480 west to Route 10. Take 10 to Route 20. At Route 58, turn left and go south 7 miles to Wellington. Turn right onto Route 18 and go west 1 mile to the boarding area.

Hours   Mid-July to October: Saturday and Sunday, 1:00 P.M., 3:00 P.M., and 5:00 P.M. Open daily during Lorain County Fair. Several departure times are available.

Fares   Adults, $3 to 6; children (ages 3 to 12), $2 to 5, children under two years of age not occupying a seat are admitted free of charge.

Contact   Lorain & West Virginia Railway, P.O. Box 1131, Elyria, OH 44036-1131. Telephone (800) 334-1673.

M A U M E E

WOLCOTT HOUSE MUSEUM COMPLEX

The Wolcott House Museum Complex includes six historic buildings from the 1800s on a seven-acre site: a building in the Federal style; a log home; a saltbox-style farmhouse; a church; a home in the Greek Revival style; and the Clover Leaf Railroad Depot. A caboose, boxcar, and 19th-century postal wagon are also on museum grounds. The depot, built in 1886, provided service to the former Toledo, St. Louis & Kansas Railroad. It then merged with another line to become the Nickel Plate Line and later became part of the Norfolk & Western Railroad in 1965.

The museum is operated by the Maumee Valley Historical Society. Future plans include restoration of the depot, caboose, boxcar, and postal wagon and creation of a small "transportation/communication" museum in the museum baggage room.

Special Events   Civil War Encampment; Old Fashioned Baseball Game; Lawn Sale; Harvest Days (especially for children); Christmas by the River.

How to Get There   From Toledo, drive west on Route 24 for 15 minutes. Turn left at Key Street to River Road. The museum is at 1031 River.

Hours   April to December: Wednesday to Sunday, 1:00 P.M. to 4:00 P.M. Closed major holidays.

Fares   Adults, $3.50; students (ages 5 to 18), $1.50; children under five years of age are free of charge.

Contact   Wolcott House Museum Complex, Maumee Valley Historical Society, 1031 River Road, Maumee, OH 43537. Telephone (419) 893-9602 (Monday to Friday, 9:00 A.M. to 5:00 P.M.).

O L M S T E D   F A L L S

TROLLEYVILLE USA

The Gerald E. Brookins Museum of Electric Railways, or Trolleyville USA, is devoted to the preservation of streetcars and their history. The collection began with four ex-Shaker Rapid cars and has grown to 28 pieces of historic streetcar equipment. An operating museum, Trolleyville USA offers visitors unlimited rides on vintage trolleys and interurbans along 2.5 miles of track through Columbia Park. Barn tours of the restoration shop are also given.

The museum has a gift shop and free parking.

Special Events   Festival of Lights.

How to Get There   From Cleveland, take I-71 south to 480 west. Then take State Road 252 (Columbia Road) into Olmsted Falls. The museum is at 7100 Columbia.

Hours   Memorial Day through September: Saturday, Sunday, and holidays, 12:00 noon to 5:00 P.M. June, July, and August: Wednesday and Friday, 10:00 A.M. to 3:00 P.M.; Saturday, Sunday, and holidays, 12:00 noon to 5:00 P.M.

Fares   Adults, $4; seniors, $3.60; children (ages 3 to 11), $2; children under three years of age are free of charge.
       The fare includes unlimited trolley rides.

Contact   Trolleyville USA, 7100 Columbia Road, Olmsted Falls, OH 44138. Telephone (216) 235-4725.

O R R V I L L E

ORRVILLE RAILROAD HERITAGE SOCIETY

The Orrville Railroad Heritage Society was founded by railroad enthusiasts interested in preserving the history of Ohio railroading. The Society's very first project was completed in 1982: saving the Pennsylvania Railroad Union Depot in Orrville, a building then owned by Conrail. A historic landmark, the depot was built in 1868. Today, it is available for touring.
       Visitors to Orrville Railroad can ride diesel-powered trains, scheduled to run in fall, spring, and during Depot Days.

Special Events   Depot Days.

How to Get There   Take I-77 south to Route 21 south. Then take State Road 585 to State Road 57 to Orrville. Turn right at the fourth stop light. The depot is on the second block after the turn.

A diesel locomotive is ready for operation during Depot Days.

A former New York Central passenger coach is one of the many historic cars on display in Orrville.

ORRVILLE RAILROAD HERITAGE SOCIETY

Static displays: a caboose and interlocking tower near the Orrville depot.

Hours   The depot is open April to October: Saturdays, 10:00 A.M. to 4:00 P.M. Train ride: call for information.

Fares   Depot: admission is free. Train ride: donations requested.

Contact   Orrville Railroad Heritage Society, P.O. Box 11, Orrville, OH 44667. Telephone (216) 682-4327 or (216) 683-2426.

PENINSULA

CUYAHOGA VALLEY SCENIC RAILROAD

The Cuyahoga Valley Scenic Railroad (CVSR) operates along a line built in 1880. The U.S. Park Service owns the tracks and the land, while the CVSR operates the trains. Originating from a restored depot in Peninsula and from Independence, CVSR operates diesel and stainless-steel coaches on a 26-mile track. Nine different tours are available, from 90 minutes to six-and-a-half hours in length, which provide spectacular sightseeing along the Cuyahoga River and through the Cuyahoga Valley National Recreation Area. Among the nine tours are opportunities to combine train rides with hiking; a stop at Hale Farm (an outdoor museum reflecting 19th-century America); and a nature trip where wildlife sightings (blue heron, fox, deer, birds) are highlighted. Park rangers are available to provide answers to questions on all excursions.

One of CVSR's newest additions is a round-end observation car, the *Saint Lucie Sound*, built in 1946. It now serves as a private car and can be rented for special occasions. Future plans include extending the track to Cleveland for a Cleveland-Akron route.

All cars are fully heated and air-conditioned.

Special Events   Fall Color Trains; Polar Bear Express; Christmas Tree Train.

How to Get There   From Cleveland, take I-77 south to exit 155 (Rockside Road). Turn east on Rockside and then left on Canal Road. Turn left again on Old Rockside. The boarding site is on Old Rockside in Independence.

Hours   May to October: Wednesday to Sunday. September: weekends only. October: seven days a week. Call for additional information.

Fares   Adults, $7 to 20; seniors, $6 to 18; children (ages 3 to 12), $5 to 12; children under three years of age not occupying a seat are admitted free of charge.

Contact   Cuyahoga Valley Scenic Railroad, P.O. Box 158, 1630 West Mill, Peninsula, OH 44264. (800) 468-4070 or (216) 657-2000; fax (216) 657-2080.

SUGARCREEK

OHIO CENTRAL RAILROAD

For a ride on the "Buckeye Route" through Amish country, the Ohio Central Railroad features a one-hour, 12-mile journey from the 1915 Sugar Creek Station Depot. The railroad has been in operation since 1989, with the only regularly operating steam locomotive in Ohio. The scenic trip offers visitors a glimpse of Amish farming life.

Special Events   Father's Day; Murder Mysteries; Fall Foliage; Double-Headed Steam; Fall Foliage; Holiday Trains.

How to Get There   From Akron, take I-77 south to exit 83. Turn right onto State Road 39 west. Drive 8 miles to Sugar Creek. Turn left onto Factory Street; the station is at 111 Factory.

Hours   May to October: Monday to Saturday, with departures at 11:00 A.M., 12:30 P.M., 2:00 P.M., and 3:30 P.M. July, August, October: same times, plus additional trains at 9:30 A.M. and 5:00 P.M.

Fares   Adults (ages 13 and above), $7; children (ages 3 to 12), $4; children under three years of age are admitted free of charge.

Contact   Ohio Central Railroad, P.O. Box 427, 111 Factory Street, Sugarcreek, OH 44681. Telephone (216) 852-4676.

OKLAHOMA

CIMARRON VALLEY RAILROAD MUSEUM

Established in 1970 by the Read family, the Cimarron Valley Railroad Museum began with the acquisition of the Santa Fe Depot from Yale, Oklahoma. Today, the museum houses a large collection of railroad artifacts and memorabilia. Outdoors, visitors will find a General Electric diesel switcher locomotive; a wooden Frisco caboose; an oil tank car; a boxcar, and other rail vehicles on display.

How to Get There   From Oklahoma City, take Highway 33 east to Cushing. Turn right onto South Kings Highway. Pass the intersection at 9th Street and drive 1 mile to the next intersection (no street name). Turn right and look for a museum sign.

Hours   The museum has no regular hours. Call ahead for hours or to make an appointment.

Fares   Free, but donations are welcome.

Contact   Cimarron Valley Railroad Museum, South Kings Highway, P.O. Box 844, Cushing, OK 74023. Telephone (918) 225-1657 or (918) 225-5335 or (918) 225-3936.

H U G O

FRISCO DEPOT MUSEUM AND HUGO HERITAGE RAILROAD

The Frisco Depot Museum, operated by the Choctaw County Historical Society, displays historical artifacts and memorabilia that help tell the history of turn-of-the-century Oklahoma. The depot originally served the St. Louis–San Francisco Railway, a line built in 1887. Fire destroyed the original depot in 1913. Today, the museum exhibits include a miniature train exhibit, railroad artifacts, miniature circus, an Oklahoma still, and a barber shop from the 1800s.

The Hugo Heritage Railroad runs regular diesel train excursions from the depot. Eighty passengers can be seated on each of the two coaches, which were built for the Norfolk & Western Railroad in 1940.

How to Get There   From Oklahoma City, take the Indian Nation Turnpike south to I-70 east, then exit Jackson Street. The depot and train are at 300 Jackson.

Hours   Museum: April through November, open Monday to Saturday from 10:00 A.M. to 4:00 P.M.

Train ride runs at 2:00 P.M. on Saturdays, April through November.

Fares   Adults, $15; children (ages 2 to 11), $10.

Contact   Choctaw County Historical Society, P.O. Box 577, Hugo, OK 74743. Telephone (405) 326-6630.

OREGON

BAKER CITY

SUMPTER VALLEY RAILROAD RESTORATION, INC.

When the Sumpter Valley Railway was created in 1890, it was designed primarily to haul logs from the Sumpter Valley Blue Mountains to the sawmill in Baker City. Today, a portion of the original Sumpter Valley Railway line is in operation, managed by the nonprofit Sumpter Valley Railroad Restoration, Inc.

Visitors can take a 5-mile steam train ride, featuring a 1915 Heisler locomotive, observation cars, caboose, and coach. The landscape includes a wildlife game habitat preserve. In the rail yard are train displays including steam locomotives. Nature trails, a park, picnic tables, restrooms, and parking are available.

Passengers can board at one of two locations: the Sumpter Depot in the town of Sumpter, or McEwen Station in Baker City.

Special Events Founders' Day Potluck Picnic; Moonlight Rides.

How to Get There   The Sumpter Depot is located off State Highway 7, on the route of the Forest Service's Elkhorn Drive Scenic Byway. The McEwen Station is located along the Oregon Trail, via Interstate 84.

Hours   Memorial Day weekend through the last weekend of September: open Saturday, Sunday, and holidays, with departures at 10:00 A.M., 12:30 P.M., and 3:00 P.M. (from McEwen Station) or 11:30 A.M., 2:00 P.M., and 4:30 P.M. (from Sumpter Depot).

Fares   Round-trip: adults, $8, children (ages 6 to 16), $6; families, $20.
One-way: adults, $5; children (ages 6 to 16), $4; families, $13.

Contact   Sumpter Valley Railroad Restoration, Inc., P.O. Box 389, Baker City, OR 97814. Telephone (541) 894-2268.

HOOD RIVER

MOUNT HOOD RAILROAD

Passengers riding Mount Hood Railroad will enjoy the spectacular views from the steep climb up the Hood River Valley. (For the first 3 miles, the railroad uses a switchback to help push the train up the 3-percent grade.) The views include beautiful Mount Hood and Mount Adams, over 11,000 and 12,000 feet high, respectively. Named the *Fruit Blossom Special,* the 1906 train travels through beautiful fruit orchards that bear blossoms or ripened fruit in spring and summer.

In addition to the 44-mile round-trip excursion from Hood River to Parkdale, visitors can explore the carefully restored **Mount Hood Railroad Depot,** built in 1911, as well as a collection of 1950s and Pullman coaches from the early part of this century.

Special Events   Easter Egg Train; Halloween Spook Train; Train Robbery and Western Celebration; Thanksgiving Holiday Train; Christmas Tree Train.

How to Get There   From Portland, take Interstate 84 to exit 63 in Hood River. Follow the AMTRAK signs. From the south, take State Highway 35 on the Mount Hood Loop.

Hours   Open April to November. Check with railroad for schedule.

Fares   Adults, $19.95; seniors (60 and above), $16.95; children, $11.95.

Contact   Mount Hood Railroad, 110 Railroad Avenue, Hood River, OR 97031. Telephone (503) 386-3556 or (800) 872-4661.

LAKE OSWEGO

WILLIAMETTE SHORE TROLLEY

The Williamette Shore Trolley, which travels between Portland and Lake Oswego, is operated by the Oregon Electric Railway Historical Society. Southern Pacific Railroad ran passenger trolleys along the route between 1914 and 1929. Later, freight was carried until 1983.

Today, visitors can take a 7-mile ride along the Williamette River in one of two trolleys: a Blackpool England double-decker type, or a Portland Traction car. Spectacular views of the river are offered as trolleys cross two trestles, including the 686-foot Riverwood. The journey also includes a trip through the 1,396-foot-long Elk Rock Tunnel and along the parallel track route of the active Southern Pacific branch.

How to Get There   To reach Lake Oswego from Portland, take Route 43 south to State Street. The depot is on the left, at 311 North State Street, between A Avenue and Foothills Boulevard.

In Portland, the terminal is located on SW Moody at Sheridan Street, three blocks south of Riverplace.

Hours March 30 to April 30: open Saturday and Sunday; Memorial Day through Labor Day: Friday, Saturday, and Sunday. Departures at 10:00 A.M., 12:00 noon, 2:00 P.M., and 4:00 P.M. (from Lake Oswego) or 11:00 A.M., 1:00 P.M., and 3:00 P.M. (from Portland).

Fares Adults, $5; children (ages 3 to 12), $3; children under four years of age accompanied by an adult are admitted free of charge.

Contact Oregon Electric Railway Historical Society, 311 North State Street, P.O. Box 308, Lake Oswego, OR 97034. Telephone (503) 222-2226.

P O R T L A N D

METRO WASHINGTON PARK ZOO

Visitors to the Metro Washington Park Zoo in Portland can enjoy a 25-minute diesel or steam locomotive ride through zoo grounds and onto mountainous terrain in nearby Washington Park. Views include a panoramic glimpse of Portland, the snowcapped and forested Cascades, and the International Rose Test Gardens.

The zoo's train collection includes three tourist trains: the *ZooLiner,* the *Steamer,* and the *Orient Express.* They travel along a 30-inch narrow gauge track for a 4-mile journey carrying four cars, traveling through a curved tunnel and stopping at two stations. The Zoo Railway is one of the last railways permitted to process and cancel U.S. mail.

Refreshments are sold at Washington Park Station.

NOTE: Due to heavy flooding, the 1996 season schedule is uncertain. Call ahead.

How to Get There   The zoo is 5 minutes from downtown Portland on westbound Highway 26. Take the first exit for the zoo.

Hours   The trains operate in spring and summer. Spring: daily departures, 10:30 A.M. to 5:15 P.M. Summer: daily departures, 10:30 A.M. to 6:15 P.M.

Fares   Adults, $1.75; children, $1.25.

Contact   Metro Washington Park Zoo, 4001 SW Canyon Road, Portland, OR 97221-2799. Telephone (503) 226-1561.

SAMTRAK

SAMTRAK offers passengers a scenic ride along Portland's Williamette River, through a bird sanctuary, and between two important Portland tourist attractions: the Oaks Park Amusement Center and the Oregon Museum of Science and Industry. The 3-mile, 1-hour round-trip excursion gives visitors the option of visiting one of the sites and returning on a later train.

A restored 1942 locomotive pulls a covered car and a caboose with a cupola and open deck seating.

NOTE: The museum station has a wheelchair ramp.

Special Events   Oktoberfest; Mother's Day; Father's Day; Friday Senior Special; Labor Day; Memorial Day.

How to Get There   Boarding is offered at three stations: at Spokane Street under the east end of Sellwood Bridge; at the Oaks Park Amusement Center at Southeast Oaks Park Drive; and at the Oregon Museum of Science and Industry at 1945 Southeast Water Avenue.

Hours   May through June: open Saturday and Sunday, 11:00 A.M. to 4:00 P.M.

July through Labor Day: open Wednesday through Sunday, 11 A.M. to 5 P.M.

September: open Friday, Saturday, and Sunday, 11 A.M. to 4:00 P.M.

Early October: open Saturday and Sunday, 12:00 noon to 4:00 P.M.

Fares   Round-trip: Adults, $4, children (ages 1 to 4), $1.50. Infants are free of charge.

One-way: Adults, $3, children (ages 1 to 4), $1. Infants are free of charge.

Cupola seats are $1 extra.

Contact   SAMTRAK, P.O. Box 22548, Portland, OR 97269. Telephone (503) 659-5452.

VINTAGE TROLLEY

Cable cars and trolleys were an important part of Portland's landscape from the late 19th to the early 20th century, but they ceased operation in 1950. Despite their long absence, public enthusiasm for trolleys never died, and in 1991 the non-profit group Vintage Trolley reintroduced the beloved cars to Portland.

Today, visitors can take free 40-minute round-trip rides between Lloyd Center and downtown Portland, operating on tracks used by Portland's light rail system. The trolleys, working replicas of vintage cars that once traveled in Portland between 1904 and 1950, feature wood interior, cane seats, original moldings, and modern electronics. Wheelchair accessible, Vintage Trolley has boarding platforms at two of its stations and a wheelchair space on each trolley.

How to Get There   Trolleys can be boarded form Portland's MAX light rail stations between Lloyd Center and downtown Portland. To reach the Lloyd Center Station from I-5 north (Eugene), take exit 302A (Weidler Street). Turn right onto

Weidler Street, right again onto 9th Avenue, left onto Mult-numah Street, and right onto 11th Avenue. The station is on the left.

Hours March through May: open Saturday and Sunday, 10:00 A.M. to 6:00 P.M.

June through New Year's Day: Monday through Friday, 9:30 A.M. to 3:00 P.M.; Saturday and Sunday, 10:00 A.M. to 6:00 P.M.

Trolleys operate every half-hour.

Fares Admission is free.

Contact Vintage Trolley, Inc., 115 NW First Avenue, Suite 200, Portland, OR 97209. Telephone (503) 323-7363.

PENNSYLVANIA

ALTOONA RAILROADERS
MEMORIAL MUSEUM

The Pennsylvania Railroad dominated the American economy in the early 20th century and made Altoona, Pennsylvania (midway between its operation systems), the busiest railroad operation in the country. The Altoona Railroaders Memorial Museum invites visitors to learn about the lives of the men and women who helped create the Pennsylvania Railroad. It presents a look at the world of the railroad worker through a variety of displays and exhibits featuring life at work and in the community.

Also included at the museum is a rich collection of steam and diesel locomotives and dining and sleeper cars. An operating model train display is also on view. The Commonwealth of Pennsylvania's official steam locomotive #1361 is currently under restoration.

The museum is undergoing a $10 million restoration project. Opening of the new museum is expected in spring of

1997. The current museum remains open until the new building's completion.

NOTE: Just 5 miles away is another train attraction, the **Horseshoe Curve National Historic Landmark** (see next entry).

Special Events   Railfest.

How to Get There   From Pittsburgh, take Route 22 to the Altoona exit and follow signs to the museum. Altoona can also be reached from Routes 220, 36, I-80, and the Pennsylvania Turnpike.

Hours   Open daily except Monday. May through October: 10:00 A.M. to 6:00 P.M. November through April: 10:00 A.M. to 5:00 P.M.

Fares   Adults, $3.50; seniors (ages 62 and up), $3; children (ages 3 to 12), $2; children under three years of age are free of charge.

Contact   Altoona Railroaders Memorial Museum, 1300 Ninth Avenue, Altoona, PA 16602. Telephone (814) 946-0834; fax (814) 946-9457.

HORSESHOE CURVE NATIONAL HISTORIC LANDMARK

To meet its goal of westward expansion, the Pennsylvania Railroad needed to cross the steep Allegheny Mountains. The 19th-century creation of the Horseshoe Curve made that possible. The curve, designed by engineer J. Edgar Thomson, is considered an engineering marvel because it enabled the railroad to connect both sides of the Allegheny Mountains. Rail workers carved an opening in the mountains with a workforce using picks, shovels, and horses. The Horseshoe Curve National Historic Landmark is a tribute to that achievement.

The landmark has a visitors center with exhibits. A single-track funicular takes visitors to a panoramic view of the curve, or visitors may climb 194 steps to the top. At the top, rail fans will enjoy the spectacular view of the more than 50 trains traveling along the track on any given day.

The landmark has a gift shop.

NOTE: The landmark is owned by the Altoona Railroaders Memorial Museum (see previous entry), a tribute to the men and women who worked on the railroad. That museum is currently undergoing a major renovation, and a new building is expected to open in 1997. The museum is still open and is a highly recommended stop for visitors of the Horseshoe Curve.

How to Get There   See the previous entry for directions to Altoona.

Hours   Open daily except Monday. May through October: 9:30 A.M. to 7:00 P.M. November through April: 10:00 A.M. to 4:30 P.M.

Fares   No admission is charged to visit the landmark. Visitors pay $1.50 for the funicular ride.

Contact   Horseshoe Curve National Historic Landmark, 1300 Ninth Avenue, Altoona, PA 16602. Telephone (814) 946-0834; fax (814) 946-9457.

A S H L A N D

PIONEER TUNNEL COAL MINE AND STEAM TRAIN

The Pioneer Tunnel Coal Mine and Steam Train, created in 1961, offers visitors two kinds of underground mine tours. One is a drift mine tour taken in battery-operated mine cars. The other tour is a "Lokie" ride on a steam locomotive called the *Henry Clay,* a 1920s narrow gauge train that takes a three-quarter-mile journey around Mahanoy Mountain to an abandoned strip mine. Mine guides explain to visitors about strip mining.

A picnic and playground facility, gift shop, snack bar, and mining museum are all in the vicinity of the tunnel. Infant seats are available and a collapsible wheelchair can be accommodated on the tours.

NOTE: The average mine temperature is 52°F. A jacket or sweater is recommended.

Special Events   Pioneer Day.

How to Get There   From I-80, take I-81 south to exit 36 west. Then take PA Route 61 north to Ashland. The museum is at the corner of 19th and Oak Streets.

From I-78, take PA Route 61 North to Ashland.

Hours   Memorial Day through Labor Day: 10:00 A.M. to 6:00 P.M. In May, September, and October: weekdays, 11:00 A.M., 12:30, and 2:00 P.M. (mine tours only), steam train tours for groups by reservation only; weekends, 10:00 A.M. to 6:00 P.M. (steam train and mine tours).

Fares   Coal mine tour: adults, $4; children (under 12), $3. Steam train: adults, $2.50; children (under 12), $1.50.

Contact   Pioneer Tunnel Coal Mine, Ashland Community Enterprises, 19th and Oak Streets, Ashland, PA 17921. Telephone (717) 875-3850; fax (717) 875-3301.

B E L L E F O N T E

BELLEFONTE HISTORICAL RAILROAD

The Bellefonte Historical Railroad, founded in 1984, carries passengers over the track formerly owned by the Pennsylvania

Railroad. The railroad operates two air-conditioned, restroom-equipped cars on the scenic excursion ride through central Pennsylvania. Riders frequently spot wild turkeys, deer, and other game along the way. Departures are from the restored Pennsylvania Railroad Station, which houses a ticket office and small railroad museum.

Special Events Ride 'n Dine; Railfan Special; Fall Excursion; Santa Express.

How to Get There From Williamsport, take I-80 west to the Bellefonte Interchange. Enter Bellefonte downtown at High Street; drive north to reach the railroad station.

Hours Memorial Day to Labor Day. open weekends. Call for hours.

Fares Saturday: adults, $6; children (ages 2 to 11), $3. Sunday: adults, $8; children (ages 2 to 11), $4.

Contact Bellefonte Historical Railroad, The Train Station, Bellefonte, PA 16823. Telephone (814) 355-0311.

CRESSON

ALLEGHENY PORTAGE RAILROAD NATIONAL HISTORIC SITE

The Allegheny Portage Railroad was created in the 19th century to further westward expansion of the American frontier. A great engineering innovation in its day, the railroad combined the use of canal boats, steam locomotives, railroad cars, and inclined planes to create the first railroad to cross the Allegheny Mountains.

The National Park Service commemorates the railroad with the Allegheny Portage Railroad National Historic Site, a

1500-acre park. Features at the park are a visitors center with exhibits, including a full-scale locomotive train model and a short film about the railroad; an incline plane; a stone quarry; and a tavern from the same period.

Many ranger activities are offered daily in the park during the summer months, including "Heritage Hikes," tours, and demonstrations. Other historical sites in the area are the Horseshoe Curve and Altoona Railroaders Memorial Museum (see previous entries).

How to Get There   Located in west-central Pennsylvania, the entrance to the park is off Route 22, at the Gallitzin exit.

Hours   Visitors center: open daily year-round, except Christmas Day, 9:00 A.M. to 5:00 P.M. (hours extended during summer months).

Fares   Admission is free.

Contact   Superintendent, Allegheny Portage Railroad Historic Site, P.O. Box 189, Cresson, PA 16630. Telephone (814) 886-6150.

GALLITZIN

GALLITZIN TUNNELS

On a trip between Altoona and Johnstown, train fans can enjoy a stop at Tunnel Park in Gallitzin. The park, created by the local community, is the location of the famous Gallitzin tunnels, which provided railroad access through the Allegheny Mountains. One tunnel was built in the 1850s by the State of Pennsylvania, and the other was built at the turn of the century by the Pennsylvania Railroad. The park viewing center has train schedules, a restored 1942 caboose available for tours, and an observation area for a view of passing trains.

NOTE: The park is handicapped accessible.

How to Get There Turn off Route 22 at the Gallitzin exit, between the Allegheny Portage Railroad and Horseshoe Curve. Follow the Path of Progress extension route signs.

Hours Open daily, 24 hours.

Fares Admission is free.

Contact Southwestern Pennsylvania Heritage Preservation Commission, P.O. Box 565, Hollidaysburg, PA 16648-9904. Telephone (814) 696-9380.

G E T T Y S B U R G

GETTYSBURG RAILROAD

For a steam train ride through Civil War country, the Gettysburg Railroad offers two excursions. The first, a 16-mile, 90-minute scenic train ride, takes visitors past the battlefields made famous in 1863 and arrives in Biglerville, the "Apple Capital of Pennsylvania." A second trip, (50 miles, five hours round-trip) takes passengers from Gettysburg to beautiful Mount Holly Springs for a dining experience at one of two restaurants (the Deer Lodge and Holly Inn). Along the way, passengers learn about train and battlefield history from the train crew.

Special Events Easter Bunny Train; Halloween Train; Civil War Train Raid; Lincoln Train; Santa Train.

How to Get There From Harrisburg, take Route 15 south to the York Street exit. Then take Route 30 west. Follow it to the center of Gettysburg and stay on it through the traffic circle. At the next stop light, turn right. Drive over the railroad tracks and look for the station.

Hours   Departure times in April: Saturday and Sunday, 1:00
P.M. and 3:00 P.M. May and June: Thursday and Friday, 10:00 A.M.
and 12:30 P.M.; Saturday and Sunday, 1:00 P.M. and 3:00 P.M.
    July and August: weekdays, 11:00 A.M. and 1:00 P.M.;
Saturday and Sunday, 11:00 A.M., 1:00 P.M., and 3:00 P.M.
    September and October: Labor Day, 11:00 A.M. and 1:00
P.M.; Thursday and Friday, 11:00 A.M. and 1:00 P.M.; Saturday
and Sunday, 11:00 A.M., 1:00 P.M., and 3:00 P.M.

Fares   Adults, $7.50; seniors, $7; children (ages 3 to 12),
$3.50; children under three are admitted free of charge.

Contact   Gettysburg Railroad, 106 N. Washington Street,
Gettysburg, PA 17325. Telephone (717) 334-6932.

GREENVILLE

GREENVILLE AREA RAILROAD MUSEUM

The Greenville Area Railroad Museum is part of a railroad park
created in 1985 and features engine 604, the last of the largest
switch engines ever made. It was built in 1936 for the Union
Railroad. Other examples of Greenville's railroading past are re-
flected in displays of coal tender, hopper car, and cabooses,
and are also depicted in exhibits housed in the reconstructed
stationmaster's quarters and dispatcher's office.

How to Get There   From Pittsburgh, take I-79 north to I-80
to Mercer. Then take Route 58 north straight into Greenville.
Turn right onto Main Street (Route 18). The museum is on the
left side at 314 Main.

Hours   May to June: Saturday and Sunday, 12:00 noon
to 5:00 P.M.
    Mid-June to Labor Day: Tuesday to Sunday, 12:00 noon
to 5:00 P.M.

September and October: Saturday and Sunday, 12:00 noon to 5:00 P.M.

Fares   Free (donations are accepted).

Contact   Shenango-Pymatuning Chapter No. 154, National Railway Historical Society, 314 Main Street, Greenville, PA 16125; telephone (412) 588-4009. Or, Greenville Area Chamber of Commerce, P.O. Box 350, Greenville, PA 16125; telephone (412) 588-7150.

H O N E S D A L E

STOURBRIDGE LINE
RAIL EXCURSIONS

Established at the Honesdale, Pennsylvania, sesquicentennial in 1979, the Stourbridge Line Rail Excursions were named in honor of the *Stourbridge Lion,* the first locomotive to run on an American railroad. The diesel excursion departs from the original site of the Delaware & Hudson Canal Company and takes visitors on weekend journeys (two to six hours in duration) throughout the year.

The **Wayne County Historical Society** museum is located nearby at 810 Main Street and contains historical artifacts and exhibits, including a replica of the *Stourbridge Lion.*

Special Events   Great Train Robbery Runs; Fall Foliage; Santa Express; Bunny Run; Bavarian Festival; Halloween Fun.

How to Get There   From Scranton, take Route 81 north to Route 380 south to I 84 east to exit 5. Turn right onto Route 348. Take it to a second red light in Hamlin. Turn left onto Route 191 north, traveling 18 miles into Honesdale. Turn left onto Main Street at the first traffic light and go four-and-a-half blocks. Look for train parking signs.

A replica of the *Stourbridge Lion,* the first locomotive to run on an American railroad.

Hours   Select theme weekends each season. Call ahead for specific dates and times.

Fares   Rides: $8 to $17.50 (dinner theater and Bavarian Festival, $26.00 to 40.00).

Museum: adults, $2; children (ages 12 to 18), $1; children under 12 years of age are admitted free of charge.

Contact   Stourbridge Rail Excursions, 742 Main Street, Honesdale, PA 18431; telephone (717) 253-1960.

Or, Wayne County Historical Society, Wayne County Chamber of Commerce, 810 Main Street, Honesdale, PA 18431; telephone (717) 253-3240.

JIM THORPE

RAIL TOURS, INC.

America's longest railroad, 9 miles long, once had its terminus in Mauch Chunk, Pennsylvania (renamed Jim Thorpe in 1954). The line hauled coal until 1870, when it began offering passenger service on the Mauch Chunk Switchback Railroad.

Today, Rail Tours, Inc. operates "Yesterday's Train Today," an 8-mile round-trip (40 minutes) excursion from the depot in Jim Thorpe to milepost 5. Longer excursions are also offered. "Hometown Trestle Special" is a 32-mile (2 hours, 30 minutes) round-trip journey; "Lake Hauto Special" is a 20-mile (1 hour, 45 minutes) round-trip ride. All trains depart downtown Jim Thorpe from the former Central Railroad of New Jersey depot on U.S. Route 209.

Special Events   Easter Bunny Train Rides; Flaming Foliage Rambles; Santa Claus Train Rides.

How to Get There   Take the Northeast Extension (Route 9) of the Pennsylvania Turnpike to exit 34. Go south on U.S. Route 209 for 6 miles to Jim Thorpe. From Northern New Jersey, go west on I-80. Exit at 4. Go south on U.S. Route 209 for 33 miles to Jim Thorpe.

Hours   "Yesterday's Train Today": May 11 to September 2, Saturday, Sunday, and holidays, 12:00 noon, 1:00 P.M., and 2:00 P.M.; July 5, September 7 to 29, Saturday and Sunday, 12:00 noon; 1:00 P.M., 2:00 P.M., and 3:00 P.M.

"Hometown Trestle Special": May 25 to August 31, Saturday, 3:00 P.M.

"Lake Hauto Special": May 26 to September 2, Sunday and holidays, 3:00 P.M.

Fares   Adults, $5 to $14; children (ages 2 to 11), $3 to $5; children under two years of age are admitted free of charge.

Contact   Rail Tours, Inc., P.O. Box 285, Jim Thorpe, PA 18229. Telephone (717) 325-4606.

KANE/MARIENVILLE

KNOX & KANE RAILROAD

The Knox & Kane Railroad offers both steam and diesel rides across what was once the highest railroad bridge in the world, the Kinzua Bridge. First built in 1882, then rebuilt in 1900 (to withstand the weight of heavier trains), the Kinzua spans 2,053 feet and is over 300 feet high.

The scenic excursion takes visitors on either a 32-mile or 96-mile ride through the beautiful hills and valleys of the Allegheny National Forest. The spectacular forest includes many varieties of trees and wildlife. The **Marienville Area Railroad and Historical Museum** is located right across the street from the Marienville Station.

How to Get There   Kane Station: From Pittsburgh take I-79 north to I-80. From I-80 take exit 8 (Shippenville) and pick up Route 66 north. Then take Route 6 east to Route 321 south into Kane. In Kane, turn right after crossing two sets of railroad tracks; the station will be in view.

Marienville Station: Take Route 66 north into Marienville; the station will be on the right.

Hours   Call ahead for specific days the trains run. Kane Station: open 10:45 A.M. to 2:25 P.M; Marienville Station: open 8:30 A.M. to 4:30 P.M.

Fares   Kane to bridge (32 miles): adults, $14; children (ages 3 to 12), $8. Marienville to bridge (96 miles): adults, $20; children (ages 3 to 12), $13. Children under three years of age are admitted free of charge.

Contact   Knox & Kane Railroad, P.O. Box 422, Marienville, PA 16239. Telephone (814) 927-6621.

L E W I S B U R G

WEST SHORE RAIL EXCURSIONS

Beautiful central Pennsylvania provides the landscape for scenic narrated journeys on West Shore Rail Excursions. Beginning at Delta Place Station, two train excursions are offered. The first, on the Lewisburg & Buffalo Creek Railroad, is a one-and-a-half-hour round-trip journey that follows the tracks of the former Reading Railroad. It travels through the Victorian town of Lewisburg, along the Susquehanna River, and past the Buffalo Mountains and Winfield before making a return trip. A longer, two-and-a-half-hour trip on the West Shore Railroad is offered on Sundays and takes visitors through Amish and Mennonite farm communities and on to the Victorian town of Mifflinburg.

The West Shore offers lunch and dinner trains. A gift shop and snack bar are available.

Special Events   Easter Bunny Express; Tourist Season Opening; Cartoon Train; Annual Motorcar and Hand Railcar Show; Fall Foliage; Haunted Train Rides; Santa Claus Express.

How to Get There   West Shore is three hours from Philadelphia. Take the Pennsylvania Turnpike to the Harrisburg east exit to Route 322. Exit at Route 15 east, drive through Lewisburg, and continue about 2 miles to the station.

Hours   Lewisburg & Buffalo Creek Railroad departures: April through May: Saturday and Sunday, 2:00 P.M. June through October: Saturday, 11:30 A.M. and 2:00 P.M.; Sunday, 11:30 A.M. June 18 through September 11: Tuesday through Sunday, 1:30 P.M.

West Shore Railroad departures: June through October: Sunday, 2:00 P.M.

Fares   Lewisburg & Buffalo Creek Railroad: adults, $7.50; seniors (over 60), $6.50; children (ages 3 to 11), $4.

West Shore Railroad: adults, $9.50; seniors (over 60), $8.50; children (ages 3 to 11), $5.

Contact   West Shore Rail Excursions, Delta Place Station R.R. 3, Box 154, Lewisburg, PA 17837. Telephone (717) 524-4337.

MERCERSBURG

JOHN B. MCFADDEN MODEL RAILROAD MUSEUM

Housed in a building on the campus of Mercersburg Academy, a secondary school, the John B. McFadden Model Railroad Museum contains a variety of Lionel trains, HO-model trains, and railroad memorabilia. The collection, first begun by the late John McFadden, was donated to Mercersburg Academy upon his death in 1973. Since 1973, the museum has received other fine additions to the collection, including brass engines, freight and passenger cars, and scale model buildings.

The town of Mercersburg, founded in 1750, was the home of President James Buchanan and is listed on the National Register of Historic Places.

How to Get There   From Harrisburg, take Route 81 south to exit #3 (Greencastle and Mercersburg). Turn right and pick up Route 16 west. Look for the Mercersburg Academy sign on the right.

Hours   Open Sunday, 1:00 P.M. to 4:00 P.M. (only when the Academy is in session). Also open on special occasions: Mercersburg House Tour, Alumni Days, Parents Weekend, some days during the Christmas season. Special tours can be arranged.

Fares   Free (donations are welcome).

Contact The John B. McFadden Railroad Museum, The Mercersburg Academy, Mercersburg, PA 17236. Telephone (717) 328-2151 or (717) 328-3511.

MIDDLETOWN

MIDDLETOWN & HUMMELSTOWN RAILROAD

The Middletown & Hummelstown Railroad, affectionately known as the "Milk & Honey Line," was part of Reading Railroad between 1890 and 1976. Today, the railroad offers a daily guided tour of its rail collection (including streetcars, snowsweeper, wooden boxcar) and a diesel train excursion with historical narration.

For the train ride, visitors depart from Race Street Station and board train coaches built in 1920 for a scenic 11-mile round-trip (1 hour, 15 minutes) ride that includes a tour along the historic Union Canal, past 100-year-old limekilns, and ultimately to the **Indian Echo Caverns.** For an additional charge, visitors can combine the train ride with a cavern tour.

Special Events Winter Wonderland Weekend (February); Easter Bunny Express (April); Railfan Day (May); Mother's & Father's Day Specials (May and June); Picnic at the Caverns (July); Chicken Barbecue at the Caverns (August); Fall Foliage (October); Halloween Special (October); Ride the Train with Santa (November and December). Also: dinner trains.

How to Get There From Harrisburg, take Route 283 east to the Middletown/Hummelstown exit. Turn right off the highway, then right onto Main Street. Turn left onto Race Street; the railroad tracks are about six blocks down.

From the Pennsylvania Turnpike, take exit 19 into Middletown/Hummelstown.

Hours   July and August: open Tuesday through Sunday. June, September, and October: open Saturday, Sunday, and Monday holidays.

Trains depart at 11:00 A.M., 1:00 P.M., 2:30 P.M., and 4:00 P.M. (from Middletown).

Fares   Train ride only: adults (12 and above), $6; children (ages 3 to 11), $3.

Train and cavern: adults (12 and above), $13; children (ages 3 to 11), $6.50.

Children under three years of age not occupying a seat are admitted free of charge.

Contact   Middletown & Hummelstown Railroad, 136 Brown Street, Middletown, PA 17057. Telephone (717) 944-4435.

N O R T H   E A S T

Lake Shore Railway Museum

The Lake Shore Railway Museum has been operated by the Lake Shore Railway Historical Society since 1970, and is committed to preserving railroad history and artifacts. Located in a brick and stone passenger station, it was built in 1899 by the Lake Shore & Michigan Southern Railway.

Among its displays are a motorized $1/10$-scale model Heisler steam locomotive; a 1922 tank car, three refrigerator cars; several freight and passenger cars; and an original fireless steam locomotive. The museum has recently restored a New York Central diesel locomotive, which is also on exhibit. Visitors may view any one of over 60 trains that operate along the line outside the museum.

The museum hosts educational programs and coordinates Society-sponsored rail trips on the **New York & Lake Erie Railroad** in Gowanda.

How to Get There   From Erie, take I-90 east to exit 11 (State Road 89). Take 89 north. Pass twin railroad overpasses and make an immediate left onto Clinton Street. Turn left again onto Robinson Street; the museum is one block away.

Hours   Memorial Day through Labor Day: Wednesday to Sunday. In September: Saturday and Sunday. Hours are 1:00 P.M. to 5:00 P.M.

Fares   Admission is free.

Contact   Lake Shore Railway Historical Society, P.O. Box 57121, Wall Street at Robinson Street, North East, PA 16428. Telephone (814) 825-2724.

OIL CITY

OIL CREEK & TITUSVILLE RAILROAD

The Oil Creek & Titusville Railroad gives scenic train rides through an area called "the valley that changed the world"—the site of the world's first oil boom and the home of the world's first oil millionaire. A two-and-a-half-hour trip makes stops at three of the railroad's four stations, where visitors can visit the railway museum, cycle along a 10-mile bike path (bicycle rentals are available), lunch at the picnic grounds, and enjoy a recreational park for fishing, hiking, camping, and hunting. Kids will enjoy having their postcards canceled and sorted on the spot at one of the last operating post office cars in the United States.

NOTE: The railroad operates rain or shine. Sponsors recommend that passengers dress accordingly, since cars do not have heat or air conditioning.

Special Events   Mystery Dinner; Applefest Excursion; Peter Cottontail; Santa Train.

How to Get There   From Pittsburgh, take I-79 north to I-80 east. Take exit 3 (Barkeyville) to Route 8 north. Route 8 leads into Titusville; in town, turn left onto St. John Street. At the end of the street turn right and cross the railroad tracks to the station.

Hours   June and September: open Saturday and Sunday. July to August, and October: open Wednesday to Sunday.

Fares   Adults, $9; seniors, $8; children (ages 3 to 17), $5. Bicycle rental, $1.

Contact   Oil Creek & Titusville Railroad, P.O. Box 68, Oil City, PA 16301. Telephone (814) 676-1733; fax (814) 677-2192.

ROCKHILL FURNACE

EAST BROAD TOP RAILROAD

One of the most appealing reasons to visit the East Broad Top Railroad (EBT) is the opportunity to tour one of the most complete and authentic narrow gauge rail complexes still in existence. A National Historic Landmark, its wide range of railroading exhibits are sure to provide an entertaining, as well as educational, experience for even the youngest train enthusiast. The EBT, in operation for over 80 years (1874–1956), provided an important transportation link to industries dependent on the coal, iron ore, timber, and other raw materials it carried. The original 33-mile line included mountainous terrain, two tunnels, and steep grades.

Today, the EBT offers a 5-mile steam train ride in original locomotive and passenger cars and an authentic railway site featuring the Orbisonia Yard, which is currently in dilapidated condition but is nearly complete with its roundhouse, six full-sized steam engines, car barn, and other railroad shops and structures. Visitors will especially enjoy watching a locomotive on the turntable and a 11:00 A.M. ritual of a passenger train being made up in the yard.

EAST BROAD TOP RAILROAD

Steam locomotive #12 in the East Broad Top Railroad yard.

The ride is a 50-minute narrated journey through scenic Aughwick Valley on 5 miles of the original track. Passengers can picnic at the turnaround point at Colgate Grove. Guided walking tours by National Park Service rangers are available, and staff members provide assistance to disabled visitors.

The **Rockhill Trolley Museum** (see next entry), which operates the Shade Gap Electric Railway, is adjacent to the EBT.

NOTE: The East Broad Top expects to be in operation June to mid-October, but call ahead for any changes in its schedule.

Special Events   Fall Spectacular Weekend.

How to Get There   The EBT is located in Rockhill Furnace on Route 522. It's 19 miles north of the Pennsylvania Turnpike (take exit 13) and 11 miles south of Mount Union.

Hours   Train rides: 11:00 A.M., 1:00 P.M., and 3:00 P.M.

Fares   Adults, $9; children (ages 2 to 11), $6; children under two years of age are admitted free of charge.

Contact   East Broad Top Railroad, Rockhill Furnace, PA 17249. Telephone (814) 447-3011; fax (814) 447-3256.

ROCKHILL TROLLEY MUSEUM

Rockhill Trolley Museum, located on the site of the former Rockhill Iron Furnace, features a narrated 2.5-mile ride in an antique trolley car where visitors learn about its trolley car collection, the museum, and the furnace. Created in 1960 and chartered in 1962 by Railways to Yesterday (a nonprofit preservation organization), its first acquisition was a Johnstown, Pennsylvania, trolley.

Twenty-six trolleys make up the museum's collection; the majority are from Pennsylvania, but other states and countries are also represented. A variety of these are operated in season (weather permitting); two or three normally run daily. Fourteen cars are operational—of these, seven make the passenger runs.

A trolley restoration shop is available for tours.

NOTE: The museum is next to the **East Broad Top Railroad** (see previous entry).

How to Get There   Rockhill Furnace is on Route 522, 19 miles north of the Pennsylvania Turnpike (take exit 13) and 11 miles south of Mount Union. From Route 522, take the Rockhill Furnace exit; the museum is adjacent.

Hours   Trolley rides: Memorial Day through October, weekends and holidays, 11:00 A.M. to 4:30 P.M.

Fares   Adults, $3; children, $1.

ROCKHILL TROLLEY MUSEUM

Visitors take a ride on the Shade Gap Electric Railway.

Contact   Railways to Yesterday, Inc., Rockhill Trolley Museum, Rockhill Furnace, Huntingdon County, PA 17249; telephone (814) 447-9576. Or, P.O. Box 1601, Allentown, PA 18105.

SCRANTON

STEAMTOWN NATIONAL HISTORIC SITE

Steamtown National Historic Site, newly opened in July 1995, is a 52-acre national park that preserves the history of steam trains. Located in downtown Scranton on the former Delaware, Lackawanna & Western Railroad yards, Steamtown offers visitors interpretive programs, a theater, two museums (history and technology), a restored roundhouse, turntable, and a rich

NATIONAL PARK SERVICE/KEN GANZ

Locomotive #26, built in 1929 by Baldwin Locomotive Works, is on display at Steamtown.

and diverse collection of trains, including 29 steam locomotives, five diesels, and passenger and freight cars. A special feature is one of the largest steam locomotives in the world, a Union Pacific *Big Boy*.

As an operating site, Steamtown provides regular steam-powered 1-mile round-trip excursion rides to the Lackawanna Station (a former station that is now a hotel) or Scranton Iron Furnaces, which supplied the iron used for railroads in the late 19th century. Other longer, scenic excursions are also offered through Steamtown and other private groups.

Steamtown includes a bookstore. An indoor food court and shopping area is adjacent to the site. Most of the site is wheelchair accessible, including excursion coaches with a wheelchair lift.

NOTE: Seating is limited on the train excursions, so reservations are recommended.

How to Get There From New Jersey and New York City, take I-80 west to I-380 west to I-81 south to exit 53 (Central Scranton Expressway). From western Pennsylvania, take I-80 east to I-81 north to exit 53 (Central Scranton Expressway).

Hours Open daily (except Thanksgiving, Christmas, and New Year's Day).
Visitors center and museum buildings: 9:00 A.M. to 5:00 P.M. Tours and programs scheduled between 9:30 A.M. and 4:00 P.M.
All excursions depart at 12:00 noon and 3:00 P.M. Memorial Day through Labor Day, and in October: trains run Friday, Saturday, and Sunday. September: trains run Saturday and Sunday.

Fares Adults, $7; seniors (62 and above), $6; children (12 and under), $3.

Contact Steamtown National Historic Site, 150 South Washington Avenue, Scranton, PA 18503. Telephone (717) 340-5204; TDD (717) 340-5207.

S H A R T L E S V I L L E

ROADSIDE AMERICA

Roadside America, an extensive indoor miniature village, is the creation of the late Laurence Gieringer, who, with his brother Paul, began whittling wood miniatures as a boyhood hobby. Laurence Gieringer pursued the hobby for over 60 years, ultimately creating a spectacular exhibit that spans a period of more than 200 years.
The display depicts life from the pioneer period to modern day. Train enthusiasts will enjoy the 250 miniature trains traveling along 2,570 feet of track, tunnels, bridges, stations, and the railway yard. A mountain-climbing trolley is also on display.

How to Get There   Shartlesville is between Allentown and Harrisburg. From Harrisburg, take I-81 east to I-78, exit 8 (Shartlesville). Roadside America is just off the exit.

Hours   July to Labor Day: weekdays, 9:00 A.M. to 6:30 P.M.; weekends, 9:00 A.M. to 7:00 P.M. September to June: weekdays, 10:00 A.M. to 5:00 P.M.; weekends, 10:00 A.M. to 6:00 P.M.

Fares   Adults, $4; children (ages 6 to 11), $1.50; children under six years of age are free of charge.

Contact   Roadside America, Roadside Drive, Shartlesville, PA 19554. Telephone (610) 488-6241.

S T E W A R T S T O W N

STEWARTSTOWN RAILROAD

The Stewartstown Railroad began operation in 1885 and includes a 1914 depot, a 1906 engine house, and an 1870 iron bridge—structures all listed on the National Register of Historic Places. It was once nicknamed "the Farmer's Railroad" because it hauled potatoes, wheat, and other farm crops that were destined for York and Baltimore.

Today, the railroad carries passengers on regular Sunday scenic countryside excursions, fall foliage trips, country breakfast trains, and during special events. The trip length varies between one hour to the village of Tolna to 1 hour and 45 minutes to New Freedom. The route offers wildlife, bridge crossings, and rolling hills through Deer Creek Valley. On regular countryside excursions, passengers are invited to bring along a lunch or snack for the train ride or to order a box lunch from Peppercorns Restaurant.

The trains operated include *Mighty Mo,* built in 1943, and passenger cars built during the same period.

The railroad also features a souvenir and gift stand.

Special Events Easter Bunny Hops; Mother's Day Special; Memorial Day Weekend; Father's Day Special; Children's Day; Labor Day; Seniors' Day; Civil War Train Ride; Haunted Train Rides; North Pole Express.

How to Get There The Stewartstown Railroad Station is on Pennsylvania Route 851. From I-83, take Pennsylvania exit 1 east for 4 miles.

Hours Countryside excursions: May 12 through September 29, and July 4: Sunday, 1:00 P.M. and 3:00 P.M.
Fall foliage trips: October, and November 2 and 3: Saturday and Sunday, 1:30 P.M. and 3:00 P.M.
Country breakfast trains: May 18, June 15, July 20, August 17, September 21, October 19, November 16. Call for departure times.

Fares Countryside excursions: adults, $6; children, $3. Country breakfast trains: adults, $14; children, $7.

Contact Stewartstown Railroad, P.O. Box 155, Stewartstown, PA 17363. Telephone (717) 993-2936.

S T R A S B U R G

CHOO CHOO BARN

Children will find Choo Choo Barn the perfect complement to a trip to the **Railroad Museum of Pennsylvania** and the **Strasburg Rail Road** (see entries following), because it's where real meets the imaginary. The barn is four separate entities in one: an elaborate model railroad display that captures the landscape of Lancaster County's Amish country; the Strasburg Train Shop, a hobby shop with thousands of model train accessories; Railroad Books and Videos, a store with over 1,000 books and videos on trains; and for fans of Thomas the Tank Engine,

Thomas' Trackside Station, a store with over 500 items featuring the popular tank engine and his friends.

How to Get There   From downtown Philadelphia, take Route 76 west (Schuykill Expressway) to exit 21. Then take Route 222 south to Route 30 east. From there, take Route 896 south, turn left onto Route 741. Signs for the Choo Choo Barn will be visible from the highway.

Hours   April to December: All stores and displays are open seven days a week, 10:00 A.M. to 5:00 P.M. June through August: Closing time is 6:00 P.M.

The barn stops admitting visitors 30 minutes before closing time.

Fares   Admission is free.

Contact   Choo Choo Barn, Inc., Route 741E, P.O. Box 130, Strasburg, PA 17579; telephone (717) 687-7911; fax 687-6529.
Strasburg Train Shop, telephone (717) 687-0464. Railroad Books and Videos, telephone (717) 687-0464. Thomas' Trackside Station, telephone (717) 687-7911.

NATIONAL TOY TRAIN MUSEUM

The historical setting for the National Toy Train Museum is the turn of the century, and the museum includes a large collection of electric trains, floor toys, and train-related accessories. Visitors are invited to view toy trains in five operating layouts, ranging from antique to modern. Guided tours of the museum are offered on weekdays, and a continuous video show on toy trains can be seen in the museum theater.

The museum is next to the Red Caboose Motel and Restaurant, which features restored train cars that have been converted into a hotel (see later entry).

How to Get There   To Strasburg, follow the directions in the Choo Choo Barn entry. From Route 741, turn left onto Paradise Lane. The museum is on the right.

Hours   May to October: open daily, 10:00 A.M. to 5:00 P.M. April, November, and December: open weekends.

Also open Christmas week (December 26–31), Good Friday, Easter Monday, and Thanksgiving Friday. Closed in January, February, and March.

Fares   Adults, $3; seniors, $2.75; children (ages 5 to 12), $1.50; children under five years of age are admitted free of charge.

Contact   National Toy Train Museum, P.O. Box 248, Strasburg, PA 17579-0248. Telephone (717) 687 8976.

RAILROAD MUSEUM OF PENNSYLVANIA

For more than 100 years, beginning in the mid-19th century, railroads were the dominant mode of transportation and commerce in Pennsylvania. The Railroad Museum of Pennsylvania, which opened its doors in 1975, presents the history of how railroads transformed the state.

The museum contains an extensive collection of railroad exhibits, including more than 250,000 railroad artifacts and over 70 locomotives and railcars; an audiovisual presentation on railroad history; a railroad yard; Steinman Station, a replica turn-of-the-century depot; and the new Railroaders Hall, a 47,200-square-foot addition that houses most of the museum's collection. The heart of that collection is the "Pennsylvania Railroad Collection," which includes a wooden combination car built in 1855 and a steam freight locomotive built in 1888.

Visitors to the museum are welcome to examine the trains up close and to sit in the engineer's seat or view the train restoration process in the railway yard.

How to Get There   To Strasburg, follow the directions in the Choo Choo Barn entry. The museum is on Route 741, east of Strasburg.

Hours   Monday through Saturday, 9:00 A.M. to 5:00 P.M.; Sunday, 12:00 noon to 5:00 P.M. Closed Mondays, November through April, and certain holidays.

Fares   Adults, $6; seniors, $5; children (ages 6 to 17), $4; children under six years of age are admitted free of charge.

Contact   Railroad Museum of Pennsylvania, Box 15, Strasburg, PA 17579. Telephone (717) 687-8628; fax (717) 687-0876.

RED CABOOSE MOTEL AND RESTAURANT

For visitors to train attraction–rich Strasburg, Pennsylvania, the Red Caboose Motel and Restaurant offers the ultimate experience for train fans: a village of converted cabooses available for overnight stays. The motel has a variety of caboose accommodations, including family sized-cabooses (sleeps a couple and up to four children), private bath, remote control cable TV, heat, and air conditioning. The motel also offers dining room coaches serving fare from local farms, simulated railroad movement, and railroad music.

The motel is a short distance from the **Strasburg Rail Road**, the **Railroad Museum of Pennsylvania**, the **Choo Choo Barn**, and the **National Toy Train Museum**.

How to Get There   To Strasburg, follow the directions in the Choo Choo Barn entry. The motel is next to the National Toy Train Museum.

Hours   Open year-round. Call for schedule.

Fares   Family caboose: $49 to $99 (depending on the season).

Contact   Red Caboose Motel and Restaurant, P.O. Box 303, Strasburg, PA 17579. Telephone (717) 687-5000.

STRASBURG RAIL ROAD

The Strasburg Rail Road has been in existence since 1832, and operates some of the oldest steam trains in the U.S. The 9-mile, 45-minute round-trip scenic journey—called "the Road to Paradise"—takes passengers through the lush farm land of Lancaster County, most of which is tended by the Amish Plains People. Pulled by coal-burning steam locomotives, passengers may ride in antique wooden coaches, open-air observation cars, the dining car *Lee Brenner*, or the parlor car *Marian*, with an attendant on duty. The railroad operates a restaurant and gift shops. Lunch and dinner trains are also offered.

The **Railroad Museum of Pennsylvania** is located across the road (see earlier entry).

Special Events   Easter Bunny Trains; Halloween Ghost Trains; Santa Claus Trains.

How to Get There   To Strasburg, follow the directions in the Choo Choo Barn entry. The railroad is directly on Route 741.

Hours   Open third Saturday of January through February (weather permitting): Saturday and Sunday, departures at 12:00 noon, 1:00 P.M., and 2:00 P.M. Monday after Presidents' Weekend, departures at 12:00 noon, 1:00 P.M., and 2:00 P.M.

March: Saturday and Sunday, departures at 12:00 noon, 1:00 P.M., 2:00 P.M., and 3:00 P.M.

April through December: call for days and times.

Fares   Regular fares: adults, $7.50; children (ages 3 to 11), $4. Season pass: adults, $30; children, $16.

STRASBURG RAIL ROAD

Visitors take a scenic journey to the town of Paradise on the Strasburg Rail Road.

Parlor car: adults, $12; children, $6. Dining car: adults, $8.50; children, $5.

Contact   Strasburg Rail Road, P.O. Box 96, Strasburg, PA 17579-0096. Telephone (717) 687-7522.

WASHINGTON

PENNSYLVANIA TROLLEY MUSEUM

The Pennsylvania Trolley Museum, a nonprofit institution, is a living history museum and a tribute to Pennsylvania's streetcar heritage. Interest in creating a museum began in the 1940s, and in 1963, it was open to the public.

The museum includes a display of over 20 trolleys from its 41 car collection and offers guided walking tours of the museum carbarn and restoration shop. Its Visitor Education Center has an interpretive trolley history display and gift shop. One exhibit, on display until 1997, is about the life of the electric railway worker.

A special feature of the museum is a scenic, 3-mile round-trip ride on a restored trolley. In 1995, the museum completed the opening of the Arden Trolley Loop.

Special Events   Trolley Fair; Membership Day; Pumpkin Trolley; The Streetcar Named Expire; Santa Trolley.

How to Get There   Washington is 30 miles southwest of Pittsburgh. Take I-79 south to exit 8 (Meadowlands) and follow signs to the museum.

Hours   April through December: open weekends, 11:00 A.M. to 5:00 P.M. Memorial Day through Labor Day: open daily, 11:00 A.M. to 5:00 P.M.

Fares   Adults, $5; seniors (65 or above), $4; children (ages 2 to 11), $3.

Contact   Pennsylvania Trolley Museum, 1 Museum Road, Washington, PA 15301. Telephone (412) 228-9256; fax (412) 228-9675.

WELLSBORO

TIOGA CENTRAL RAILROAD

The Tioga Central Railroad operates on track dating from 1839. All operating trains were built between the 1920s and 1940s. The one-and-a-half-hour, 24-mile round-trip passenger ride was inaugurated as an excursion trip over the Wellsboro and Corning Railroad freight line in 1994. The Tioga Central includes five diesel-electric locomotives, a switcher, a few former Canadian National Railways coaches, an open-air observation car, and a 68-seat diner car. The oldest piece in the collection, *Car 54,* is an open-platform business car built in 1894 now used as a ticket and crew office.

The Tioga departs from the Wellsboro Junction Passenger Station. It takes passengers on a scenic journey, crossing bridges and passing deer and marshland that attracts geese and blue heron, and a lake that draws ospreys (fish hawks).

Children are welcome to visit the engine cab to ring the bell or operate the whistle (if time permits). The Tioga operates a gift shop and snack bar on the train. The town of Wellsboro is home to Pennsylvania's "Grand Canyon," which is 50 miles long and 1,000 feet deep.

Special Events   Fall Foliage Trains; Wellsboro Rail Days; Thanksgiving Day; Wellsboro's Dickens of a Christmas.

How to Get There   The station is 3 miles north of Wellsboro, on State Route 287. It's 35 miles south of Corning, New York, and 50 miles north of Williamsport, Pennsylvania.

Hours   Regular trains operate May 11 to October 20: Saturday and Sunday departures at 11:00 A.M., 1:00 P.M., and 3:00 P.M. Dinner trains operate June 1 to October 19: Saturday departure at 5:30 P.M. The ride lasts 2 hours and 30 minutes.

Fares   Adults, $10; seniors (60 and above), $9; children (ages 6 to 12), $5; children under six years of age accompanied by an adult are free of charge.

Contact   Tioga Central Railroad, P.O. Box 269, Wellsboro, PA 16901. Telephone (717) 724-0990.

W I L L I A M S P O R T

LYCOMING COUNTY HISTORICAL SOCIETY MUSEUM

The Lycoming County Historical Society is dedicated to preserving the history of north central Pennsylvania. Its museum includes two levels of more than 35 exhibits, beginning with the Frontier Room, the General Store, Lumber Gallery, and the Hall of Farming, Crafts, and Industry.

Train enthusiasts will especially enjoy the Shempp Model Train Display (named after LaRue Shempp, a model-train collector), an exhibit that features both American and European trains, with over 300 complete toy train sets and two operating layouts.

Other attractions in the neighboring area are the **Little League Hall of Fame Museum, Reptileland,** and **Little Pine Creek State Park.**

How to Get There   From Harrisburg, take Route 15 north to Williamsport. Then take Route 220 south to the Maynard Street exit. Turn right at the first stop sign after the exit, then left onto 4th Street. The museum is at 858 West Fourth.

Hours   May to October: Tuesday to Friday, 9:30 A.M. to 4:00 P.M.; Saturday, 11:00 A.M. to 4:00 P.M.; Sunday, 1:00 P.M. to 4:00 P.M.

Fares   Adults, $3.50; seniors, $3; children, $1.50.

Contact   Lycoming County Historical Society, 858 West Fourth Street, Williamsport, PA 17701-5824. Telephone (717) 326-3326.

RHODE ISLAND

NEWPORT

OLD COLONY & NEWPORT SCENIC RAILWAY

Beautiful Narragansett Bay—with its sailing ships, rocky beaches, and wildlife—is the backdrop for the Old Colony & Newport Scenic Railway. Passengers taking the one-hour, 10-mile ride or the three-hour, 21-mile round-trip diesel excursion can travel in an open-platform coach built in 1912 or an 1895 parlor car. Trains depart from both Melville and Newport.

How to Get There   Take Route 238 south (America's Cup Avenue) to downtown Newport. Look for signs to the railway.

Hours   Early May through June: open Sunday and holidays. July through Labor Day: open Wednesday, Thursday, Saturday, Sunday, and holidays.
    Early to mid-September: open Saturday and Sunday. Mid-September to mid-November: open Sunday.

Departures at 11:00 A.M., 12:30 P.M., and 2:00 P.M. (one-hour ride), and 12:30 P.M. (three-hour ride).

Fares   One-hour ride: adults, $5; seniors, $4; children (14 or younger), $3; parlor car, $7 per person. There is no family rate for one hour.

Three-hour ride: adults, $6; seniors, $5; children (14 or younger), $4; families (two adults and children 14 or younger), $15; parlor car, $9 per person.

Contact   Old Colony & Newport Scenic Railway, P.O. Box 343, Newport, RI 02840. Telephone (401) 624-6951.

SOUTH CAROLINA

W I N N S B O R O

SOUTH CAROLINA RAILROAD MUSEUM

On the National Register of Historic Places, the South Carolina Railroad Museum was created in 1973 by railroad enthusiasts; by 1982, the museum had acquired 11.5 miles of the former Rockton and Rion Railway. The Rockton line was built in the 1890s and hauled stone for the Winnsboro Granite Company. The line was renamed the Rockton, Rion and Western Railroad (RR&W) in 1990.

The museum's collection includes freight and passenger cars, a steam locomotive from the Hampton and Branchville Railroad, diesel engines, and several cabooses.

From May to October the museum offers diesel-powered train excursions to the Anderson Quarry, known for its world famous blue granite.

Future plans include educational train excursions for the complete 11.5-mile route, related exhibits and displays, and a railroad library.

Special Events   Railfan Weekend; Festival in the Park; Ride with Santa.

How to Get There   From Columbia, take I-77 north to exit 34. Go west on South Carolina Highway 34 for 6.5 miles towards Winnsboro. Turn left onto Industrial Park Road. The museum is on the right.

Hours   Mid-May to mid-October: open first and third Saturday of the month, with departures at 10:00 A.M., 11:00 A.M., 1:00 P.M., 2:00 P.M., 3:00 P.M., and 4:00 P.M.

Fares   Adults (ages 12 and above), $4; children (ages 2 to 12), $2.50; infants not occupying a seat are admitted free of charge.

Contact   South Carolina Railroad Museum, P.O. Box 7246, Columbia, SC 29202-7246. Telephone (800) 968-5909, (803) 796-8540, (803) 776-8856, or (704) 313-0335.

SOUTH DAKOTA

HILL CITY

BLACK HILLS CENTRAL RAILROAD

The tracks used by the Black Hills Central Railroad were first used by the Chicago, Burlington & Quincy Railroad to accommodate the mine and mill industries of the late 1800s. Today, visitors can take the steam locomotive *1880 Train* on a two-hour, 20-mile round-trip ride through the Black Hills National Forest to Harney Peak—at an elevation of 7,242 feet, it's the highest point between the Swiss Alps and the Rocky Mountains. Two boarding points are available for departure: Hill City and Keystone Junction.

The railroad's train collection includes locomotive #7, built in 1919 and seen on TV and in motion pictures. A gift shop and snack bar are open to visitors.

Special Events   Annual Railroad Days (September).

How to Get There   Black Hills Central Railroad is 15 minutes from Mount Rushmore National Memorial. Hill City is at the junction of Highways 16 and 385; Keystone is the town nearest the other boarding point.

Hours   Open mid-May to September. Extra evening trips are available in July and August.
From Hill City: four departures daily, 8:00 A.M. to 4:30 P.M.
From Keystone Junction: four departures daily, 9:00 A.M. to 5:30 P.M. (No 8:00 A.M. or 9:00 A.M. rides on Saturday or Sunday.)

Fares   Adults, $14; children (4 to 14), $9; children under four are free of charge.

Contact   Black Hills Central Railroad, P.O. Box 1880, Hill City, SD 57745. Telephone (605) 574-2222.

M A D I S O N

PRAIRIE VILLAGE

Prairie Village is a living museum with more than 40 restored buildings and exhibits that reflect pioneer life in the United States. Train fans will particularly enjoy visiting two authentic depots on site and viewing *Wilhelmine VII*, a 1927 German-made steam locomotive.
The last weekend of August, Prairie Village offers a Jamboree featuring three full days of activities including tours of the area's original buildings. These include a log cabin, churches, and a bank. Locomotive train rides are offered.

Special Events   Prairie Village Steam Threshing Jamboree.

How to Get There   The village is 43 miles from Sioux Falls, 2 miles west of the Hardee's corner at the junction of highways 34 and 81 in Madison.

Hours   Memorial Day through Labor Day: open daily, 9:00 A.M. to 6:00 P.M.

Fares   Adults, $5; seniors (55 and above), $4.50; children (ages 6 to 12), $2; families, $12.50; children under six years of age are free of charge.

Contact   Prairie Village, P.O. Box 256, Madison, SD 57042. Telephone (800) 693-3644 or (605) 256-3644.

M I L B A N K

MILBANK TRAINFEST

The Milbank Trainfest is an annual two-day celebration held the second weekend in August to honor the railroad and its history in the region. The event features train rides, exhibits, model train displays, a train car open house, and other train memorabilia. Other events include an arts show, a rodeo, and live music entertainment.

How to Get There   From Sioux Falls, take I-29 north to the Toronto exit. Then take Highway 15 north, through Clear Lake, to Milbank. Milbank is about two hours from Sioux Falls.

Hours   Second weekend of August: Friday, check for schedule; Saturday, 10:00 A.M. to 6:00 P.M.; Sunday, 10:00 A.M. to 6:00 P.M.

Fares   Train ride: adults, $6; children, $4. With dinner: adults, $15; children, $13. Pizza Run: $6 per person.

Contact   Milbank Chamber of Commerce, 401 South Main Street, Milbank, SD 57252. Telephone (605) 432-6656.

TENNESSEE

CHATTANOOGA

CHATTANOOGA CHOO-CHOO

Chattanooga Choo-Choo, a 1909 train terminal and architectural design winner restored by the Holiday Inn Hotel in 1973, was once an important railway center, servicing almost every train heading south. Listed on the National Register for Historic Preservation, the complex has over 300 rooms, including 48 suites that are converted train cars; a restored 1880 Baldwin steam locomotive with a wooden tender, last used by the Great Smoky Mountains Railroad in the 1940s (visitors are free to climb aboard); the Chattanooga Area Model Railroad Club's operating railroad display, with more than 3,000 square feet, 100 locomotives, 600 freight and passenger cars, and over 100 miles of track; and a collection of railroad photographs.

Visitors will especially enjoy two rail rides offered at the Choo-Choo. The *New Orleans Trolley* takes passengers on a 20-minute trolley ride around the terminal complex. The *Downtown Arrow*, the city's only regularly scheduled passenger train, takes visitors to the Grand Junction Depot at the **Tennessee Valley Railroad Museum** (see next entry), where railroad artifacts and exhibits are on display.

How to Get There   Eastbound: take I-24 to exit 178 to Broad Street South and follow the signs to the Choo-Choo (eight blocks).
Westbound: take I-24 to exit 178, turn right on Market Street (north) and drive six blocks to the station.

Hours   Complex open and trains run year-round. Call ahead for specific times.

Fares   Trolley: adults, $1; children, $.50 (hotel guests ride free of charge).
For the *Downtown Arrow*, check the Tennessee Valley Railroad (next entry).

Contact   Chattanooga Choo-Choo, Terminal Station, Chattanooga, TN 37402. Telephone (423) 266-5000.

TENNESSEE VALLEY RAILROAD

The Tennessee Valley Railroad became the Tennessee Valley Railroad Museum in 1961 to help preserve operating steam passenger trains. Today, the railroad offers visitors an opportunity to explore its train exhibits, reflecting the 1890s to the present day; take a guided tour of railcars on display; see the train repair shop; and take a steam train ride in a 1930s-era locomotive, on tracks near the original East Tennessee, Virginia & Georgia Railroad right-of-way built in 1852. Rides originate from Grand Junction Station (an 1888 replica of an Alabama depot) and the East Chattanooga Depot, a station resembling a small town depot of the 1890s.

The journey takes passengers on a 6-mile excursion through historic Missionary Ridge Tunnel and crosses Chickamauga Creek, from Grand Junction to East Chattanooga.

During the summer months, the *Downtown Arrow* takes passengers on a longer, 15-mile round-trip excursion from East Chattanooga and the **Chattanooga Choo-Choo,** a hotel complex in a historic train terminal (see previous entry). On selected days, the railroad also offers "Dixie Land" excursions through rural northwest Georgia hills, a four- to eight-and-a-half-hour journey.

A dining room, gift shop, restrooms, and air conditioning are available at the Grand Junction Depot.

NOTE: The railroad is handicapped accessible, although there are steps to climb and some walking is required for exhibits.

How to Get There For Grand Junction, from I-75 take exit 4 (Chickamauga Dam) to Highway 153. Drive north on 153 to Jersey Pike (fourth exit). Follow signs to Tennessee Valley Railroad Museum (TVRM) on Cromwell Road, one-third of a mile.

For East Chattanooga Depot, from downtown Chattanooga go east on Main Street, turn left on Holtclaw Avenue, then drive north to Wilcox Boulevard. Turn right on Wilcox, go to the third light, and turn left on North Chamberlain; go 16 blocks to TVRM depot on right.

Hours Trains run at 75-minute intervals. *Downtown Arrow* service to Chattanooga Choo-Choo runs weekends June to August.

April to November: open Saturday, 10:00 A.M. to 5:00 P.M.; Sunday, 12 noon to 5:00 P.M.

April, May, September, and October: open weekdays, 10:00 A.M. to 2:00 P.M.

June, July, and August: open weekdays, 10:00 A.M. to 5:00 P.M.

Fares East Chattanooga and Grand Junction: adults, $8.50; children (ages 3 to 12), $4.50.

Downtown Arrow: adults, $13.50; children (ages 3 to 12), $9.50.

Children under three years of age are admitted free of charge.

Contact   Tennessee Valley Railroad, 4119 Cromwell Road, Chattanooga, TN 37421-2119. Telephone (800) 397-5544 or (615) 894-8028; fax (615) 894-8029.

C O W A N

Cowan Railroad Museum

Located in the heart of the Cumberland Mountains is the Cowan Railroad Museum. There, visitors can view a restored depot, a steam locomotive, flatcar, caboose, an HO-gauge railroad display of the Cowan Pusher District, and railroad memorabilia. Parks are adjacent to the museum.

How to Get There   The museum is located at the intersection of Highways 64 and 41-A.

Hours   May through October: Thursday, Friday, and Saturday, 10:00 A.M. to 4:00 P.M.; Sunday, 1:00 P.M. to 4:00 P.M.

Fares   Donations are welcome.

Contact   Cowan Railroad Museum, P.O. Box 53, Cowan, TN 37318. Telephone (615) 967-7365.

J A C K S O N

Casey Jones Home
and Railroad Museum

The Casey Jones Home and Railroad Museum is a tribute to Jonathan Luther Jones of Cayce, Kentucky. Jones lost his life in

April 1900 after his heroic attempt to prevent a railroad colli-
sion involving his locomotive and railcars stuck on a railroad
track. (See the entry for the Casey Jones Railroad Museum and
State Park in Vaughan, Mississippi.)

The home and museum are located in Casey Jones Village, a complex that includes a gift shop, an inn featuring a caboose and 1890-period railcar rooms, a country store, and a
miniature train ride that carries up to 46 adults and children
along a quarter-mile track. The home and museum can be
toured and include a model train exhibit housed in a 19th-cen-
tury railcar as well as a brief video about the hero's life. A
replica of Jones' locomotive #382 is on display, and children
may get on board and ring the bell.

How to Get There   The museum is just off I-40 at exit 80A.

Hours   Museum: open daily (closed Easter, Thanksgiving,
and Christmas), 8:00 A.M. to 9:00 P.M. Train rides operate late
spring through October.

Fares   Museum: $2 per person (children under six years of
age are admitted free of charge).

Train rides: adults, $3; children (ages 6 to 12), $2; children under six years of age are admitted free of charge.

Contact   Casey Jones Home and Railroad Museum, Casey
Jones Village, Jackson, TN 38305. Telephone (901) 668-1222
or (800) 748-9588; fax (901) 664-7782.

M E M P H I S

MAIN STREET TROLLEY

Vintage trolley cars are featured on the Main Street Trolley. The
route follows the same path that mule-drawn cars once followed—along Main Street from Auction Avenue to Calhoun

Avenue—and today serves downtown Memphis sites, including **Beale Street, South Main Historic District,** and the **National Civil Rights Museum.**

The restored trolleys were built between 1912 and 1940 and include many of their original features, including antique light fixtures and hand-carved mahogany detailing.

How to Get There   The Main Street Trolley can be boarded at any of the 20 station stops located in the heart of Memphis.

Hours   Open Monday through Friday, 6:30 A.M. to 11:00 P.M. (departures every 10 minutes); Saturday, 9:30 A.M. to 12:00 midnight (departures every 20 minutes); Sunday, 10:00 A.M. to 6:00 P.M. (departures every 20 minutes).

Fares   Regular fare, $.50 each way. Seniors and disabled persons, $.25 each way.

Lunchtime fare (Monday to Friday, 11:00 A.M. to 1:30 P.M.), $.25 each way. All-day pass, $2; three-day pass, $5.

Contact   Main Street Trolley, 547 North Main Street, Memphis, TN 38103. Telephone (901) 577-2640.

PIGEON FORGE

DOLLYWOOD

Originally created in 1961 as "Rebel Railroad," this East Tennessee entertainment park became Dollywood in 1986 when singer and entertainer Dolly Parton became one of its owners. The theme park today features musical shows, amusement park rides, an eagle habitat, a Dolly Parton Museum, and the Dollywood Express Train.

Two Baldwin steam locomotives—*Klondike Katie,* built in 1943, and *Cinderella,* built in 1939—were originally built for the U.S. Army, and hauled troops and lumber in Alaska during World War II. The seven open-air cars, which have a 550-passenger capacity, depart from the depot and take visitors on a 30-minute, 5-mile ride throughout the Dollywood complex.

NOTE: Wheelchairs (manual and electric) and strollers are available for rental at Dollywood.

Special Events Fantasy Express (during Smoky Mountain Christmas).

How to Get There Dollywood is in Pigeon Forge, 35 miles southeast of Knoxville, off I-40, exit 407, in the foothills of the Great Smoky Mountains.

Hours Late April to December: 10:00 A.M. to 6:00 P.M. Check for schedule updates.

Fares Adults (12 and above), $23.99 plus tax; seniors (60 and above), $20.99 plus tax; children (ages 4 to 11), $15.99 plus tax.

Contact Dollywood, 1020 Dollywood Lane, Pigeon Forge, TN 37863-4101. Telephone (423) 428-9488.

TEXAS

AUSTIN

AUSTIN STEAM TRAIN ASSOCIATION

Since 1992, the nonprofit Austin Steam Train Association has operated the *Hill Country Flyer*, a restored 1915-vintage steam train that travels over the former route of the 19th-century Austin & Northwestern Railroad. With a landscape that includes canyons and creeks and the South San Gabriel River, the scenic 33-mile journey includes a three-hour layover in Burnet. Visitors can have lunch or take a town tour.

The steam train, locomotive #786, was retired in 1956 and restored between 1990 and 1992. The passenger coaches are from the 1920s and were built by the Pennsylvania Railroad. The *Flyer* offers first-class amenities, which include heating and air conditioning, compartment seating options, and free snacks and beverages.

A "Twilight Flyer" operates on selected Saturdays, 7:00 P.M. to 8:45 P.M., and includes a complimentary basket of fruit and cheese. The train departs from Cedar Park, near Austin.

NOTE: Reservations are required, due to limited seating.

How to Get There From Austin, take I-35 north to Round Rock. Then drive west on Road 1431 to Cedar Park. Watch for signs.

Hours Saturday and Sunday: 10:00 A.M. departure from Cedar Park; three-hour layover in Burnet; 5:30 P.M. return.

Fares Coach: adults, $24; children (ages 3 to 13), $10. Children two years of age and under are admitted free of charge.
First-class: adults, $38; children (ages 3 to 13), $19.

Contact Austin Steam Train Association, Box 1632, Austin, TX 78767-1632. Telephone (512) 477-8468.

D A L L A S

AGE OF STEAM RAILROAD MUSEUM

The Age of Steam Railroad Museum invites visitors of all ages to experience the rich history of railroading. Owned and operated by the nonprofit Southwest Railroad Historical Society, the museum is housed in Dallas' oldest depot, Houston and Texas Central Depot, built at the turn of the century.

Nearly 30 pieces of historic railroad equipment are on display, including locomotives such as the Union Pacific's *Big Boy* #4018 and *Centennial* #6913, elegant Pullman sleeping cars, and streamliners. The museum features hands-on displays and visitors are encouraged to climb aboard the trains for closer inspection.

A gift shop is on the premises. Tours are available for groups of 15 or more.

How to Get There From downtown Dallas, take I-30 east to the Second Avenue exit. Turn left onto Parry Avenue, then right at the Washington Street entrance to Fair Park.

From I-30 westbound, take the First Avenue exit around to Exposition Avenue, then left on Parry Avenue to the Washington Street entrance.

Hours   Open year-round: Thursday and Friday, 10:00 A.M. to 3:00 P.M.; Saturday and Sunday, 11:00 A.M. to 5:00 P.M.

Fares   Adults, $3; children (12 and under), $1.50.

Contact   Age of Steam Railroad Museum, 1105 Washington Street, P.O. Box 153259, Dallas, TX 75315-3259; telephone (214) 428-0101.

GALVESTON

RAILROAD MUSEUM

The Railroad Museum has over 20,000 items among its exhibits, including railcars and steam locomotives, an operating model train layout of the Port of Galveston, railroad history displays, Pullman sleepers, cabooses, and a restored 1930s railway depot, where visitors can hear from the "ghosts" of former travelers. The museum is also a boarding point for Galveston's rail trolley. Visitors can ride through the downtown, beach, and historic Galveston neighborhoods.

How to Get There   From Houston, take I-45 east to Galveston Island. (I-45 becomes Broadway when you reach Galveston Island.) Go to 26th and Broadway. Turn left onto 26th Street and go eight blocks to Santa Fe Place. Look for a train on a platform outside the museum.

Hours   Open daily, 10:00 A.M. to 5:00 P.M. Closed Thanksgiving, Christmas Eve and Day, and Mardi Gras weekend.

Fares   Museum: adults, $5; children (ages 4 to 12), $2.50. Rail trolley: $1.

Contact   Railroad Museum, 25th Street and The Strand, Galveston, TX 77550. Telephone (409) 765-5700.

H O U S T O N

GULF COAST RAILROAD MUSEUM

The Gulf Coast Chapter of the National Railway Historical Society (NRHS) is involved in the collection, preservation, and maintenance of rail equipment and other artifacts related to the railway history of Houston and the United States. The chapter operates the Gulf Coast Railroad Museum, which has an extensive collection of railcars and locomotives in its possession, including a 1940 observation car, a 1949 caboose, a 1938 post office car, and a 1942 Pullman car. Occasional train excursion rides are also sponsored by the chapter during the year.

How to Get There   In Houston, take exit East Loop 610 at McCarty Drive and go east toward Liberty. Go 1 mile to Mesa Road (first traffic light) and turn left. Go another mile until reaching the museum on the right.

Hours   April to October: open Saturday, 11:00 A.M. to 4:00 P.M.

Fares   Adults, $3; children, $1.50.

Contact   Gulf Coast Railroad Museum, 7390 Mesa Road, Houston, TX 77001; telephone (713) 631-6612. Or, Gulf Coast Chapter, NRHS, Inc., P.O. Box 457, Houston, TX 77001-0457.

R U S K

TEXAS STATE RAILROAD

In 1996, the Texas State Railroad celebrates its 100th birthday. Railroad construction began in 1896, when prison laborers completed the first 5 miles of track. The line was then used to help transport iron to a foundry in Rusk.

By 1972, the railroad was in disrepair, and the Texas Parks and Wildlife Department was commissioned to assist. The department helped preserve steam locomotive history by incorporating the railroad into a state park with tourist passenger service. In 1976, the railroad reopened, offering a 50-mile round-trip excursion between Rusk and Palestine in historic steam-powered engines. The railroad owns five steam locomotives built between 1901 and 1927.

The route follows a stretch of forest and the picturesque East Texas countryside, crossing 30 bridges. Visitors can begin their journey from either of two turn-of-the-century-style depots: Rusk or Palestine. Tours of the engine cab are offered prior to departure, and questions to the engineer and fireman are welcome. Refreshments, gifts, and souvenirs are sold at both depots and during the trip.

Special Events   Autumn Color Run; Buffalo Soldiers Reenactment; Easter Sunrise Drama; 100th Anniversary Celebration (1996).

How to Get There   From Tyler, take Highway 69 south, to Highway 84 to Rusk. Drive 3 miles west of town and look for a train monument at the entrance to the railroad.

Hours   Open most weekends and some weekdays throughout summer; call ahead for dates.

Rusk train: departure at 11:00 A.M. (return to Rusk at 3:00 P.M.). Palestine train: departure at 11:00 A.M. (return to Palestine at 3:00 P.M.).

Fares One-way: adults, $10; children (ages 3 to 12), $6. Round-trip: adults, $15; children, $9.

Special summer fares in June, July, and August (tickets are discounted $2).

Contact Texas State Railroad, Highway 84, Rusk, TX 75785. Telephone (903) 683-2561.

S A N   A N T O N I O

TEXAS TRANSPORTATION MUSEUM

The Texas Transportation Museum, located on a 37-acre site, displays a variety of exhibits related to transportation, including a large section on railroading. The museum collection is a mixture of small and large items, and it also features a half-mile train ride and static displays of ore cars, a business car, a Pullman sleeper car, steam engine, a narrow gauge mine train, caboose, railroad station (all of which can be toured), an outdoor miniature garden railroad, and a 100-foot-long HO-gauge model railroad layout.

How to Get There In San Antonio, go north to Broadway, which dead-ends. Make a right on Wetmore, and go 200 feet past the overpass. The museum is on the left.

Hours Open Thursday, Saturday, and Sunday, 9:00 A.M. to 4:00 P.M.

Fares Donations are requested: adults, $3; children, $1.

Contact   Texas Transportation Museum, 11731 Wetmore Road, San Antonio, TX 78247-3606. Telephone (210) 490-3554.

TEMPLE

RAILROAD AND PIONEER MUSEUM

The Railroad and Pioneer Museum offers visitors a chance to learn about the rich heritage of Bell Temple County, Texas, through museum collections on farming, ranching, business, and the railroad. A 1907 Santa Fe depot houses the collection of artifacts, including a restored steam engine. Personal tours of the exhibits are offered and visitors are welcome to climb on board the steam engine and ring the bell.

Special Events   Texas Train Festival (third weekend of September); Traveling Trunk Educational Programs ("touchable history") are available to schools.

How to Get There   From San Antonio, take I-35 north to exit 300 (service road). Get in the far right lane to turn right on Avenue H. Turn left onto 31st Street; the depot is half a block away.

Hours   Open Tuesday to Friday year-round, except major holidays, 1:00 P.M. to 4:00 P.M.; Saturday, 10:00 A.M. to 4:00 P.M.

Fares   Adults, $2; seniors, $1; children (ages 5 to 12), $1; children under five years of age are admitted free of charge.

Contact   Mary Irving, Director, Railroad and Pioneer Museum, 710 Jack Baskin, Temple, TX 76504. Telephone (817) 778-6873.

UTAH

BRIGHAM CITY

GOLDEN SPIKE
NATIONAL HISTORIC SITE

Not long after the first railroads began operating in America, the idea was launched for a national railroad. That idea was realized in May 1869 when the Central Pacific and Union Pacific Railroads completed 1,776 miles of track at Promontory Point, Utah. A transcontinental railroad had been built and Golden Spike National Historic Site commemorates the achievement.

The site houses a visitors center with slide programs and displays on the history of the railroad's development. In the summer, park guides (often dressed in period costumes) give presentations and instructions for self-guided walks and auto tours.

A special feature between late April and the beginning of October is a steam demonstration, featuring two replicas of the *Jupiter* and locomotive #119, two wood-burning steam engine locomotives that pulled the presidents of Central Pacific and

Union Pacific Railroads to the Golden Spike Ceremony to commemorate the great event.

Special Events Anniversary Celebration; Railroader's Festival.

How to Get There Golden Spike is 32 miles west of Brigham City, Utah, via Highways 13 and 83 through Corinne.

Hours Visitors center is open daily, Memorial Day weekend through Labor Day, 8:00 A.M. to 6:00 P.M. Rest of the year: 8:00 A.M. to 4:30 P.M., except holidays.

Steam locomotive displays are open daily April 29 to May 26 and September 5 to October 9, 9:30 A.M. to 4:00 P.M.; daily, September 5 to October 9, 9:30 A.M. to 5:00 P.M.

Fares April 29 through October 9: $2 per person; $4 per vehicle.

Contact Golden Spike National Historic Site, P.O. Box 897, Brigham City, UT 84302. Telephone (801) 471-2209.

H E B E R   C I T Y

HEBER VALLEY HISTORIC RAILROAD

The Heber Valley Historic Railroad offers two-hour and three-and-a-half-hour excursions on authentically restored steam and diesel locomotives. The shorter trip takes passengers through beautiful farmlands and travels along Deer Creek Lake. The longer journey includes a continuation of the trip, descending into a canyon and along a river, with the final destination at a park. Visitors can spend time touring the park and using park facilities before the return trip.

Passengers are free to bring along a picnic, reserve a train box lunch, or purchase snacks on board.

Special Events   Presidents' Day Excursion; Santa Claus Express.

How to Get There   Heber City is 44 miles southeast of Salt Lake City at Highways 40 and 189.

Hours   May to October: 10:00 A.M. to 6:00 P.M. In May: Saturday and Sunday only until Memorial Day.

Fares   Adults, $16 to 18; seniors (65 or above), $12 to 14; children (ages 3 to 12), $8 to $10; children under three years of age are admitted free of charge.

Contact   Heber Valley Historic Railroad Authority, 450 South 600 West, P.O. Box 641, Heber City, UT 84032. Telephone (801) 654-5601 (Heber City) or (801) 581-9980 (Salt Lake City).

T O O E L E

TOOELE COUNTY MUSEUM

The Tooele County Museum features exhibits and artifacts that tell the story of railroading, mining, and smelting operations in the western Utah region. The museum was created in 1983, when a 1909 railroad depot (formerly part of the Tooele Valley Railroad) and railroad equipment were donated by the Atlantic Richfield Company.

Exhibits include a 1910 steam locomotive, two woodside cabooses, passenger coaches, and snowplows, as well as photos of railroad and smelting operations. Train enthusiasts will particularly enjoy the miniature train that tours around the museum grounds.

How to Get There   From Salt Lake City, take I-80 west to exit 99. Take Highway 36 south for 10 miles to Tooele.

Hours   Open Memorial Day to Labor Day: Tuesday to Saturday, 1:00 P.M. to 4:00 P.M.

Fares   Call for information.

Contact   Tooele County Museum, 35 North Broadway, Tooele, UT 84074. Telephone (801) 882-2836 or (801) 882-8133.

Vermont

BELLOWS FALLS

GREEN MOUNTAIN RAILROAD

Named after a former Vermont passenger train, the *Green Mountain Flyer* is owned and operated by the Green Mountain Railroad, a freight and passenger line that runs on a 50-mile portion of the former Rutland Railway. Departing from Bellows Falls Station or Chester Depot, visitors take a 26-mile round-trip excursion through beautiful southern Vermont countryside, pulled by 1950s diesel locomotives in restored, enclosed open-window coaches built in the late 19th and early 20th century.

The scenic route includes a nesting habitat for geese, cranes, herons, and eagles, and it passes over covered bridges, flowing waters, and seven crossings of the Williams River before reaching its destination. Day-long excursions are also offered on special weekends.

The 25-minute layover at Chester Depot allows passengers to tour the restored 1872 station and a 1941 Bessemer & Lake Erie Railroad bay window caboose on display nearby.

GREEN MOUNTAIN RAILROAD

The *Green Mountain Flyer* crosses a stone bridge near Brockway Mills.

A lunch coach offers sandwiches and soft drinks during the trip.

Special Events   Valentine's Ride; Maple Sugar; Easter Bunny; Mother's Day; Sunset Special; Ludlow Foliage Rides.

How to Get There   From Burlington, take I-89 south to I-91 south to exit 6. Then take Route 5 south into the village of Bellows Falls. Turn left onto Depot Street and look for signs for the train.

Hours   Late May and June: open weekends. July through September: open Tuesday through Sunday. Late September through late October: open daily. Call ahead for specific hours.

Fares   Adults, $11; children (ages 3 to 12), $7; children under three are free of charge when not occupying a seat.

Contact   Green Mountain Railroad, Depot Square, P.O. Box 498, Bellows Falls, VT 05101-0498. Telephone (802) 463-3069.

M I D D L E B U R Y

SUGARBUSH/VERMONT EXPRESS

The summer of 1995 marked the inaugural journey of the Sugarbush/Vermont Express, which offers scenic passenger service between Burlington and Middlebury, Vermont. Now managed by Vermont Rail Excursions, a six-car passenger train makes stops in Vergennes and Shelburne before arriving at destinations in Burlington and Middlebury. Passenger cars include vintage lounge, dining, and baggage cars formerly operated by the Atchison, Topeka and Santa Fe, Smoky Mountain, and Indiana Railroads.

How to Get There   From Middlebury, take Route 7 north to the train (just south of Burlington).
From Burlington, go south on Route 7 to the train.

Hours   June and early September: open weekends. July through August: open Wednesday to Sunday. Late September through Late October: open daily.
Hours are 8:30 A.M. to 7:30 P.M, both directions. Three departures daily in either direction.

Fares   Adults, $10; seniors (65 and above), $8; children (ages 3 to 12), $5; children under three years of age are admitted free of charge.

Contact   Paula Palmer, c/o Sugarbush Vermont Express, P.O. Box 243, Middlebury, VT 05753. Telephone (802) 388-0193 or (800) 707-3530.

SHELBURNE

SHELBURNE MUSEUM

The Shelburne Museum presents early American life and culture in Vermont through a rich variety of historical exhibits, including ones focusing on transportation. Among the train-related displays at the museum are the Shelburne Railroad Station built in 1890, which once served the Rutland Railroad; a freight shed containing railroad workers' tools; *Old #220*, a 1915 steam locomotive known as "the Locomotive of the Presidents" because it pulled the presidential cars of Presidents Coolidge, Hoover, Roosevelt, and Eisenhower; *Grand Isle*, an elegantly appointed luxury rail car, circa 1890; and other railroad equipment and memorabilia.

NOTE: Comfortable walking shoes are recommended.

How to Get There   From Burlington, take Route 7 south to Shelburne. Look for signs to the museum.

Hours   May 18 through October 31: open daily, 10:00 A.M. to 5:00 P.M. Winter hours: 1:00 P.M. guided tour only (weather permitting).

Fares   Entrance (two-day pass): adults, $17.50; children, $8.75. Winter guided tour: adults, $7; children, $3.

Contact   Shelburne Museum, U.S. Route 7, P.O. Box 10, Shelburne, VT 05482. Telephone (802) 985-3346; fax (802) 985-2331.

VIRGINIA

U.S. ARMY TRANSPORTATION MUSEUM

Displaying historical artifacts and exhibits on the Army's transportation history, this comprehensive museum covers the colonial period through the present. The six-acre complex contains both interior and exterior exhibits, including dioramas, videos, models, and full-sized equipment.

Beginning with World War I, Fort Eustis provided railway artillery training demonstrations; by World War II, Fort Eustis was the central training site for the Army Transportation Corps. Among the railway exhibits are steam locomotives, ambulance cars, boxcars, tank cars, flatcars, and a caboose.

The museum has a gift shop and is handicapped accessible.

How to Get There   The museum is off I-64 on Route 105, 11 miles south of colonial Williamsburg.

Hours   Open daily (except Mondays and federal holidays), 9:00 A.M. to 4:30 P.M.

Fares   Admission is free.

Contact   United States Army Transportation Museum, Building 300, Besson Hall, Fort Eustis, VA 23604-5260. Telephone (804) 878-1115.

R O A N O K E

VIRGINIA MUSEUM OF TRANSPORTATION

The Virginia Museum of Transportation is the official transportation museum of the Commonwealth, with a strong focus on the railroad. Located in a restored railway freight station next to Norfolk Southern Corporation track, the museum has one of the largest diesel locomotive collections in the United States and features steam and electric locomotives, automobiles, carriages, airplanes, and other vehicles that help trace transportation developments from the Industrial Revolution to space flight.

Many of the exhibits are hands-on, and visitors may climb on board many of the trains in the railway yard to learn more about the golden age of railroading. Weekend visits to the museum include guides by costumed historical interpreters who provide information on artifacts. Model railroad exhibits also make up the displays. An added attraction of the museum is that visitors may safely watch trains in operation at the Norfolk Southern site next door.

Several educational programs with rail themes designed for preschool, kindergarten, and elementary school children are offered throughout the year.

Future plans include construction of an amphitheater and observation tower for viewing Norfolk Southern trains. The museum has a souvenir shop and a picnic area.

How to Get There　The museum is located in downtown Roanoke. From I-81, take the airport exit to I-581, to downtown exit 5 to Williamson Road. Turn right on Church and right again onto Third Street. The street will dead end onto Norfolk Avenue near the museum entrance.

Hours　Monday through Saturday: 10:00 A.M. to 5:00 P.M.; Sunday, 12:00 noon to 5:00 P.M. Closed Mondays in January and February.

Fares　Adults, $5 plus tax; seniors, $4 plus tax; children (ages 3 to 18), $3 plus tax; children under three years of age are free of charge.

Contact　Virginia Museum of Transportation, 303 Norfolk Avenue, Roanoke, VA 24016. Telephone (540) 342-5670.

WASHINGTON

ANACORTES RAILWAY

A beautifully restored, Queen Anne–style former Great Northern depot station built in 1911 serves as the passenger station for the Anacortes Railway. It is on the National Register of Historic Places. A family-owned 18-inch narrow gauge steam train takes passengers on a scenic three-quarter-mile trip along the waterfront and parkways. Comfort and elegance characterize the railway's cars: red velvet cushions, thick carpeting, cherrywood interiors, an Italian marble fireplace, and spacious seating are all part of the design. An observation platform and an open summer car enhance the view.

The steam train uses fir bark for fuel, and it is rotated on a turntable at the end of the line for the return. Upon request, the railway invites visitors to ride in the engineer's cab and ring the bell. Music is played on the railway's Tangley air calliope.

How to Get There   From Seattle, take I-5 north to Burlington. Get off at the Anacortes exit (Highway 20). Travel west for 17 miles to Anacortes. At the first traffic light, take a right onto R Avenue. Turn right onto 9th Avenue and look for the W.T. Preston Steam Paddle Museum. The station is next door.

Hours   Mid-June through Labor Day: open Saturday, Sunday, and holidays, 12:00 noon to 4:30 P.M.

Fares   Admission is $1.

Contact   Anacortes Railway, 387 Campbell Lake Road, Anacortes, WA 98221. Telephone (360) 293-2634.

S E A T T L E

WATERFRONT STREETCAR

Seattle's scenic waterfront streetcar rides, which give visitors a wonderful view of Elliott Bay, began in 1982 with two 1927 Australian vehicles; three cars were added in 1990. Up to 52 seated and 40 standing passengers can be accommodated on each of the streetcars, which operate through three Seattle neighborhoods: the Waterfront, Pioneer Square, and the International District. Museums, specialty shops, boat rides, restaurants, and an aquarium are all among the sites to visit along the way.

Each ticket enables passengers to board from any one of nine stops during a 90-minute period.

The streetcars and stations are handicapped accessible.

How to Get There   Take I-5 north to the Madison Street exit. Go over Freeway, turn left onto Madison and go down the waterfront to a trolley stop.

Hours   Open May to September: weekdays, 7:00 A.M. to 10:40 P.M.; Saturday and Sunday, 9:00 A.M. to 10:40 P.M.

Fares   Adults, $.85 to $1.10 (cheaper fares offered in off-peak periods); seniors and disabled patrons, $.25; youth (ages 5 to 17), $.75, children under five are free of charge.

Contact   Waterfront Streetcar, King County, 821 Second Avenue, Seattle, WA 98104-1598. Telephone (800) 542-7876 or (206) 553-3000; TDD (206) 689-3413.

SNOQUALMIE

SNOQUALMIE VALLEY RAILROAD/ NORTHWEST RAILWAY MUSEUM

The Snoqualmie Valley Railroad Company and Northwest Railway Museum offer railroad excursions over former Seattle, Lake Shore, and Eastern Railway tracks built in the 1880s. The locomotives used by the railroad are Alco or Fairbanks-Morse diesels and carry enclosed coach, coach/baggage, or an open car with a roof. The site features an 1890 depot, listed on the National Register of Historic Places, a collection of railroad displays, and a museum store.

Special Events   Santa Trains.

How to Get There   The railroad and museum are 30 miles east of Seattle. From I-90 east, take exit 27 to reach Snoqualmie, or exit 31 to reach North Bend.

From I-90 west, take exit 31, follow Highway 202 to Snoqualmie or North Bend.

Hours   In April: open Sunday, 11:00 A.M. to 4:00 P.M. (Snoqualmie Station, King Street and Highway 202); 11:30 A.M. to 3:30 P.M. (North Bend Station, 205 McClellan Street).

Memorial Day through summer: open Saturdays and Sundays. Same hours.

Fares   Adults, $6; seniors, $5; children (ages 3 to 12), $4; children under three years of age are admitted free of charge.

Contact   Northwest Railway Museum, P.O. Box 459, Snoqualmie, WA 98065. Telephone (206) 746-4025.

TOPPENISH

YAKIMA VALLEY RAIL AND STEAM MUSEUM

The Yakima Valley Rail and Steam Museum Association was formed in 1989 to save and restore Northern Pacific Railroad's 1911 depot. Today, the Association oversees the **Toppenish Depot,** a museum featuring railroad displays, restoration of Northern Pacific's Steam Engine #1364, and 45 miles of track for the **Toppenish, Simcoe & Western Railroad.** The railroad offers a two-hour, 20-mile narrated tour through scenic farm country. On a clear day, Mount Rainier and Mount Adams can be seen.

Special Events   Santa Claus Express.

How to Get There   From Seattle, take I-90 to Ellensburg. Turn onto I-82 to Yakima and take exit 50 into Toppenish (Route 22). Go toward the railroad tracks, but don't cross. Turn left on to Asotin Avenue. Go through the intersection and straight to the depot.

Hours   Museum is open daily May to September and weekends October through December. Call ahead for specific hours.
    Train runs June to October, Saturday and Sunday, 2:00 P.M.

Fares   Museum: adults, $2; seniors and children (ages 17 and younger), $1.
    Train: adults, $5; children (ages 3 to 12), $3.

Contact   Yakima Valley Rail and Steam Museum Association, 10 Asotin Avenue, P.O. Box 689, Toppenish, WA 98948. Telephone (509) 865-1911.

W I C K E R S H A M

LAKE WHATCOM RAILWAY

The scenic Lake Whatcom Railway travels along a Northern Pacific branch line built in 1902. It takes passengers on a 7-mile, one-and-a-half-hour steam train excursion that goes through a tunnel, past a lake, and through a forest. The railway's equipment includes a Pullman coach built in 1912, a 1920 Pullman parlor car, a coffee shop coach built in 1925, a 1926 Pullman business car, and a baggage car. The steam locomotive was built in 1907. A wooden caboose, track motorcars, and a handcar are used on special occasions.

Special Events   Valentine Train; Easter Bunny Train; Independence Day Train; Autumn Train; Santa Train.

How to Get There   From Seattle, take I-5 north to Burlington to exit 232 at Cook Road. Pick up Highway 20 through Sedro Wooley to Highway 9 north. Take NP Road to the railroad tracks. The entrance to the railway is about 200 feet ahead.

Hours   July 1 to August 31: departures on Saturday and Tuesday, 11:00 A.M. and 1:00 P.M.

Fares   Adults, $10; children (under 18), $5.

Contact   Lake Whatcom Railway, NP Road, Sedro Wooley, WA 98284. Telephone (360) 595-2218 or (360) 236-2857. Or, P.O. Box 91, Acme, WA 98220.

Y A K I M A

YAKIMA ELECTRIC RAILWAY MUSEUM

The Yakima Electric Railway Museum, located in a 1910 build-ing, is run by the Yakima Interurban Lines Association, which operates a living museum of electric railroading. Electric street railway service began in the Yakima area in 1907 by Yakima businessmen; the Union Pacific Railroad expanded it before dis-continuing freight service in 1985. Among the current displays are a 1909 Line Car A, a 1923 Steeplecab #298, 1930 Master Unit streetcars #21 and #22, and two wooden Brill streetcars.

The museum offers trolley excursions (1 hour, 40 min-utes) from Yakima to Selah, that travel through orchard coun-try, over a truss bridge, and along vertical cliffs before reaching

KENNETH G. JOHNSEN

One of the Yakima Electric Railway trolleys outside the museum.

the final destination. There is a 30-minute layover in Selah, but passengers may return on a later car.

How to Get There From Yakima, drive west on Yakima Avenue to Third Avenue. The museum is three blocks south at Third and Pine Street.

Hours Early May to mid-October: Saturday, Sunday, and holidays, Yakima departures at 10:00 A.M., 12:00 noon, 2:00 P.M., and 4:00 P.M.; Selah departures at 11:00 A.M., 1:00 P.M., 3:00 P.M., and 5:00 P.M.

July and August: weeknight evening rides, Yakima departure at 7:00 P.M.; Selah departure at 7:45 P.M. Call ahead for confirmation.

Fares Adults, $4; seniors, $3.50; children (ages 6 to 12), $2.50; families (two adults and two children, ages 6 to 12), $12; children five years of age and under not occupying a seat are free of charge.

Contact Yakima Interurban Lines Association, 306 West Pine Street, P.O. Box 649, Yakima, WA 98907. Telephone (509) 575-1700.

WEST
VIRGINIA

C A S S

CASS SCENIC RAILROAD
AND STATE PARK

Cass Scenic Railroad and State Park is a living museum that tells the history of West Virginia's logging industry. Cass was a logging center in the early 20th century, when timber was hauled from the woods to mountain summits. Shay steam locomotives, equipped to carry heavy loads and navigate steep and curved terrain, performed the task.

Today, the railroad takes tourist excursions through spectacular scenery along 11 miles of track first built in the early 1900s. Visitors may choose a 1.5-hour round-trip excursion to Whittaker Station or a 4.5-hour trip to Bald Knob, the second highest point in West Virginia at an altitude of nearly 5,000 feet.

The park has a fine historical museum with logging artifacts (including Shay locomotives) and photos; a wildlife

UNITED STATES

museum; and an audiovisual show with the town of Cass, circa 1920, depicted in a miniature model. Visitors to the railroad may find accommodations in refurbished turn-of-the-century cottages or bed-and-breakfast inns.

NOTE: Track conditions due to weather may prevent the Bald Knob trip until late 1996. Call ahead.

Special Events Memorial Day; Independence Day; Labor Day; Halloween Train.

How to Get There Take SR 28/92 between Dunmore and Green Bank in Pocahontas County. An 11-mile connector route, WV 66, links Cass to U.S. 219 at Slatyfork.

Hours Cass to Bald Knob: departures at 12 noon. Summer season: Tuesday to Sunday; fall season: Friday to Sunday; fall color schedule (September 29 to October 15): Tuesday to Sunday.
   Cass to Whittaker Station. Summer season and special fall color schedule (September 27 to October 15): departures daily at 11:00 A.M., 12:00 noon, 1:00 P.M., and 3:00 P.M.

Fares Whittaker Station: adults, $10 (weekday) and $12 (weekend); children (ages 5 to 12), $6 (weekday) and $8 (weekend). Bald Knob: adults, $8 (weekday) and $16 (weekend); children (ages 5 to 12), $8 (weekday) and $10 (weekend). Ticket includes train ride, Cass Showcase, wildlife museum, and historical museum.
   Dinner trains: adults, $25; children, $15. Reservations are required. Price includes barbecue, live entertainment, and train ride. Call for schedule.

Contact Cass Scenic Railroad State Park, Box 107, Cass, WV 24927. Telephone (304) 456-4300 or (800) CALL-WVA.

HARPERS FERRY

HARPERS FERRY TOY TRAIN MUSEUM AND JOY LINE MINIATURE RAILROAD

The youngest train enthusiast will particularly enjoy the offerings at the Harpers Ferry Toy Train Museum and Joy Line Miniature Railroad. From the Joy Line Miniature Railroad, adults and children can take a ride on a 1953 miniature locomotive and admire the train station, formerly a B & O Railroad section car house, that once stood in Hagerstown, Maryland. The museum features the antique toy train collection of the late Robert E. Wallich, Sr., which consists of trains of every size and make (most built before 1939) and a 75-foot-long operating standard gauge layout.

How to Get There   From West Virginia, take 340 west, 1 mile past Harpers Ferry. Turn right onto Bakerton Road, and drive 1 mile to the museum.

Hours   April to October: open weekends and holidays (weather permitting), 9:00 A.M. to 5:00 P.M.

Fares   Train, hand car, and museum fares are all $1 per person.

Contact   Harpers Ferry Toy Train Museum, Harpers Ferry, WV 25425. Telephone (304) 535-2291 or (304) 535-2521.

KINGWOOD

WEST VIRGINIA NORTHERN RAILROAD

West Virginia coal country, complete with mountainous landscape, white-tailed deer, and wild turkey provides the backdrop for riders of the West Virginia Northern Railroad. The line began in 1882 as the Kingwood Railway Company. It received its present name in 1894. The railroad once carried coal, timber, fertilizer, and flour as well as passengers. Today's railroad takes a 10.7-mile, three-hour diesel excursion ride through the mining country of Preston County, West Virginia.

Special Events   Memorial Day; Grandparents' Day; Veteran's Day; 4th of July; Labor Day; Northern Nightmare Express; Fall Foliage; Santa Express.

How to Get There   The West Virginia Northern Railroad is less than 30 minutes from I-68 or I-79.

Hours   Mid-May to October: Saturday, Sunday, and holidays, 11:00 A.M. and 3:00 P.M. and October weekdays at 12:00 noon.

Fares   Adults and teenagers, $10; seniors, $8; children (ages 3 to 12), $5; children under three years of age are free of charge.

Contact   Kingwood Northern, Inc., 156 Sisler Street, P.O. Box 424, Kingwood, WV 26537. Telephone (304) 329-3333.

R O M N E Y

POTOMAC EAGLE

"Where eagles fly" and "the Route of Eagles" are phrases used by Potomac Eagle Scenic Railroad sponsors, and that's because nearly every diesel excursion provides an opportunity for passengers to see such birds soaring above the train. The three-hour narrated trip features travel through a beautiful valley called "The Trough," where river and wildlife offer a peaceful and picturesque setting. The Potomac provides two kinds of seating: regular coach and the *Classic Club*, a luxury lounge car serving afternoon lunch and a free glass of West Virginian wine for adults. Refreshments are available on trains.

NOTE: Except for the Classic Club car, heating is limited on trains, so dress accordingly.

Special Events All-day excursions to Petersburg; Railfan Day; Ronald McDonald Day; Hampshire Heritage Days (Civil War).

How to Get There From Cumberland, Maryland, take Route 28 south toward Romney. The station is 1 mile south of Romney on Route 28.

Hours Memorial Day through September: open Saturday with departures at 10:00 A.M. and 2:00 P.M.; Sunday with a departure at 1:00 P.M.
     October: open weekdays with a departure at 1:00 P.M.; Saturday and Sunday with departures at 10:00 A.M. and 2:00 P.M.

Fares May to September: adults, $16; seniors, $15, children (ages 3 to 12), $10; Classic Club, $35; Season Coach Pass, $75.
     October: adults, $19; seniors, $17; children (ages 3 to 12), $12; Classic Club, $42; Season Coach Pass, $50.
     Children under three years of age accompanied by an adult are admitted free of charge.

Contact Potomac Eagle, P.O. Box 657, Romney, WV 26757. Telephone (800) 223-2453 (tickets) or (304) 822-7464 (information).

W H E E L I N G

MINIATURE RAILROAD AND VILLAGE AT OGLEBAY

The Miniature Railroad and Village at Oglebay is a 1,200-square-foot O-gauge model railroad depicting early-20th-century life in Wheeling. Oglebay, a resort named after an industrialist who willed his estate to the community, is more than 1,500 acres with a variety of amenities: golf courses, ski slopes, riding stables, fishing, paddleboats, 10 tennis courts, an outdoor Olympic-sized pool, and a state-of-the-art planetarium.

The train exhibit was created by the staff at Oglebay to help complement family visits to the resort's own children's zoo. Featured among the displays are three main line tracks, steam trains, replicas of a coal mine and steel mill, trestle bridges, two operating steamboats, a logging operation, an amusement park, carousel, and merry-go-round, all placed against the backdrop of mountainous terrain.

A 1.5-mile train ride is also offered.

Special Events   Oglebay Model Railroad Show (January 13 and 14).

How to Get There   The Oglebay Resort and Conference Center is 3 miles off I-70. Take the Oglebay exit and follow Route 40 east for half a mile, then take State Route 88 north for 2.5 miles. The exhibit is on the lower level of the children's zoo (main building).

Hours   Open daily. February through April: 11:00 A.M. to 5:00 P.M. May through October: 10:00 A.M. to 6:00 P.M. November through January: 10:00 A.M. to 9:00 P.M.

Christmas Eve and New Year's Eve: 10:00 A.M. to 4:00 P.M. Christmas and New Year's Days: 4:00 P.M. to 9:00 P.M.

Fares   Adults, $4.25; children, $3.75. Train ride is $1.

Contact   Oglebay, Wheeling, WV 26003. Telephone (304) 243-4034; fax (304) 243-4070; CompuServe address: 72467, 2051.

WISCONSIN

GREEN BAY

NATIONAL RAILROAD MUSEUM

One of the oldest and largest railroad museums in the United States, the National Railroad Museum features more than 70 locomotives and railroad cars in its collection, including a Union Pacific *Big Boy*, the world's largest steam locomotive. The museum offers visitors an exhibit hall with dioramas on railroad history, Hood Junction Depot, an HO-scale model railroad layout presented by the Green Bay Area Model Railroaders Club, a large theater, gift shop, library, and visitors center.

Children will especially enjoy the train ride around the museum grounds on a former short-line steam locomotive (converted to diesel power) that pulls two 1920s coaches on a 1-mile loop, giving passengers a good view of the Fox River. A miniature train is also on display and can be boarded by visitors.

How to Get There   From downtown, take Walnut Street to Broadway. After crossing the bridge on Broadway make a left. Look for the museum on the left.

Hours   Open 9:00 A.M. to 5:00 P.M. daily, May through October; weekdays only, November through April. Closed Thanksgiving, Christmas, and New Year's Day.

Fares   May through October: adults, $6; seniors (62 and above), $5; children (ages 6 to 15), $3; Immediate Family Pass (two adults and two children), $16.

November through April: adults, $4; seniors (62 and above), $3; children (ages 6 to 15), $2. Immediate Family Pass (two adults and two children), $10.

Contact   National Railroad Museum, 2285 S. Broadway, Green Bay, WI 54304-4832. Telephone (414) 435-7245 or (414) 437-7623.

L A O N A

Camp 5 Museum

The Camp 5 Museum Foundation, a nonprofit organization, operates the Camp 5 Museum complex, a multifaceted site that presents a variety of fun and educational attractions. Among the offerings at the complex are a logging museum and blacksmith shop with historical artifacts; railroad memorabilia; animal barn; nature center; forestry tour; transportation and agricultural artifacts; and a hayrack/pontoon boat ride along the river.

A special highlight for train fans is a steam train ride on the Laona & Northern Railway. The railway runs the *Lumberjack Special,* a 1916 steam locomotive, during the summer months. The train features a prairie-style Vulcan locomotive, two coaches, and three antique cupola cabooses. It departs from a yellow 19th-century depot on Highway 8 to the Camp 5 Museum complex.

The complex has a restored turn-of-the-century gift shop.

Special Events   Camp 5 Heritage Celebration (first weekend of August) and Fall Color tours.

How to Get There   From Milwaukee, take Highway 41 north to Green Bay. Then take Highway 32 to Laona. Camp 5 is adjacent, look for signs.

Hours   Open mid-June through last Saturday of August. Laona to Camp 5: departures at 11:00 A.M., 12:00 noon, 1:00 P.M., and 2:00 P.M. Camp 5 to Laona: departures at 11:30 A.M., 12:20 P.M., 1:20 P.M., 2:45 P.M., and 4:00 P.M.

Fares   Adults, $14; students (ages 13 to 17), $9; children (ages 4 to 12), $4.75; families, $38. Hayrack/pontoon trip: adults, $2.50; children, $1.25.

Contact   Camp 5 Museum, RFD #1, Laona, WI 54541. Telephone (800) 774-3414 or (715) 674-3414.

MANITOWOC

PINECREST HISTORICAL VILLAGE

The Pinecrest Historical Village is a 60-acre outdoor history museum owned and operated by the Manitowoc County Historical Society. Celebrating its 25th anniversary, the village depicts Manitowoc in 1900. Dedicated to the men and women of early Manitowoc County, the site is composed of over 20 authentically researched and renovated buildings and period artifacts. Special exhibits and demonstrations are often featured.

Train fans will enjoy visiting the Collins Depot, a former Soo Line station built in 1896, which handled both passenger and freight service; the 44-ton steam locomotive 321 and coal tender, built in 1887; a 16-ton caboose built in 1886; and a flatcar on display. Other exhibits include a granary, blacksmith and wagon shop, barn, school and a host of other structures that typified 1900 village life.

The village has a picnic area.

How to Get There   Take I-43 to exit 152. Go west on County Trunk Highway JJ for 3 miles and turn left on Pine Crest Lane. From the Lake Michigan car ferry, take U.S. Highway 10 west to County Trunk Highway JJ.

Hours   May 1 through Labor Day: 9:00 A.M. to 4:30 P.M. Fridays, Saturdays, and Sundays through mid-October: 10:00 A.M. to 4:00 P.M. Last weekend in November and first weekend in December: 11:00 A.M. to 4:00 P.M.

Fares   Adults $4; youth (ages 6 to 17), $2; children under six are free of charge; family rate is $10 (for a family of two adults and children under 12).

Contact   Manitowoc County Historical Society, P.O. Box 574, Manitowoc, WI 54221-0574. Telephone (414) 684-5110 or (414) 684-4445.

NORTH FREEDOM

MID-CONTINENT RAILWAY MUSEUM

The Mid-Continent Railway Museum gives visitors a chance to learn about the role of the short line railroad and small-town life. The Mid-Continent Railway Historical Society, which sponsors an outdoor museum, also offers a 50-minute excursion on a steam locomotive along 7 miles of track built in 1903 for the Chicago & NW Railroad.

Departures take place in North Freedom at Chicago & NW's historic and restored depot built in 1894. Visitors to the museum can take a tour of the railway yard and view many displays and exhibits, including restored turn-of-the-century

MID-CONTINENT RAILWAY

Mid-Continent Railway's locomotive #1385 steams along the track between North Freedom and La Rue.

wooden passenger and freight cars and modern 20th-century
railcars.

Special Events Snow Train; Autumn Color Train; Santa Express Train.

How to Get There From Highways 12, 33, and 136 in West
Baraboo, turn west onto Highway 136. Turn south on County
PF to North Freedom. Mid-Continent is half a mile west of the
four-way stop in North Freedom.

Hours Museum hours: 9:30 A.M. to 5:00 P.M. May to August:
open daily. Late April, late October, and holidays: open weekends only.
    Train rides depart at 10:30 A.M., 12:30 P.M., 2:00 P.M., and
3:30 P.M.

Fares   Museum admission is free. Train fares: adults, $8; seniors (62 and above), $7; children (ages 3 to 12), $4.50; families (four or more), $22.

Contact   Mid-Continent Railway Historical Society, Inc., E8948 Diamond Hill Road, North Freedom, WI 53591-0358. Telephone (800) 930-1385 or (608) 522-4261.

N O R T H   L A K E

KETTLE MORAINE RAILWAY

The Kettle Moraine Railway takes passengers on a 50-minute, 8-mile round-trip steam train ride, originating at the North Lake Depot. The tour goes through two moraine cuts, crosses a 125-foot wooden trestle and up an incline west before making its return to North Lake. Snacks and gifts can be purchased at the depot.

NOTE: Advance reservations are not required, but the railway recommends that passengers arrive half an hour before departure time.

How to Get There   From Minneapolis, take I-94 east to exit 287 to Highway 83 north to North Lake. Turn right on Kilbourne and follow the signs to the depot.

Hours   June to September: Sundays and Labor Day, departures at 12:30 P.M., 2:00 P.M., and 3:30 P.M.
    October (first three weekends): Saturday departures at 12:30 P.M., 2:00 P.M., and 3:30 P.M. Sunday departures at 11:00 A.M., 12:30 P.M., 2:00 P.M., and 3:30 P.M.

Fares   Adults, $7.50; children (ages 3 to 11), $4; children under three years of age are admitted free of charge.

Contact   Kettle Moraine Railway, P.O. Box 247, North Lake, WI 53064. Telephone (414) 782-8074.

P L A T T E V I L L E

THE MINING MUSEUM

Photographs, artifacts, dioramas, and models on display at the Mining Museum tell visitors the story of lead and zinc mining in the Upper Mississippi Valley. Featured in a visit to the museum are guided tours of an 1845 lead mine and a train ride above ground on museum property in ore cars led by a 1931 Whitcomb locomotive. The museum shares the same building with the **Rollo Jamison Museum**, which houses a collection of more than 20,000 items reflecting turn-of-the-century American life. Tours of both museums and the train ride take one-and-a-half hours. Train ride operates weather permitting.

NOTE: Both museums are handicapped accessible. Ninety steps take visitors to the lead mine, and there are nine landings at regular intervals. The mine temperature is 52°F. Comfortable shoes and jacket or sweater are recommended.

How to Get There   The museum is half an hour from Dubuque and three hours from Milwaukee. Two blocks north of Highway 151.

Hours   May to October: open daily, 9:00 A.M. to 4:00 P.M. Tours given November to April, Monday to Friday, 9:00 A.M. to 4:00 P.M. (no mine visit).

Fares   Fare includes tours of both museums and the train ride. Adults, $4; seniors, $3.50; children (ages 5 to 15), $2; children under five years of age are admitted free of charge. Train only: $.50 per person.

Contact   City of Platteville, Museum Department, 405 East Main, P.O. Box 780, Platteville, WI 53818-0780. Telephone (608) 348-3301.

W A U K E S H A

EAST TROY ELECTRIC RAILROAD MUSEUM/WISCONSIN TROLLEY MUSEUM

Trolleys once dotted southeastern Wisconsin's landscape, providing dependable transportation for passengers traveling between towns. The East Troy line was one of five interurban lines, operating from 1907 to 1939. The rich history of this interurban railway is captured at the East Troy Electric Railroad Museum and Wisconsin Trolley Museum, jointly operating since November 1995.

The East Troy Electric Railroad Museum operates a 10-mile round-trip ride between East Troy and Elegant Farmer, along original track that is the longest of any museum-operated interurban railway in the United States. Over 20 historic trolleys are on display, featuring nearly every style ever made. Visitors are invited to watch cars undergoing restoration.

A gift shop and exhibit area is housed in the passenger station. Dinner trains and charters are available.

Future plans include development of a Wisconsin Trolley Heritage Center.

How to Get There   From Milwaukee, take I-43 west and exit at East Troy (State Road 20). Drive west on State Road 20, go through the stop sign, and turn left three-quarters of a mile after the stop. Look for signs.

Hours   May 25 to October 27: open weekends and holidays, departures at 11:30 A.M., 1:00 P.M., 2:30 P.M., and 4:00 P.M. Museum: 11:00 A.M. to 5:00 P.M.

June 19 to August 16: open Wednesday, Thursday, and Friday, departures at 11:00 A.M. and 1:00 P.M. Museum: 11:00 A.M. to 3:00 P.M.

Fares Museum is free. Adults, $8; children (ages 3 to 11), $4. Dinner trains: $40 per person.

Contact Wisconsin Trolley Museum, Friends of East Troy Railroad Museum, P.O. Box 556, Waukesha, WI 53187-0556. Telephone (414) 548-3837.

CANADA

ALBERTA

Note: All fares are given in Canadian dollars.

CALGARY

HERITAGE PARK

Opened in 1964 and located on 66 beautiful acres, Heritage Park is a historical village depicting western Canadian life from the 19th-century fur trade and railway development to the beginning of World War I. Featured are Heritage Park staff dressed and performing in period costumes, over 150 exhibits, and more than 40,000 artifacts that help re-create the past.

The park also features a railway and a variety of train displays, including train stations built at the turn of the century, a water tower, a six-stall roundhouse replica built in 1981, an original turntable, narrow gauge mine cars, and a replica of a horse-drawn streetcar. Visitors may take rides on two steam-powered locomotives, #2023 or #2024.

Other offerings are rides on an antique Ferris wheel, boat rides, and ample play areas for children.

Special Events Twelve Days of Christmas.

How to Get There From downtown Calgary, take the McCloud Trail Highway. Turn west onto Heritage Drive, which leads straight into Heritage Park.

Hours Late May to beginning of September: open daily. September to October: open weekends and holidays. Call for hours of operation.

Fares Adults, $10 (basic fare), $16 (with rides); children (ages 3 to 16), $6 (basic fare), $12 (with rides). Children two years of age and under are free of charge.
    Family rates and season passes are also available; call for information.

Contact Heritage Park, 1900 Heritage Drive SW, Calgary, Alberta T2V 2X3. Telephone (403) 259-1900; fax (403) 252-3528.

EDMONTON

FORT EDMONTON PARK

A historical settlement situated on 158 acres of parkland, Fort Edmonton Park includes over 60 period buildings reflecting four important eras in Edmonton's history. Dressed in period costumes, park staff demonstrate Edmonton life during each era and serve as historical interpreters and visitor guides. Also featured are rides on a 1919 steam train, streetcars, a stage-coach, wagon, and ponies.
    There are souvenir and period shops throughout the park. From the 1885 period: McDougall's General Store, Daly's Drug Store, and Lauder's Bakery; from the 1905 period: Ernest Brown Photo Studio; from the 1920 period: the Ukranian Bookstore.

NOTE: Gravel and dirt roadways make wheelchair access difficult, and access is available only in portions of the park. Additional portable ramps provide access. Adult and children's strollers are available.

How to Get There Fort Edmonton Park is 10 minutes from downtown and West Edmonton Mall.

Hours Late May to late June: open weekdays, 10:00 A.M. to 4:00 P.M.; weekends and holidays, 10:00 A.M. to 6:00 P.M. Late June to early September: open daily, 10:00 A.M. to 6:00 P.M.
  In September: open Sunday, 10:00 A.M. to 6:00 P.M. Guided tours: Monday to Saturday, at 11:00 A.M., 12:00 noon, 1:00 P.M., and 2:00 P.M.

Fares General admission: adults, $6.50; seniors/youth, $5; children, $3.25; families, $19.50.
  September guided tours: adults, $4.25; seniors/youth, $3.25; children, $2; families, $12.50.

Contact Fort Edmonton Park, P.O. Box 2359, Edmonton, Alberta T5J 2R7. Telephone (403) 496-8797.

S T E T T L E R

ALBERTA PRAIRIE RAILWAY EXCURSIONS

The Alberta Prairie Railway Excursions offers more than 60 steam and diesel trips through scenic central Alberta between May and October. The excursions last from four-and-a-half to nine hours. Among the cars used on trips are an open-air observation car, a wooden cupola caboose, Pullman coaches, deluxe sleeper cars, and a 1919 combination baggage and passenger car.

The 1996 season will feature live entertainment on most runs and a complete and hearty buffet-style dinner. A children's play area and entertainment car may be included on selected trains.

Special Events   Fall Colours; Halloween Ball; Harvest Special; Teddy Bear Special; Family Specials; School Specials.

How to Get There   Stettler is about three hours from Calgary. Take Highway 2 north to Highway 12 east, straight into Stettler. Look for signs to the depot (on the right).

Hours   Open May to October. Departure times vary; call or write for more information.

Fares   Adults, $53; seniors (60 and above), $49; students (ages 11 to 18), $36; children (ages 4 to 10), $29.50.
    Children three years of age and under not occupying a seat are admitted free of charge. One-way fares, with and without meals, are available on request.

Contact   Alberta Prairie Railway Excursions, 4611 47th Avenue, Stettler, Alberta T0C 2L0. Telephone (403) 742-2811.

BRITISH COLUMBIA

D U N C A N

BRITISH COLUMBIA FOREST MUSEUM

The British Columbia Forest Museum was established as a Historical Site in 1974, and presents the rich history of logging in British Columbia with displays of forest industry artifacts and a steam train ride over a 100-acre park. Visitors travel through forested areas, cross a trestle, and take self-guided tours throughout the area to see displays depicting logging tools and techniques. Trails throughout the park include steam locomotives, steam donkeys, and other logging equipment.

A large picnic area and snack bar are available.

Special Events   National Forestry Week; Canada Day; Celebration of Steam.

How to Get There   From Victoria, take Highway 1 north for about 60 kilometers. Just past the town of Duncan, turn right onto Drinkwater Road. The museum is at 2892 Drinkwater.

Hours   Museum is open daily. April 5 to May 3 and September 4 to October 14: 10:00 A.M. to 5:00 P.M.; May 5 through September 3: 9:30 A.M. to 6:00 P.M.

Steam train rides operate May 4 to May 17 (weekends only) and May 18 through September 3 (daily), 9:30 A.M. to 6:00 P.M.

Fares   Adults, $7; seniors, $6; students (ages 13 to 18), $6; children (ages 5 to 12), $4; children under five years of age are admitted free of charge. Family Day Pass (two adults and three children): $25. Fares do not include tax.

Contact   British Columbia Forest Museum, R.R. #4, 2892 Drinkwater Road, Duncan, B.C. V9L 3W8. Telephone (604) 746-1251.

K I M B E R L E Y

BAVARIAN CITY MINING RAILWAY

The Bavarian City Mining Railway was created by a group of volunteers and had its first official run in 1984. The rolling stock originated with the (now-closed) H. B. Mine in Salmo. Operating in the Happy Hans Campground in Kimberley (a town modeled after a Bavarian village), the railway operates a 20-minute, 2.5-kilometer narrated ride, featuring beautiful mountain views while going across a timber trestle approximately 7.5 meters high and 60 meters long, a tunnel, and one of the world's largest lead and zinc mines. Igor the gold prospector, animal cutouts, an old mining schoolhouse, and mining artifacts are featured. The train station houses photographs depicting the early mining days and history of the railway.

The camping area includes a variety of amenities: a picnic area with playground and swings, washrooms, pool, and a mini-golf attraction. Future plans include extending the line to downtown and adding a grade to the railway.

How to Get There   From Vancouver, take Highway 1 east. At Hope, turn onto Highway 3 east (toward Salmo). At Cranbrook, take Highway 95A (toward Kimberley). In Kimberley, turn left at the stop light, left again onto J. Sorensen Way, and look for signs to the recreation area.

Hours   Mid-May: open weekends, 1:00 P.M. to 5:00 P.M. Late June to Labour Day: open daily, 1:00 P.M. to 9:00 P.M.

Fares   Adults, $3; seniors (60 and above), $2.50; youth (ages 13 to 18), $2.50; children (ages 6 to 12), $1; families, $8. Children six years old and younger are free of charge.

Contact   Bavarian City Mining Railway, Kimberley Chamber of Commerce, 350 Ross Street, Kimberley, B.C. V1A 2Z9. Telephone (604) 427-3666 or (604) 427-2929 (campground); fax (604) 427-2917.

NORTH VANCOUVER

ROYAL HUDSON STEAM TRAIN/BC RAIL

BC RAIL offers a variety of train excursions, among them a steam train ride on the antique *Royal Hudson 2860* (featured on the book cover) from North Vancouver to Squamish, British Columbia. Built in the 1900s, BC RAIL was originally the Pacific Great Eastern Railway, designed to connect a Prince George rail line to the Vancouver port. The scenic excursion, which departs from the BC RAIL station in North Vancouver at 10:00 A.M., travels over trestles, rolls past waterfalls, and goes through six tunnels before arriving in Squamish at 12:00 noon. Passengers can lunch in Squamish or tour the area for two hours before making the return trip at 2:00 P.M.

Special luxury travel is offered on the Mount Cascade, a refurbished parlor car. The car features large observation windows, an open observation platform, and nickelodeon piano. Outbound, a light lunch is served on linen-covered tables; tea and dessert are offered on the return trip. Other options include a train and boat combination, which enables passengers to depart on the Royal Hudson and return to North Vancouver by boat.

BC RAIL provides shuttle bus service from downtown and the North Vancouver SeaBus Terminal to the rail station.

Special Events   Halloween Haunt; Jingle Bell Express.

How to Get There   The BC RAIL station is at the foot of Pemberton in North Vancouver.

Hours   June to September: departs North Vancouver Wednesday to Sunday (and Monday holidays), 10:00 A.M. to 4:00 P.M.

Fares   Train (round-trip): adults, $36; seniors (60 and above), $31.50; youths (ages 12 to 18), $31.50; children (ages 5 to 11), $10. Parlor car: $69 per person.

Train/boat combination: adults, $62.06; seniors (60 and above), $52.43; youths (ages 12 to 18), $52.43; children (ages 5 to 11), $17.12.

Children under five years of age are admitted free of charge.

BC RAIL offers other daylong and extended trips by rail. Check with the company for further information.

Contact   BC RAIL, 1311 W. First Street, North Vancouver, B.C. V7P 1A7. Telephone (800) 663-8238 or (604) 984-5500; fax (604) 984-5505.

SQUAMISH

WEST COAST RAILWAY HERITAGE PARK

The West Coast Railway Association was created in 1961 to help preserve and interpret British Columbia's rich railway history. The West Coast Railway Heritage Park, operated by the Association, is housed on 12 acres and represents a typical mid-20th-century railway facility. Visitors can view over 50 pieces of historic railway equipment, memorabilia, and artifacts at different stages of restoration.

The Association also operates rail tours in British Columbia.

How to Get There   From Vancouver, drive 1 hour north on Highway 99 to Squamish. Go 3 kilometers past the first stoplight to Centennial Way. Turn west from Highway 99 onto Centennial Way. Centennial Way turns into Government Road. Follow it until cross BC RAIL tracks. Entrance is on the right.

Hours   April to October: 10:00 A.M. to 4:00 P.M.

Fares   Adults, $4.50; seniors, $3.50; children under 12, $3.50; families, $12.

Contact   West Coast Railway Association, Box 2790, Vancouver, B.C. V6B 3X2. Telephone (604) 524-1011 or (800) 722-1233.

MANITOBA

PRAIRIE DOG CENTRAL

The nonprofit Vintage Locomotive Society operates the Prairie Dog Central, a vintage steam train that makes a 36-mile, two-hour round-trip journey between Winnipeg and Grosse Isle.

Departing from St. James Station, a 1910 structure built by Canadian Northern, the Prairie Dog Central is pulled by *Old Number 3*, a Scottish-made steam locomotive built in 1882.

The five wooden passenger coaches are open-window, prairie-air-conditioned cars, and were made between 1901 and 1913. The Society also has a hopper car, boxcars, bunk car, caboose, and a business car originally built in 1903.

The station sells souvenirs, and refreshments can be obtained on the train. Free parking is available.

How to Get There   From downtown Winnipeg, take Portage Avenue west to the St. James CNR station, located by the Polo Park Shopping Center.

Hours   June through September: Sunday, departures at 11:00 A.M. and 3:00 P.M. (daylight savings time). Train capacity is limited, so visitors are urged to arrive early. No reservations taken. Ticket office opens at 9:00 A.M. for the 11:00 A.M. trip; 12:00 noon for the 3:00 P.M. trip.

Fares   Adults, $13; seniors (65 and above), $11; youths (ages 12 to 17), $11; children (ages 2 to 11), $7; children under two years of age accompanied by an adult and not occupying a seat are admitted free of charge.

Contact   The Vintage Locomotive Society, P.O. Box 33021, RPO Polo Park, Winnipeg, Manitoba R3G 3N4. Telephone (204) 832-5259.

NEW BRUNSWICK

HILLSBOROUGH

SALEM & HILLSBOROUGH RAILROAD

The Salem & Hillsborough Railroad is an operating museum offering one-hour coach excursion and dinner trains along 10 miles of track originally laid in the 19th century. The journey takes visitors through scenic countryside from Hillsborough to Salem Station. Passengers have a 10-minute stop and can watch the train crew unhook the engine for the return trip.

The railroad recently acquired a 1959 Canadian National diesel locomotive and is recovering from a 1994 fire that caused damage and loss to its fine collection of rolling stock. Housed on the site of a former gypsum mining operation, the rail yard also includes a display of steam and other diesel engines, a baggage car, flatcar, snowplow, and a variety of tools and equipment.

The railroad has a gift shop.

Special Events Blueberry Festival; Thanksgiving Turkey Runs; Fall Foliage Train; Canada Day; Homecoming Days.

Canadian Pacific steam locomotive #29.

How to Get There   From Moncton, take Route 114 south to Hillsborough. Look for signs to the railroad.

Hours   Train rides: early June to early September, Sunday, 1:30 P.M. and 3:00 P.M.

Museum and gift shop: late June to early September, open 10 A.M. to 8 P.M.

Fares   Adults, $6.50; seniors, $5.50; children (ages 6 to 12), $3.25; families, $20.

Contact   Salem & Hillsborough Railroad, P.O. Box 70, Hillsborough, New Brunswick E0A 1X0. Telephone (506) 734-3195 or (506) 734-3100.

NEWFOUNDLAND

CORNER BROOK

RAILWAY SOCIETY OF NEWFOUNDLAND

Created in 1987 to help preserve Newfoundland Railway history and heritage, the Railway Society of Newfoundland provides guided tours of its railway displays. Located on two acres (a former Newfoundland Railway terminal site), displays include 1,500 feet of main-line narrow gauge track and features the *Newfie Bullet*—a Baldwin steam locomotive #593—two baggage cars, a passenger car, diner car, and sleeper. Other exhibits include a snowplow, caboose, and an operating diesel electric locomotive that visitors can board for a closer look.

Future plans include conversion of a 90-year-old freight shed into a museum.

How to Get There From Porte Basques, take the Trans Canada Highway to Corner Brook. Once in Corner Brook, look for signs to the society.

Hours   June, July, and August: 10:00 A.M. to 6:00 P.M. and also by appointment.

Fares   Admission is free.

Contact   Railway Society of Newfoundland, P.O. Box 673, Corner Brook, Newfoundland A2H 6G1. Telephone (709) 634-6089 (president) or (709) 634-5658 (secretary/treasurer).

NOVA
SCOTIA

LOUISBOURG

SYDNEY & LOUISBURG RAILWAY

The Sydney & Louisburg Railway (S & L) Historical Society celebrates railroading and mining history in Nova Scotia with its operation of the Sydney & Louisburg Railway Museum. The 1895 completion of the Sydney & Louisburg Railway, among the most modern of its day, helped link the transport of coal by rail between Sydney and the harbor at Louisbourg. Thirty-one steam locomotives traveled over 100 miles of track by the 1950s. Because coal remained so plentiful, the operation of steam trains remained viable until 1966.

Today, visitors to the museum complex can view the 1895 station, the original freight shed, and a new roundhouse used to protect two passenger cars from 1881 and 1914. Seven kinds of handcars, a boxcar, tank car, caboose, and the passenger cars make up the museum's rolling stock. (Supervised children may explore the passenger cars and handcars.) Also featured are railroad memorabilia, artifacts, and model trains

SYDNEY & LOUISBURG RAILWAY MUSEUM

A front view of the museum.

and stations. Watercolor paintings of ships at ports around the world are featured in the Marine Room. Souvenirs are sold.

Future plans include a complete layout model of the S & L line in 1996.

How to Get There   From Halifax, take Highway 102 east to Truro to Highway 104. Take 104 to Route 4 to Sydney. Then take Route 22 to Louisbourg. Look for signs to the museum.

Hours   April through early June: 9:00 A.M. to 5:00 P.M. Mid-June to October: 9:00 A.M. to 7:00 P.M.

Fares   Donations are welcome.

Contact   Sydney & Louisburg Railway Museum, Box 225, Louisbourg, Nova Scotia B0A 1M0. Telephone (902) 733-2720.

ONTARIO

COCHRANE

COCHRANE RAILWAY AND PIONEER MUSEUM

Cochrane Railway and Pioneer Museum, launched in 1970, was designed to preserve the history and heritage of the pioneering and homesteading era in northern Ontario. Among the exhibits are a steam locomotive, Canadian National caboose, baggage car and coach, a model train display, and photographs. The museum has a gift shop.

Special Events   Polar Bear Express Trains (call for details).

How to Get There   From Timmins, take Highway 11 north to Cochrane. Turn right onto Railway Street; the museum is across from Union Station.

Hours   Late June to mid-September: open Friday to Wednesday, 11:00 A.M. to 7:00 P.M.

Fares   Families, $3; seniors, $1; students (ages 12 to 18), $1.50; children (ages 3 to 12), $1. Children under three are free of charge.

Contact   Cochrane Railway and Pioneer Museum. P.O. Box 490, Cochrane, Ontario POL 1C0. Telephone (705) 272-5378 or (705) 272-4361.

K O M O K A

KOMOKA RAILWAY MUSEUM

The Komoka Railway Museum opened in 1986 and was formerly the Komoka Railway Station. Now restored, the building includes a number of exhibits, including early railway equipment and artifacts, a three-wheel velocipede and an HO-gauge model railroad room with a large Lionel train collection.

Currently underway is restoration on a 1913 Shay locomotive (used for logging) and a 1939 baggage car. The museum also uses multimedia presentations to tell visitors about the station's restoration process and the history of railroading in Canada.

Future plans include opening a gift shop in the museum.

Special Events   Model Railroad Flea Market and Operating Display.

How to Get There   The museum is 13 kilometers west of London, on Middlesex County Road 14.

Hours   June through September: Tuesday and Thursday, 7:00 A.M. to 9:00 P.M.; Saturday, 9:00 A.M. to 12:00 noon; Sunday, 1:00 P.M. to 4:00 P.M.

Fares   Adults and youths (12 and over), $2; children under 12 are admitted free of charge.

Contact   Komoka Railway Museum, Inc., P.O. Box 22, 133 Queen Street, Komoka, Ontario N0L 1R0. Telephone (519) 657-1912.

O T T A W A

NATIONAL MUSEUM OF SCIENCE AND TECHNOLOGY

The National Museum of Science and Technology has a rich collection of exhibits showcasing the full range of scientific and technological subjects, including agriculture, astronomy, broadcasting, space, communications, computer technology, physics, printing, and land and marine transportation.

In 1995, the museum greatly added to its rail exhibits when Canadian National Railways donated a major collection of its historic rail equipment and artifacts. Among the contributions are four steam locomotives, an electric locomotive, four passenger cars, an 1895 caboose, and nearly 1,000 smaller artifacts. The collection helps to illustrate the important role played by the railroad in Canada's 19th-century development.

The museum encourages visitor participation, and guided tours and demonstrations are given throughout the day. Special educational programs geared to primary and secondary school children are offered between October and June. Visitors are free to climb on board a steam locomotive. Picnic areas, a gift shop, and a museum cafeteria are located on site.

NOTE: The museum is wheelchair accessible.

How to Get There   The museum is 10 minutes from downtown Ottawa. Take the Queensway exit at St. Laurent South. Turn left at the lighthouse on Lancaster Road.

Hours   May through early September: open daily, 9:00 A.M. to 6:00 P.M.; Friday until 9:00 P.M. Early September through April: Tuesday to Sunday, 9:00 A.M. to 5:00 P.M. Closed Monday.

Fares   Adults, $6; students and seniors, $5; children (ages 6 to 15), $2; children under six years of age are free of charge. Free general admission: Monday through Friday, 4:00 P.M. to 5:00 P.M.

Contact   National Museum of Science and Technology, 1867 St. Laurent Boulevard at Lancaster Road, Ottawa, Ontario K1G 5A3. Telephone (613) 991-3044; TTY (613) 991-9207.

R O C K W O O D

HALTON COUNTY RADIAL RAILWAY

The Halton County Radial Railway, operated by the nonprofit Ontario Electric Railway Historical Association, was originally created to save a streetcar in 1953. Today it consists of an operating electric railway and a museum housed on 38 acres of land. The site includes a visitors center, with gift shop, snack bar, the 1912 Rockwood Station, car houses, and other facilities.

HALTON COUNTY RAILWAY

Halton County Railway trolleys, stationed at Car House #3.

An all-day pass enables visitors to take a ride on 1.5 kilo-meters of streetcar track. Featured is a collection of full-sized streetcars and radial cars that once ran in and outside the province of Ontario. A gift shop, ice cream parlor, and picnic grounds are on site.

NOTE: A wheelchair ramp is available for boarding.

Special Events Neighbours Evening; Spring Extravaganza and Yard Sale; 75th Birthday Anniversary; Night Show and Public Corn Roast; Fall Colour Cavalcade; Christmas Fiesta; Light Show.

How to Get There The railway is located 15 kilometers north of exit 312 off Highway 401, or 5 kilometers south of Highway 7 via Wellington Road 44.

Hours May, September, and October: Saturday, Sunday, and holidays. June: Wednesday through Saturday. July and August: daily. 10:00 A.M. to 5:00 P.M.

Fares Adults, $6.50; seniors, $5.50; youths (ages 3 to 17), $4.50; families (two adults and up to three persons under 17, or one adult and up to four persons under 17), $17.50.

Contact Halton County Radial Railway, R.R. #2, Rockwood, Ontario NOB 2KO. Telephone (519) 856-9802.

SAULT STE. MARIE

ALGOMA CENTRAL RAILWAY, INC.

The Algoma Central Railway Company, a predecessor of today's Algoma Central Railway, Inc., was created in 1899 to help trans-port resources needed to open up a once-inaccessible region of North America. Today's railway offers train rides on the Agawa

Canyon and Snow Train, two train excursions that take visitors on a rail trip through the heart of the Canadian wilderness. The journey is 184 to 193 kilometers north of Sault Ste. Marie (depending on tour), complete with spectacular views, tall trestles, granite formations, and a descent to the bottom of Agawa Canyon Wilderness Park (on the Agawa Tour) for a two-hour stop. At the park, travelers can take hikes, marvel at cascading waterfalls, or enjoy a picnic lunch. On hand during the trip are tour hosts and park rangers to answer questions and to identify highlights.

Passengers travel in refurbished coaches with large picture windows. Dining cars are also available.

Special Events   "Canyon Quest" (June) is open to school groups up to the eighth grade, with organized activities in Agawa Canyon and lunch. Families may enter the railway's family vacation contest worth $5,000 in 1996.

How to Get There   The railway is at the terminus of I-75, across from the international bridge in Sault Ste. Marie. It's one hour north of the Mackinac Bridge in Michigan.

Hours   Agawa Canyon tour operates daily, June 3 through October 14, 7:00 A.M. to 6:30 P.M. (office hours); 8:00 A.M. departure and 5:00 P.M. return. Snow train operates on Saturdays and Sundays, December 30, 1995 through March 17, 1996, 8:00 A.M. departure and 4:00 P.M. return.

Fares   Agawa Canyon Tour: adults, $49 (June 3 to September 8) and $55 (September 9 to October 14); seniors, $40 (June 3 to September 8) and $30 (September 9 to October 14); children/high school students, $15 (June 3 to September 8) and $30 (September 9 to October 14); children (ages 5 and under), $10; infants in arms are admitted free of charge.

Snow Train Tour (September 9 to October 14): adults, $49; children/high school students, $25; children (ages 5 and under), $10; infants in arms are admitted free of charge.

Contact   Algoma Central Railway, P.O. Box 130, 129 Bay
Street, Sault Ste. Marie, Ontario P6A 6Y2. Telephone (800)
242-9287 or (705) 946-7300.

SMITHS FALLS

SMITHS FALLS RAILWAY MUSEUM

The Smiths Falls Railway Museum is housed in a railway station
once used by the Canadian Northern and Canadian National
Railway lines. Until 1979, the station served trains traveling between Ottawa and Toronto. Threatened by plans for demolition,
the 1914 station was saved in the 1980s by the volunteer efforts
of the Smiths Falls Railway Museum Association.

Restoration efforts have yielded a collection that includes
artifacts, exhibits, a museum library, and thousands of photographs, all related to local railway history. Special features
include a steam locomotive (under restoration), a diesel locomotive, five cabooses (including one dating back to 1891), a restored dental car from the 1900s (open for tours every
Tuesday), and a 1919 Pullman combination car. Two Wickham
inspection cars provide rides to visitors. Each visitor has the
choice of a guided tour or a self-guided visit (informational
booklets available).

The museum encourages children to pump an antique
handcar, check out the engineer's seat on a diesel train, and explore the five cabooses and the home and office of a traveling
dentist.

A museum gift shop, restrooms, parking, and picnic areas
are available.

How to Get There   The museum is located halfway between
Ottawa and Kingston, at the intersections of Highways 43, 15,
and 29.

Hours May through October: daily, 10:00 A.M. to 4:00 P.M. September through April: by appointment only.

Fares Museum: adults, $2; seniors, $1.50, children (12 and under), free. Wickham car rides: adults and seniors, $2; children (12 and under), $1.

Contact Smiths Falls Railway Museum, 90 William Street West, P.O. Box 962, Smiths Falls, Ontario K7A 5A5. Telephone (613) 283-5696.

QUEBEC

H U L L

HULL-CHELSEA-WAKEFIELD RAILROAD

The Hull-Chelsea-Wakefield Railroad offers half-day trips in one of Canada's last steam trains. Swedish-built engine 909 was built in 1907. The coaches, also from Sweden, were built in 1940. Each coach can seat 68 passengers, for a maximum capacity of 536. Guides are on board to respond to visitors' questions and provide singing and storytelling entertainment.

Beginning in Hull and traveling through the Gatineau Valley, the journey is 32 kilometers (1 hour, 20 minutes) each way, with a two-hour stop in Wakefield. During the layover, passengers can watch the crew turn the locomotive around for the return trip, take walking tours of the village, or visit local craft shops.

NOTE: Reservations are required. Check-in time is 30 minutes prior to departure.

Special Events   Mother's Day; Canadian Tulip Festival; Tulip Sunset Journey; Father's Day; Canada Day Excursion; Family Month; Fall Foliage.

How to Get There   From downtown Ottawa, take King Edward Street North to cross Macdonald-Cartier Bridge. Follow Highway 5, and take the Casino Boulevard exit. Off the ramp, stay on your right and make a right turn onto Casino Boulevard, then turn left immediately onto de la Carriere Boulevard. Note the blue and white signs for the station route. At the second four-way stop, turn left on Deveault Street.

Hours   All departures are at 1:30 P.M. Call ahead for dates open.

Fares   Adults, $23 plus tax; seniors, $21 plus tax; students, $19.50 plus tax; children (12 and under), $11 plus tax.
    One-way (all ages): $19.50 plus tax.

Contact   Hull-Chelsea-Wakefield Railroad, 165 Rue Deveault Street, Hull, Quebec J8Z 1S7. Telephone (819) 778-7246; fax (819) 778-5007.

ST. CONSTANT

CANADIAN RAILWAY MUSEUM

More than 100 pieces of railway equipment and 6,000 artifacts are featured at the Canadian Railway Museum, an institution established in 1961 and one of the largest museums of its type in North America. Among the displays are steam, diesel, and electric locomotives, freight and passenger cars, streetcars, and interurbans. Special attractions include an operating replica of the *John Molson,* an 1849 steam locomotive, and two large and powerful steam locomotives, CPR 5935 and CNR 4100.

Children will especially enjoy train rides on the *John Molson* on special weekends and on the streetcar and caboose rides (offered on Sundays in the summer). Other exhibits include the 1882 Barrington Station, a locomotive turntable, Montreal's first electric streetcar, *The Rocket,* and an operating O-gauge model railroad layout.

A picnic area is available at the site.

How to Get There   The museum is on St. Pierre Street in St. Constant, off Route 209.

Hours   May through Labour Day: daily, 9:00 A.M. to 5:00 P.M. Also open weekends through October.

Fares   Adults, $5.75; seniors, $4.75; students (ages 13 to 17), $3.25; children (ages 5 to 12), $2.75; children under five years of age are admitted free of charge.

Contact   Canadian Railway Museum, 120 Rue St. Pierre, St. Constant, Quebec J5A 2G9. Telephone (514) 632-2410; fax (514) 638-1563.

SASKATCHEWAN

RUSTY RELICS MUSEUM

Dedicated to the pioneer days of Saskatchewan, Rusty Relics Museum (open since 1980), is housed in a former Canadian National Railway station built in 1910. Displays on site include a 1943 Canadian Pacific Railway caboose, which visitors are free to tour, a Canadian National Railway motorcar, and tool shed. A country school built in 1905 is also offered as part of the museum visit.

How to Get There The museum is located near Moose Mountain Provincial Park and White Bear Lake. Carlyle is about 96 kilometers north of the U.S. border and 65 kilometers west of Manitoba.

Hours June to Labour Day: daily, 10:00 A.M. to 5:00 P.M.

Fares   Adults, $2; students, $1; preschoolers are admitted free of charge.

Contact   Rusty Relics Museum, Box 840, Carlyle, Saskatchewan S0C 0R0. Telephone (306) 453-2266.

BIBLIOGRAPHY

Information about the train attractions in this book was derived largely from the train sites themselves. Additional background information was drawn from the following sources:

Drury, George. *Guide to Tourist Railroads and Railroad Museums.* Waukesha, Wis.: Kalmbach Publishing, 1995.

Live Steam. Traverse City, Mich.: Village Press, Jan./Feb. 1996.

Locomotive & Railway Preservation. Pasadena, Calif.: Pentrex, Inc., 1995–96.

Model Railroading. Englewood, Colo.: Wiesner Publishing, 1996.

Thirtieth Annual Steam Passenger Service Directory. Waukesha, Wis.: Great Eastern Publishing, 1995.

TourBooks (United States and Canada). Heathrow, Fla.: American Automobile Association (AAA), 1995.

Trains. Waukesha, Wisc.: Kalmbach Publishing Company, 1995–96.

INDEX

386